The Civil War in

STRATFORD-
UPON-AVON

Publications of
The Shakespeare Birthplace Trust
in association with
Alan Sutton Publishing Limited

Robert Bearman
Shakespeare in the Stratford Records
1994

Joan Lane
John Hall and his Patients:
The Medical Practice of Shakespeare's Son-in-Law
1996

Philip Tennant
The Civil War in Stratford-upon-Avon:
Conflict and Community in South Warwickshire 1642–1646
1996

Jeanne Jones
Family Life in Shakespeare's England:
Stratford-upon-Avon 1570–1630
1996

General Editors' Preface

The objects of The Shakespeare Birthplace Trust, as defined by the Act of Parliament under which it operates, are:

a)   to promote in every part of the world the appreciation and study of the plays and other works of William Shakespeare and the general advancement of Shakespearian knowledge;

b)   to maintain and preserve the Shakespeare birthplace properties for the benefit of the nation;

c)   to provide and maintain for the benefit of the nation a museum and a library of books, manuscripts, records of historic interest, pictures, photographs and objects of antiquity with particular but not exclusive reference to William Shakespeare, his life, works and times.

It is from these objectives that the series of publications, of which this volume is part, derives. The central focus of the series is Shakespeare: his plays and their performance, his life, and the environment, historical, topographical, and domestic, in which he lived; and the raw material for volumes in the series is derived largely from the rich Shakespearian holdings of the Trust's Library and Records Office, in the form of printed books and archival and pictorial material relating to Shakespeare's life in Stratford, to the history of the town, to scholarship and criticism on his writings, and to the performance history of his plays. Such a collection of volumes, covering a wide range of topics – theatrical, literary and historical – cannot, of course, observe rigid editorial uniformity. To a considerable extent, therefore, treatment and approach from volume to volume are determined by the aims and needs of individual authors and editors. Within this rather broad scope, however, we seek to produce a series of volumes that will be of interest to the general reader while maintaining a high standard of scholarship in the furtherance of that basic objective of The Shakespeare Birthplace Trust, 'the general advancement of Shakespearian knowledge'.

Robert Bearman
Robert Smallwood

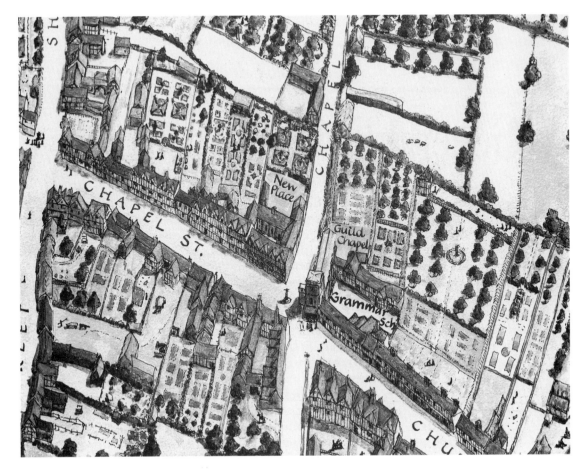

Shakespeare's Stratford. *A detail taken from the panoramic reconstruction by Dr Pat Hughes in 1995. At the crossroads stand New Place, Shakespeare's old home, frequently occupied by military commanders during the Civil War and, perhaps, by Queen Henrietta Maria on her visit of July 1643; the ancient Guild Chapel, a focus for puritan activity in pre-war days; and the grammar school, whose master, John Trapp, as an uncompromising Puritan, fled the town during the war to escape royalist victimization. The houses, barns, closes and orchards were all frequently invaded by soldiers and their horses during the war.*

(The Shakespeare Birthplace Trust)

Introduction

Despite the routine barbarities of Elizabethan and Stuart times which we prefer to forget, the myth of Merry England dies hard, and perhaps nowhere more so than in the 'Shakespeare Country'. Yet as that great civil war historian Dame Veronica Wedgwood has reminded us, Shakespeare himself had grown up under the shadow of disturbing changes, and by the time of his death almost every ingredient of future conflict was already in place.[1] Even in his own day, the rural tranquillity was largely illusory, as the many echoes of contemporary dramas in the plays hint to us. The Forest of Arden was continuing to shrink under new commercial pressures, lands in which he had interests were being enclosed, and the regular toll of natural disaster – plague, flood, failed harvest – continued unabated, alternating as ever with the more human creations of persecution, destitution, corruption, intrigue and crime. Underlying all were the deep-seated religious tensions, the inexorable rise of puritanism, the beginnings of entrepreneurial and speculative ventures, the widespread rural malaise. Any glance at Stratford's council records or those of its church courts shows the unreality of the much-cherished idyll.[2]

Three years after Shakespeare was buried in the dilapidated chancel of Holy Trinity Church, what little harmony existed among the town's ruling elite was shattered by the appointment of an obstreperous zealot as the new vicar. His reign coincided with a darkening national scene, which by the time of his death in 1638 seemed set to degenerate further into open conflict, into the civil war which Shakespeare himself had so much dreaded and, as it were, indirectly foreseen.[3] Although, as war approached, probably a majority of the town's elders were conservatives and therefore soon portrayed as 'Royalists', like many other communities Stratford was in fact fairly evenly divided and reluctant to get involved in the coming conflict, giving generously to public subscriptions 'for the safety of the county' in the period of the phoney war of 1642 in the hope of averting tragedy. But once the real war came, situated in what almost instantly became a frontier zone between opposing spheres of influence, uncomfortably close to rival garrisons and lines of communication, it was powerless to avoid being sucked into the conflict. Indefensible, without ancient walls or towers, open to the fields on all sides, and temptingly prosperous for ravenous and ruffianly soldiers, it inevitably found itself occupied and reoccupied by troops of both sides, often in no great hurry to move on. Although ultimately it was to escape the wholesale destruction seen elsewhere and it witnessed no real atrocities, harassment and violence became almost daily realities for most of its citizens. Stratford offers, consequently, a fairly representative case-study of typical civil war features. Yet although much happened here, the town has attracted scarcely a mention in standard Civil War works, and even those with a regional bias make only brief passing (and sometimes even misleading) reference to it. The conclusion which an unwary reader might reasonably draw is that the war simply passed by at some distance.

How far this is from the truth is apparent from even a cursory glance at the relevant Warwickshire archives. It was, after all, unlikely that a conflict, whose dramatic opening moves and subsequent course affected the Midlands particularly, should leave unscathed a busy market centre at an important road junction, situated on a navigable river becoming commercially viable for the first time and within easy raiding distance of predatory garrisons (see Map 1, page xiii). The archives in question do not, of course, offer anything like a complete narrative. However talkative in street or council chamber, none of Stratford's citizens was obliging enough to keep a diary for posterity, and many important pieces are missing from the jigsaw puzzle which is all we have. But what survives, patchy, deficient and occasionally unreliable though it appears, constitutes nonetheless a substantial mass of material from which a reasonably full picture may emerge. This book attempts, by drawing on that material, to reconstruct, as far as possible in a continuous narrative, the main lines of that picture. The intention is twofold: firstly, to explain for the first time in detail what actually happened in and around Stratford between the years 1642 and 1646; and secondly, to lay emphasis throughout less on ideology than on the day-to-day effect of events on the countless ordinary people unavoidably caught up in them. After long ignoring the wealth of local evidence of the civil war, preferring instead to concentrate on its 'causes', underlying political issues and, if necessary, a few great battles which in fact accomplished surprisingly little, historians are now beginning to recognize the sheer extent of the disruption it caused across the countryside. This aspect is not what the war was 'about', but is its human subtext, what the conflict came to mean for ordinary people as well as the leading gentry, and it is on the burdens of war rather than its ideology that the following chapters focus particularly. It is as well to remember, in any case, a remark made by the reluctant royalist the Earl of Berkshire at the end of the war, that 'noe body can tell what we have fought about all this whyle'.[4]

The basic sources used are contemporary manuscript ones, and among these two in particular are of outstanding value. These are the vast hotchpotch of newsletters and reports collected by the London bookseller George Thomason preserved in the British Library, and the almost equally large collection of parish and military accounts scattered among the so-called Commonwealth Exchequer Papers in the Public Record Office.[5] The former provide an up-to-the-minute unending commentary on events as the fighting washed across the countryside. Admittedly, much of this tabloid-style journalism is blatantly biased, but, carefully and critically read and checked wherever possible against other sources, its unreliability can be minimised and its unique importance becomes evident. Any serious account of the civil war is today unthinkable without the 'Thomason

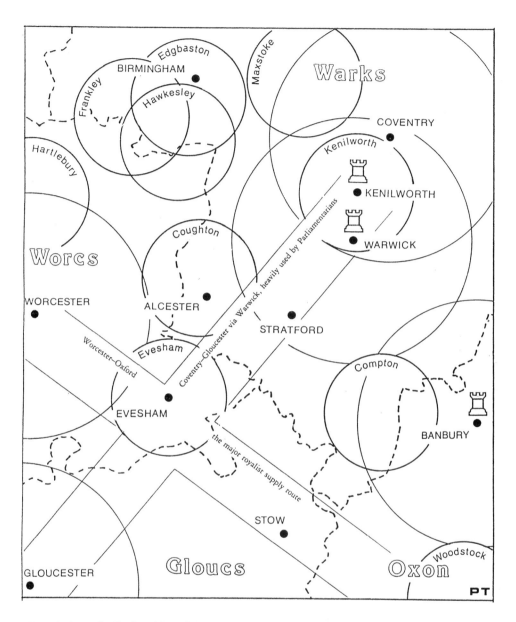

Map 1. Stratford's Civil War Position.
Throughout the war, Stratford was hemmed in on all sides by rival garrisons competing for territorial domination, the most important being parliamentary Warwick, as well as being situated near rival supply lines crossing near Evesham. All the garrisons collected taxes and provisions throughout wide, overlapping areas. Large circles represent approximate raiding and collecting orbits of the major permanent garrisons, all of which were besieged by the enemy at some point. Small circles represent minor or intermittent garrisons. All frequently initiated local conflicts besides providing reinforcements to field armies passing through the district, as shown on the maps for 1642–6.

Tracts'. The parish accounts, the second source, call for particular emphasis since they are still relatively ignored by historians and virtually unknown to the general public. They were compiled, usually with great care, at the end of the war by local officers, often the constable or, in a town like Stratford, the town clerk or his deputy, when the parliamentary authorities, in a praiseworthy exercise in open and fair government, instructed each community to submit claims for compensation for losses and damage suffered at the hands of their troops during the previous four years of war. For Warwickshire, unlike some counties, the survival rate for these returns is surprisingly good, and particularly so for the Stratford district where over half are extant. Stratford's own submission, of which two similar but not identical original copies survive,[6] is unfortunately incomplete, the title 'Stratford upon Avon's First Booke' being a clear indication that, as was usual for the larger parishes (and even some smaller ones), at least one further book was intended – or was actually completed but has since been lost. The information contained was evidently hurriedly collated between the end of January, which appears to be the Stratford deadline for the submission, and 14 March 1646, when the whole return was due to be 'brought in' to the county authorities at Coventry. Some of the individual bills were evidently handed in late, being dated early February, and entries often refer to events taking place almost simultaneously, hinting at the immediacy and urgency of what was clearly a rushed operation. As said, this document is incomplete, not only because the 'first booke' alone has survived, the 123 names included (see Appendix 2) representing less than half of the householders,[7] but because even that includes the names of only 'such persons of the said Burrough as have put in their Bills'. Consequently, some well-known Stratford names like the Sadlers and the Quineys are missing, as are many other surnames figuring in the parish registers and other sources over the war years. There are separate returns for Old Stratford and Shottery, but these are numerically even more disappointing, since they represent a mere fifteen homes from a large area which comprised not only Shottery and Old Stratford but Bridgetown, Clopton and Welcombe, all within the parish but outside the borough, of which there is no mention. In spite of these obvious deficiencies, however, the returns, particularly when complemented by the many similar ones sent in by neighbouring parishes, provide unique and substantial information on events and their impact on leading residents in the district and clearly must form the basis of any attempt to evaluate Stratford's civil war experience. As such, they provide much of the account of individual fortunes and those of the town described in the following chapters. While there is no objective means of testing the accuracy of the records or of eliminating the possibility that some claims may have been inflated by the outraged villagers, it is as well to remember the context. The exercise of submitting the claims, far from being private or secret, was one carried out in the full glare of neighbourly publicity in small communities by a respected elected official, and focused mainly on either personal belongings, livestock and crops, items whose precise values were common knowledge, or on the cost of providing board and lodging for a soldier at a precise rate set by the local authorities. Certainly memories were defective, and occasionally admitted to be so – as in some Stratford cases – and

A Stratford Compensation Claim. Typical of many bills of expenses submitted by the town's residents to the county authorities in Coventry in the spring of 1646 in the hope of receiving eventual reimbursement. Headed 'A Bill of presentment of contribution and other damages sustained by John Beddome of Stratford by the Parliament forces', it details taxes, loans of money, provision and charges for quartering soldiers, including those of Sir Thomas Fairfax after Naseby. Beddom, who lived in the High Street, was Stratford's deputy town clerk, and as such was responsible for drawing up the citizens' returns; this manuscript appears to be in his own handwriting.

(The Shakespeare Birthplace Trust)

often claims were quite openly rounded up to a figure described subjectively as 'at the least'. But there is little or no evidence that the county authorities considered abuse a major problem, and their treasurer, Thomas Basnet, was no country bumpkin but a wary and experienced professional who could be relied upon to scrutinize submissions critically and, no doubt, cross-check them against information on troop movements submitted by the military. Certainly the issue is not clear-cut; but although it would be naive to assume total honesty on one side and modern standards of accounting on the other, the likelihood is that those village claims made, and quoted in the following chapters, were not far from the truth. Moreover, it must not be forgotten that other factors guaranteed that claims made actually fell short of the overall reality rather than exaggerating it. Most communities, including Stratford, suffered at the hands of the Royalists too, for which little documentation survives, so that the existing returns – the parliamentary ones – inevitably paint only half the picture except where occasionally, as with Ashow, near Kenilworth, a village thought it worthwhile to submit claims for royalist plunder as well as parliamentarian. The villagers' returns are incomplete for other reasons too. Shuckburgh's 'acquittances' (receipts for soldiers' billeting) were 'carryed away and torne to peeces' by plundering Royalists, so that 'wee sett downe lesse than we have paid, and farr lesse for free quarter than it would amount to'. Tysoe, while submitting substantial numbers of claims, noted that the constable had lost 'both his warrants and acquittances', so that 'how much the somes are we cannot certifie'. Dunchurch pointed out that 'the whole number wee cannot well remember, by reason of our frequent quartering of souldiers, our Towne lying in the Rode way', while Stretton-on-Fosse made the same point. At Ashow, Burmington and Temple Grafton the constables died and their accounts were lost, and in any case, as Temple Grafton was careful to stress, 'the Inhabitants, not knowing that these things were to be accountable hereafter, did not beare the same in mynd soe well as they might have done'. This human dimension is perhaps most touchingly illustrated by John Wilton, the vicar of Great Wolford:

> for as much as the most part of the sayd Inhabitants are husbandmen and unlearned men, and have kept no Accompt of theyr great charges and losses for these fower or five yeares last past, nor can possibly so call to mynd the sayd charges, . . . therfore they desyre to be excused for making any further Account.

Many simple folk must indeed have adopted the down-to-earth attitude of Alcester's Richard Yarnell, who gloomily noted: 'I have kept no account, never expecting any thing for any such Charges.' For all these reasons, the village submissions, far from being unrealistically inflated, must in effect have fallen far short of reality. None of this, however, should obscure the main point: that incomplete though the picture undoubtedly is, the surviving contemporary archives comprise a substantial mass of material for south Warwickshire. When used in conjunction with the contemporary news sheets already mentioned, standard sources like the state papers and, wherever possible, by rare personal testimony in correspondence, such a wealth of material offers a graphic insight into the impact of the war at a local level. It may be only the tip of a vast submerged iceberg; but even that tip is huge.

Naturally, the use of contemporary manuscripts – hurriedly produced in unprecedented circumstances, of varying format, erratically spelt, near-illegible in places, unpunctuated and with unfamiliar vocabulary and abbreviations – poses certain problems of how best to transmit their information to the modern non-specialist reader. Some editing is unavoidable if clarity is to be retained, and the following compromises have accordingly been adopted. In all contemporary quotations the original spelling has been kept except very occasionally where to have done so might have resulted in unnecessary confusion. For the same reason, standard abbreviations have usually been expanded ('pish' into 'parish', 'Lop' into 'Lordship', 'Maty' into 'Majesty' and so on). For clarity again, modern punctuation has been inserted, and in transcribing monetary values the £ sign substituted for the usual abbreviated Latin, though pre-decimal currency has been kept. The 1640s £ would be roughly equivalent to £100 today – though such a comparison, of course, ignores transformed values, assumptions and life-styles. The maps are intended as nothing more than graphic simplifications of a complex reality and, in each, the limitation of space has allowed only a selection of events to be represented. The marches of the major field armies are numbered so that they can be read chronologically for each year, but it must be remembered that these armies often recrossed the district barely weeks later, taking an almost identical route, so that the local community could suffer the same regiments more than once within a short space of time. The study is largely confined to Stratford and its immediate neighbourhood, taken (though not too strictly) to mean that within an approximate ten mile radius of the town, though events are of course related throughout to the wider context without which they would appear largely meaningless. For accounts of events which took place just outside this limit, like the major battles of Edgehill and Cropredy or the sieges at Banbury, and fuller treatment of events inside the limit but for reasons of space only briefly mentioned here, the interested reader is referred to my previous work, *Edgehill and Beyond* (Alan Sutton, 1992). To Martyn Bennett, Bernard Capp, Peter Gaunt, Colin Hey, Christopher Hill and Ronald Hutton, who wrote generous reviews of that work, I am deeply grateful. I owe a particular debt to the general editors of this series of publications, Robert Smallwood and Robert Bearman, who wear their enviable scholarship so lightly and who as always offered friendship as well as unassuming expertise; and to my wife Thelma, for her invaluable practical help, patience and support. All in their various ways gave the encouragement to pursue a fascinating subject further. The Civil War puzzle can never be completed, but the search for its lost pieces is an unending and absorbing one.

NOTE ON REFERENCES TO PARISHES

Unless otherwise stated in the notes, all references to events and people in individual parishes are to the series of Commonwealth Exchequer Papers, classed SP.28, preserved in the Public Record Office. To avoid unnecessary repetition the respective piece numbers are given in Appendix 7. Photocopies of the two separate surviving Stratford books, sometimes difficult to decipher, may be consulted at The Shakespeare Birthplace Trust Record Office, Stratford-upon-Avon.

Local Civil War Chronology, 1642–7

1642

Jan   King flees London after abortive attempt to arrest five rebellious MPs (4th). Stratford Corporation and county as a whole fearful of insurrection following papist scares.

Mar   Parliament issues Militia Ordinance to wrest control of armed forces from king, and appoints Lord Brooke to replace Earl of Northampton as Lord Lieutenant of Warwickshire. Lord Brooke fortifying Warwick Castle.

Jun   King at York issues Commission of Array instructions to muster Warwickshire forces under Earl of Northampton. Vicar and bailiff of Stratford accused of betraying town by approving billeting of soldiers (3rd). Shottery and Old Stratford manors sold to pay off Sir Charles Smith's debts (10th).

Jun–Jul   Citizens donate money and plate to Warwick Castle to safeguard county from violence. Military rallies held at Stratford, Warwick and elsewhere by Lord Brooke for Parliament and Earl of Northampton for king. Armed confrontation between the two peers near Warmington (30 Jul).

Aug   Royalists unsuccessfully besiege Warwick Castle (c. 4th–22nd). King arrives Stoneleigh, launches abortive assault on Coventry (20th) and withdraws to Nottingham as parliamentary force under Lord Brooke approaches. Royalists routed by Brooke near Southam (23rd), day after king raises standard at Nottingham. Stratford Corporation votes Lord Brooke a further £100 (29th).

Sep–Oct   Military build-up and sporadic pillaging as parliamentary army under Earl of Essex twice crosses district to and from Worcester and Royalists march through Kenilworth to Southam. Stratford invaded by large contingents of parliamentary troops. Officers billeted at New Place.

Oct   County law sessions suspended after soldiers disrupt proceedings at Warwick (4th). Battle of Edgehill (23rd), first major battle of civil war, indecisive.

Nov   Many wounded soldiers scattered throughout district, others crossing county to join king at Oxford; continued pillaging. Royalists capture Broughton Castle and Banbury Castle (*c.* 27th), establishing major garrison at Banbury.

Dec–Jan   Lord Brooke appointed head of parliamentary security association combining Warwickshire and Staffordshire. Violent skirmishing about Banbury involving Prince Rupert.

1643

Jan   Parliamentary force from Warwick refused entry to Stratford by aldermen (7th). Lord Brooke sends Capt. John Needham to occupy town and collect all arms (*c.* 10th).

Feb   Stratford aldermen visit Col. John Bridges, governor of Warwick Castle. Royalists under Col. Joseph Wagstaffe attempt to occupy Stratford. Vicar Henry Twitchet leaves town; curate William Hawling becomes acting vicar. Lord Brooke routs Royalists at Stratford (25th), during which market hall is severely damaged by explosion and Henley-in-Arden is plundered.

Apr   Prince Rupert twice passes through Stratford, to and from storming of Birmingham and Lichfield, to keep open communications between Oxford and York. On return journey, Stratford supplies his men with beer.

May   Stratford and district begin paying regular war taxes to parliamentary authorities at Coventry and Warwick, and intermittently to Royalists at Banbury too.

Jun   Widespread tension as Queen Henrietta Maria approaches Stratford from York. Beauchamp Chapel at Warwick vandalized by Parliamentarians under Col. William Purefoy (14th).

Jul   Queen stays two nights at Stratford (11th–12th), possibly at Shakespeare's New Place, accompanied by Prince Rupert, on way to rejoin king at Kineton and Oxford. Schoolmaster John Trapp briefly imprisoned by Royalists.

Nov–Dec   Parliamentary forces from Warwick occupy Coughton Court, capture Aston Hall (28 Dec) and storm Beoley House, near Redditch, killing catholic inmates (31 Dec).

1644

Feb–Mar   Intense military activity throughout district over Gloucester convoys. Halford bridge destroyed. Stratford occupied by Parliamentarians under Col. Hans Behr, who lodges at New Place twice (mid-Feb; *c.* 6th Mar). Local skirmishing and plundering.

May   Royalist vicar of Welford-on-Avon seized, imprisoned in Warwick Castle, and replaced by John Trapp.

Jun   Col. William Purefoy imposes new tax on Stratford on way to capture Earl of Northampton's seat at Compton Wynyates (8th). Armies of king and Sir William Waller pass twice nearby in build-up to battle of Cropredy (29th).

Jul–Aug Parliamentary regiments of Cols. Thomas Stevens and Thomas Archer under Earl of Denbigh occupy Stratford and Alcester districts on Worcester campaign. First parliamentary siege of Banbury begins (abandoned 25 Oct).

Sep–Oct Continued violence in district. Royalists retaliate against John Trapp in Welford church, who takes refuge in Warwick Castle as garrison chaplain.

Nov   Continued skirmishing as Royalists raid Stratford and invade New Place. Maj. Abraham Pont killed near Pershore (11th), funeral cortège passes through Stratford to Coventry.

Dec   Parliamentary force under Col. Joseph Hawksworth burns Milcote House to the ground (5th) as Royalists garrison Chipping Campden (end Dec).

1645

Jan   Increased royalist presence in district. Sir William Compton's Banbury Royalists fail to recapture Compton Wynyates from Maj. George Purefoy (30th).

Feb   Parliamentarians under Col. John Bridges storm and destroy Lark Stoke House near Ilmington (c. 7th).

Spring   Royalists raiding at Loxley (Feb), Halford (Mar) and Sherbourne (Apr), when they rampage through Stratford extorting money. Outbreak of plague in Stratford.

May   Parliamentary forces of Maj. Anthony Buller, under Gen. Oliver Cromwell, occupy Stratford district, with Cromwell at Southam, Warwick and Kenilworth, in build-up to Naseby. Col. Edward Massey storms and occupies Evesham (26th).

Jun   Decisive parliamentary victory at Naseby (14th). District flooded with troops under Sir Thomas Fairfax and Cromwell, who lodge at Clifford Chambers (23rd).

Jul–Aug District twice invaded by Scots under Earl of Leven marching to and from Hereford, then more Parliamentarians under Cols. Sydenham Poyntz and Edward Rossiter marching to pursue king in Worcestershire.

Sep   Vicar of Adderbury killed in ambush (12th). Cross-country royalist raiding from Rugby (27th) to Charlecote and Stratford (28th).

Dec   Stratford bridge broken at request of Worcestershire Parliamentarians to cut communications between Oxford and the west.

1646

Jan   Citizens compile claims for compensation for war losses to submit to authorities at Coventry. Royalists destroy Wormleighton House (7th).

Mar   Sir William Brereton lodges at New Place (*c.* 20th) on way to defeat last royalist army under Lord Astley at Stow-on-the-Wold (21st). Troops of Col. Thomas Morgan quartering and looting in district.

May   King surrenders to Scots at Newark (5th). Banbury Royalists surrender to second long parliamentary siege (9th).

Jun–Jul   Stratford again on transit route for parliamentarian siege of Worcester (mid-Jun). Successive royalist capitulations of Oxford (25 June) and Worcester (23 Jul) signal end of war.

Aug   Parliament orders disbanding of all troops except at Warwick and Coventry.

Sep   Curate William Hawling leaves Stratford to make way for Puritan Alexander Bean. Horse fair thriving (24th).

1647

Feb–Mar   Church authorities belatedly confirm expulsion of Stratford vicar Henry Twitchet, replaced by Alexander Bean.

CHAPTER 1

A Divided Community

In the spring of 1636, Thomas Wilson, the puritan vicar of Stratford-upon-Avon, on one of his periodic London visits, was staying at the house of a merchant in Milk Street, near Shakespeare's old lodging. Embittered by recent personal experience at home but uplifted by contacts with the celebrated Blackfriars preacher William Gouge, he wrote fervently to his 'very much honor'd friend', the devout parliamentarian Sir Robert Harley, on the theme of godly duties in a corrupt society:

> Worship God in spirit and truth, hating vaine fictions and inventions and loving God's law. Shun now as pernicious the errors of the wicked and the spots of the world . . . Save your selfe from this untoward generation; 'tis a contending age. Love not the world![1]

Wilson was one of a significant minority of clergy across the south Midlands convinced that their church and country were facing a deepening crisis. Civil war was six years away and unthinkable, but a dangerous polarization in political and religious circles was increasingly evident and popular discontent was rising. Evidence of moral decay was only too easy to find for a puritan vicar surveying the district he had served for the past seventeen years. The Stratford countryside had for years been plagued by lawless vagrants, and the town itself, despite the affluence of its leading citizens and the prosperity of its trade, was overburdened with a huge destitute underclass which it repeatedly refused to support. Ungodly actors had been wandering through the country, performing at Solihull, Meriden, Coventry, Kineton, Wormleighton, Charlecote and Stratford itself, some being imprisoned at Banbury in 1633. Near Chipping Campden the brutish Cotswold Games continued as popular as ever, condemned by the godly as an epitome of vice yet mischievously celebrated by the poet laureate and Puritan-baiter Ben Jonson. Outside Stratford, poets and drinkers caroused at the Rainsfords' Manor House at Clifford Chambers, while even nearer, across Clopton Bridge, minstrels and dilettantes amused idle minds in the great Tudor hall of the disgraced Earl of Middlesex's mansion at Milcote. The nation's leaders themselves set no example. The flighty young catholic queen loved the theatre, the king was preoccupied with artistic patronage and, it was later said, read Shakespeare more frequently than the Bible, while even the good Sir Thomas Lucy entertained wandering players at Charlecote and had dubious French and Italian books in his library.

The Forest of Arden to the north had long been, according to a recent commentator, 'a lurking place of mad squires of extreme conservatism', while to the south, powerful reactionary landowners like the Earl of Northampton and great catholic gentry like Robert Throckmorton and William Sheldon effectively obstructed the spread of enlightened social ideals on their vast estates scattered across the countryside.[2]

Nor was Stratford likely to have become a model of virtue since the catalogue of misdemeanour dealt with by the church courts since the 1590s. Although not specifically accused, like Rugby, of harbouring bear-baiters and prostitutes as sabbath alternatives to the pulpit, of being a haunt of depravity like Alcester, or of relishing morris dancing 'and other heathenish customs' like Henley-in-Arden, it had until recently possessed a maypole, still had a bull-ring and bowling alley, had broken its own ban on the performance of plays and, as a thriving market and brewing centre, contained many large and flourishing taverns, always a focus for disorder and blasphemy, as when a Worcestershire man tippling in a Stratford alehouse declared that 'our Saviour Christ was a bastard and our Virgin Mary a whore'. Unchristian wrangling encouraged by the town's very commercial success embittered daily life as controversy and sometimes violence dogged issues as diverse as the encroachment on its commons, the enclosures at Welcombe, the completion of the new market hall, the management of the mills on the River Avon, the exploitation of the river for commercial navigation, the appointment of the vicar and, as ever, the vexed question of church seating, as self-important townsmen competed for the best pews. In 1637, in a bitter legal dispute with Shakespeare's daughter Susanna, the prominent alderman Baldwin Brooks (later to become the town bailiff) had the doors and the poet's 'Study of books' at New Place broken and books seized. Like most small communities at the time, Stratford was certainly no stranger to petty violence.[3]

It was inevitably, however, the purely religious question which caused Wilson his deepest anxiety, at both local and national levels. Although Stratford had a long puritan tradition which had caused trouble in the past, the neighbourhood as a whole had been a permanent haunt of catholic families, some wealthy and influential, many more inoffensive artisans and labourers, but all, lumped together, easily seen as potentially subversive, as at the time of the not-too-distant Gunpowder Plot, which had indeed implicated some of the leading families in the district. Although by now the title of lord of the manor carried few actual rights, the local situation was far from healthy. Stratford was held by the disgraced old Earl of Middlesex, permanently absent from his nearby seat at Milcote and politically suspect, while the manors of Old Stratford and Shottery were about to pass from the debt-ridden catholic Sir Charles Smith of Wootton Wawen, busy felling all his timber to support his family and soon to be a leading suspect in a further papist scare, to an equally dubious catholic relative resident in Sussex.[4]

The town's elders had become largely hostile to Wilson, as he had recently found to his cost. His initial appointment in 1619 had been marked by abuse, rioting and smashed church windows, and libellous doggerel had been distributed in taverns, events culminating in a Star Chamber investigation. Like his friend Samuel Clarke, the reforming vicar of nearby Alcester, Wilson had followed his father's example by attempting to wage a moral crusade among his flock, enforcing church discipline more vigorously than before, removing the maypole, attacking drunkenness and condemning those who profaned the sabbath. The situation had deteriorated to the point where his own church had excommunicated him for nonconformity – a measure he had treated with contempt – and, more recently, another bitter climax had come when the visitation by Archbishop Laud's representative in June 1635 had ended in a damning personal indictment and temporary suspension from office. A petition against him signed by many townspeople had been submitted, his own bishop had condemned him and he had scandalized notable members of his congregation by outspoken personal attacks in sermons. As if that were not enough, he had displayed his contempt for the false vanity of outward reverence by keeping his dog and farmyard animals in the Guild Chapel and allowing his children to play ball there. The result was that, only days before his trip to London in May 1636, his request for an increased allowance to minister to his large parish of two thousand communicants had been refused. Outside the circle of his clergymen friends he had found a few staunch allies, like William Combe, the prominent Justice of the Peace and the one notable puritan landowner in Stratford, and his doctor, John Hall, Shakespeare's son-in-law, who had treated him for an eye infection, supported him in the council chamber and had himself been ejected as a troublemaker. Wilson was evidently dealt with leniently by the church authorities because he was acknowledged as being conscientious, learned and the son of a respected dean of Worcester – and because he had promised to mend his ways. But his position was becoming untenable. 'Wearied with suits', as he admitted in 1637, he would not live to see his country slide into civil war; but had he done so there is no doubt that he would have taken up the parliamentary cause with fervour or, like many godly commentators, attributed its horrors to divine retribution on an ungodly people.[5]

During this long, unhappy period the vicar of Stratford had kept up morale by regular contacts with a wide circle of radical, zealous clergy in the district, 'gadding to sermons', (as the scoffers described the puritan habit of travelling to hear as many as possible) and by attending lectures by visiting celebrity preachers. Among such were Thomas Dugard, Master of Warwick school, elderly scholars like the brothers-in-law William Whateley of Banbury and Robert Harris of Hanwell, both of whom visited Stratford periodically to preach, and John Poynter, who lectured at Wootton Wawen in 1630 and later at Hornton and lived at Warwick – not forgetting more distant allies like, as we have seen, his 'reverend friend' William Gouge when in London. Above all he had the constant comfort of discussing sermons and scriptures with his three closest clergymen friends, John Bryan, vicar of Barford and soon to become chaplain to Warwick's parliamentary garrison, Samuel Clarke, the radical vicar of Alcester, and John Trapp, the well-respected Stratford schoolmaster who was also minister of Weston-on-Avon. In these anxious, contentious times, even moderate conservatives like Sir William Dugdale were tempted to see in such circles, perhaps with some justice, a kind of holy mafia engaged in systematically subverting orthodox belief and stirring up the public against rightful authority. Wilson's dilemma vividly illustrates aspects of the deepening religious divide of the immediate pre-war years in an area already marked by a profound spiritual diversity and much mutual intolerance. To the west, in neighbouring Worcestershire, bigotry would soon force the moderate Puritan Richard Baxter to flee for his life, while in the opposite direction the Puritans themselves violently confronted their own outspoken vicar, John Howes, at Banbury, who was actually forced into prison for a time. Archbishop Laud's unpopular directives, widely if unjustly seen as paving the way for a return to Catholicism identified with idolatry and even, perhaps, the ultimate horror of foreign invasion, were alienating even moderate opinion and making religious uniformity more elusive than ever. In places, as at tiny Barcheston in 1635, altar rails were being obediently installed while in others they were being removed or smashed. At Stratford, the lurid wall paintings in the Guild Chapel had already proved contentious, as they were to prove at Alcester too. Voicing the fears of many moderates, Wilson's young neighbour Thomas Warmstry at Whitchurch condemned Laud's policies in 1640, arguing that images, altars and crucifixes brought the church 'into suspition of inclination to Popery, the poyson of the Church', while reports from adjacent counties claimed that, there too, 'Altar-Priests [i.e. ultra-conservative, High Church] have poysoned the people'.[6]

Perhaps the most dramatic evidence of puritan frustration was the exodus of a significant minority in the Pilgrim Fathers movement to find refuge in the New World, begun in 1620 and now given fresh impetus by Laud's divisive policies of the 1630s. In this national movement, two godly local peers took the lead: the uncompromising young radical Robert Greville, Lord Brooke, of Warwick Castle, who hated Laud almost as much for being a social upstart as for his religious views; and his elderly parliamentarian colleague, Lord Saye and Sele, of Broughton Castle near Banbury. Both consistently resisted Court-and-Church policies in the 1630s. Brooke had pointedly absented himself from home when Charles I visited Warwick in August 1636 and allied himself with Lord Saye, both in opposing Ship Money and in refusing the Oath of Allegiance. Each found himself in prison at York in April 1639. But even before, both peers had been busily placing godly protégés in local parishes in order to further a reformist programme and allying themselves with others soon to play prominent roles on Parliament's side in the war, like Sir Arthur Haselrig, John Pym and Sir William Waller, in establishing puritan colonies in New England. Both had themselves originally intended emigrating there. At least two contacts of the vicar of Stratford left the district to make the hazardous journey: in 1638, George Willis, a wealthy landowner from Fenny Compton with estates in Stratford, Clopton, Welcombe and Bishopton, who had twice married into Stratford families, was related to the Puritan William Combe and maintained a regular correspondence from Connecticut with Stratford relatives, including Wilson's ally John Trapp; and in 1639, Ephraim Huitt, minister of Wroxall, a small refuge of puritanism in a largely catholic district, who was 'driven out', according to friends, 'by the Tyranny of the Prelaticall Party'. Stratford's vicar would have been fully conversant with these thrilling yet ominous developments.[7]

The defiance of Wilson and his more celebrated colleagues stemmed from the conviction that the reform of the English Church, begun in the sixteenth century, was now dangerously undermined by Archbishop Laud's retrograde policies, a situation made even more desperate by its local dimension. For, unlike neighbouring Northamptonshire and Oxfordshire, Warwickshire conspicuously lacked both a major puritan centre like Northampton and Banbury and any substantial number of nonconformist gentry willing to combat the supposed slide to popery, let alone anything resembling an organized opposition movement. Isolated puritan families like the Purefoys in the extreme north of the county and the Burgoynes of Wroxall, or odd individuals like Clement Throckmorton of Haseley, Thomas Lucy of Charlecote, William Combe of Stratford and Anthony Stoughton of Warwick, could hardly provide a counterweight to the status of the great interrelated catholic landowners like the Coughton Throckmortons, the Sheldons, Smiths and Morgans. Although in Warwickshire as a whole the number of Catholics was small – no more than two per cent of the total population – these were mostly concentrated in the south and south-west, as Ann Hughes has pointed out: 'a cohesive, much inter-married group, and in the villages they dominated, recusancy flourished in all ranks of society'. Long before the Gunpowder Plot involved the Stratford neighbourhood, when the prominent Henley Street Catholic George Badger was found receiving incriminating relics from Clopton House, the whole district, including the adjacent parts of Worcestershire and Gloucestershire, had been recognized as a veritable haven for Catholics. Under Elizabeth, the Bishop of Worcester had admitted that his diocese, which included most of this area of Warwickshire, was 'as dangerous as any place that I know', with scores of recusants being regularly reported to the authorities, 'besides retainers, wanderers and secret lurkers dispersed in forty several parishes . . . many of them not only of good wealth but of great alliance'. Some were doubtless actively propagating their faith: the wealthy Lady Alice Dudley, daughter of Sir Thomas Leigh of Stoneleigh, presented many locally manufactured silver-gilt Gothic revival chalices and communion plate to churches in her patronage, six being donated in 1638 alone, to Ashow, Kenilworth, Leek Wootton, Monks Kirby, Ladbroke and Stoneleigh. Such news must have seemed to Wilson and his allies confirmation of their worst fears. Certainly, when war came no simple equation between Catholicism and militant royalism could be made, since the majority of catholic families were too impoverished and alienated by Charles's punitive taxation policies of the 1630s to take up arms for him. But the major catholic landowners in Warwickshire did indeed champion the king's cause and provided sons and relatives for his army. Catholics had long been seen as politically unreliable, fears of popish plots were widespread, and at times of crisis Catholics, real or suspected, could be seen, however unjustly, as an easily identifiable enemy within. Once the war began, they therefore became automatic targets for puritan anger.[8]

For their part the conservatives' fear of leading Puritans like Lord Brooke and Lord Saye was equally strong; they were popularly viewed as extremists, 'strangely tainted', as Sir William Dugdale put it, 'with fanatic principles used to stir up all persons'. By encouraging butchers, bakers and candlestick-makers to become preachers they were furthering social anarchy. In a much-publicized incident in November 1643, Lord Brooke's former miller and a grocer friend preached to a large congregation, including many women who clearly ought to have been engaged in seemly domestic duties, in an open-air conventicle in Humbridge quarry at Coten End, outside Warwick, a scandal only to be expected, a caustic royalist journalist commented, of those like Lord Brooke who 'made their Stable-grooms Preachers' and encouraged the desecration of churches. Such fears were confirmed at the very outset of the war by the deliberate vandalism by Parliament's soldiers in the district in the name of godly reform, and were before long to fuel the persecution of the Quakers, seen in their turn as subversive troublemakers likely to usher in what one of the war's most popular ballads termed 'a world turned upside-down'.[9]

It is against this ominous background of national and local disharmony and apprehension that a new stage in Stratford's own problems must be seen, when in December 1638 its controversial vicar suddenly died, possibly of the plague which had returned to the district, and, ironically, just as the long disputes seemed to be resolved and his maintenance allowance restored. This event evidently threw the Stratford elders into disarray. A chaotic eighteen months elapsed before the vacancy was filled, during which rival claimants and interested parties lobbied various authorities amid renewed attempts by the corporation to gain the legal right to appoint their minister themselves. Their own immediate choice of successor – suggesting that anti-puritan sentiment was neither unanimous nor narrowly doctrinaire – was the much-respected Robert Harris of Hanwell, near Banbury, whom Wilson had succeeded in 1629 in engaging to lecture regularly at Stratford, where Sir Thomas Lucy and 'a great confluence of the chiefest Gentlemen and choicest Preachers and Professors in those parts' would travel to hear him. The lord of the manor, the elderly Earl of Middlesex, was appealed to by the corporation to exert influence on Harris's behalf. But although thought at first to be sympathetic, he was evidently non-committal – understandably, since the earl was a life-long friend of the near-catholic Godfrey Goodman, Bishop of Gloucester, was related to the dilettante courtier Sir John Suckling, and had expressed strong views against nonconformists in the past. Harris, in any case, was elderly and reluctant to leave Hanwell. At the same time, two other local vicars travelled to London to try to secure the incumbency, both with puritan credentials: Thomas Warmstry of Whitchurch, young but already controversial, and John Salisbury of nearby Clifford Chambers – probably the 'Mr Salisbury' harassed by Laud over a sermon bemoaning the 'shipwreck of faith' in 'our deplorable England' threatened by popery, and recently in trouble over the more mundane matter of highway repairs from Clifford to Stratford.[10] Both candidates were strongly opposed in a petition signed by the bailiff and twenty leading citizens who, while complaining about being left 'destitute a full yeare or more', were presumably anxious, after Wilson's turbulent regime, to avoid further contention, and in April 1640 the Crown authorities in London nominated an obscure Hertfordshire clergyman, Henry Twitchet, to the Stratford living. Twitchet, who had recently been given the incumbency of a Huntingdon parish but had no known Warwickshire connections, had a wife and family to support, and the town corporation promptly approved a comprehensive restoration programme, in effect a rebuilding, for the long-unused vicarage before the new vicar moved in. Shortly after, he took leases of the churchyard and the chapel orchard opposite Shakespeare's old garden, arranged for furniture to be made by local craftsmen, approved urgent repairs to the church roof and tower and had its windows restored by the glazier John Scriven. At first, Twitchet seems to have settled in to a harmonious relationship with some of his predecessor's puritan friends like Thomas Dugard and John Trapp the schoolmaster, and to have successfully combined Stratford with his Huntingdonshire duties. But a crisis was now looming nationally, and his reign at Stratford was to be a short one.[11]

CHAPTER 2

The Coming of War

National events were now building up a sombre momentum of their own, and both Stratford and its new vicar were soon to be caught up in them. But England in the mid–1630s was not yet a country on the verge of civil war. In 1636 the king was lavishly entertained at Warwick Castle (though not by its puritan owner, Lord Brooke, who managed to be elsewhere), and the following year he declared himself the happiest ruler in Europe. Life and business continued much as usual. From Myton, Lord Conway's bailiff wrote to his master in London with news of his estates around Alcester and Stratford: whether William Combe was to take out the new lease or not, which horses were to be sold at the fair, how good brick-making clay had been found at Luddington, and whether William Sandys's controversial scheme for making the Avon navigable might affect the mills. The elderly Earl of Middlesex would still come down to spend an occasional Christmas amid a whirl of activity and excitement at Milcote, and to be reminded gently by the Stratford bailiff, Nathaniel Duppa, of his promise to present him with a prime buck from Kenilworth Park. The London coaches still clattered out of Warwick, Stratford and Kineton several times a week, bound for the Queen's Head at St Giles or the Rose and Crown in High Holborn. The summer fields were filled with new crops of woad for the local dyers, and coal from north Warwickshire was stocked at Barford Wharf awaiting transport to Lady Lucy's at Charlecote.[1] Later, during the austere Commonwealth years, Lord Clarendon and other elderly conservatives were to recall the decade as a halcyon period when civilized social values still flourished, the age of Inigo Jones and Van Dyck, of courtly poets and lutenists, of aesthetes and philosophers discoursing at idyllic Great Tew across the county border in Oxfordshire. Yet nearer Stratford, at Broughton Castle, Lord Saye was presiding over a very different kind of gathering, of radicals plotting in a secret roof-top chamber, it was rumoured, comprising a roll call of implacable Parliamentarians like Pym and Hampden and the Lords Brooke, Holland, Essex, Bedford and Warwick. Deprived by the king's dissolution of Parliament of any forum for discontent, such men provided a hint of organized opposition, which coexisted, for the moment, with the old order. The potential for conflict clearly existed: the Milton of the courtly masque *Comus* was also the admirer of Lord Brooke who could write sardonically, 'I shall beleeve there cannot be a more illboding signe to a Nation then when the Inhabitants, to avoid unsufferable grievances at home, are inforc'd by heaps to forsake their native Country'.[2] All that was required was a further deterioration of the political climate; and that was exactly what was provided at the end of the 1630s by a whole catalogue of ill-considered or mismanaged royal initiatives, exploited by shrewd political operators like Pym and Hampden able to tap popular discontent. Of these, the widespread resentment of the king's money-raising policies, and particularly Ship Money, over which Stratford's corporation, like many other local communities, evidently agonized, Charles's humiliation by the Scots over his religious policy, and his complicity in the Army Plot, were only the most obvious. When to these were added sporadic violence in the summer of 1640 (some in Warwickshire, where a planned rendezvous of 600 local recruits for the ill-fated Scottish venture turned nasty and Stratford's council voted to share out the town's gunpowder and shot among its chief citizens), the shock waves produced by the arrest of Laud and the execution of the king's favourite, Strafford, and, above all, the hysteria unleashed by the massacre of English protestant settlers in Ulster by Irish Catholics in November 1641, the point of no return had almost been reached. By any standard these were crisis years.[3] The shrewd Midland observer Richard Baxter later recalled the Irish rebellion as a watershed in pushing the country towards a state of war; and one of the first public duties of Stratford's new vicar, as destitute refugees from Ireland began to appear in the district, was to act as official receiver for the generous charity donations which flooded in from rich and poor to help 'the distressed Protestants in Ireland'.[4]

This disastrous national sequence coincided, moreover, with more unsettling developments in Warwickshire and in Stratford itself – some accidental, others less so. Local religious dissension came out into the open as a series of county petitions, well organized by puritan gentry, flooded in to Parliament. Two from Warwickshire submitted on 12 February and certainly approved, if not actually masterminded by Lord Brooke, highlighted the county's 'sad condition' over the last ten years. Warwickshire, it was claimed, was 'swarming' with Catholics, good people everywhere were in constant fear of insurrection and drastic measures were needed: papists should be disarmed, 'scandalous' clergy removed in favour of 'godly, able, painfull preaching Ministers', all relics of superstition and idolatry rooted out. Then in March 1641, compounding (as always in such cases) widespread suspicion of divine retribution, another of Stratford's periodic fires ravaged the affluent Bridge Street area, causing an estimated £20,000 worth of destruction. In August of the same year the ambitious Lord Brooke replaced Sir Thomas Lucy, who had recently died, as Recorder of Stratford, a position which would have made confrontation with the recusant lord of the manors of Shottery and Old Stratford, Sir Charles Smith, and with at least some members of the town's corporation, inevitable sooner or later had the war not intervened. Then dramatically, in November 1641, coinciding exactly with the horrific news from Ireland, Parliament was informed that, as in 1605, south Warwickshire was at the heart of more dangerous catholic subversion, with a plot 'to take away the lives of some members of this House and to disturb the peace of the kingdome', with Robert Throckmorton, William Sheldon, Thomas Morgan and Sir Charles Smith suspected as ringleaders. No matter that the plot turned out to be imaginary; in an increasing atmosphere of panic, deepened further by the king's rash and illegal attempt to arrest five rebellious members on the floor of the

House of Commons in January 1642 before fleeing from a capital which seemed on the brink of revolution, orders were given to prevent 'unlawful assemblies' and to double the watch throughout the county, 'upon the motion of divers inhabitants and consideration had of the present time'.[5] As in Worcestershire, where militiamen were warned to be ready at an hour's notice – armed – Stratford's corporation thought it advisable to replenish the town's armoury: 'Itt is ordered thatt 1c waite of powder shall be forthwith bought for the use of the Chamber.' In January 1642 the curate Simon Trapp died and was replaced by William Hawling, who was to serve the town throughout the war years. A worsening economic climate added to the general discontent as merchants and traders everywhere complained of threats to livelihood and land values continued to fall. Recalling Falstaff's memorable comment on the economic effects of civil war, that 'you may buy land now as cheap as stinking mackerel', George Willis had already reported to his father from Warwickshire in April 1640 that 'the times are so ill and things so unsettled that I cannot sell any land except for an extreme under value', and the complaint was to be echoed repeatedly throughout the war years. The vicar of tiny Whatcote protested to Parliament at what was fast becoming a national scandal – the disappearance of building timber due to irresponsible tree-felling in ancient woods. At Kenilworth, popular resentment was voiced at illegal evictions blamed indirectly on the queen. Apprehension was spreading. From near Stratford the vicar of Whitchurch, Thomas Warmstry, warned that desperate remedies to the country's ills were needed: 'It is no time to stand discussing of niceties, to stand upon ceremonies and formalities, when a whole Church and Kingdome is under a desperate disease.' Reading the signals, the astute Lord Brooke began fortifying Warwick Castle, raising walls, constructing ramparts, buying gunpowder. When the king, having despatched his wife to Holland to collect soldiers and war supplies, moved north to establish his court at York, a critical impasse had clearly been reached. Charles had lost control, and had abandoned his capital to the opposition. The resort to arms seemed only a short step away.[6]

Religious divisions, too, were hardening, but not yet to the point where consensus was impossible in the face of the national emergency presented by the news from Ireland. As elsewhere, those digging deep into their pockets at Stratford in response to the public appeals to help the Irish victims came from all sides of the town's political and religious spectrum and represented virtually every household. Thus while the wealthy Puritan William Combe headed the list of donations with by far the biggest contribution of £13 6s. 8d., other notable donors included the future Royalists, bailiff John Woolmer and chief alderman Baldwin Brooks. The puritan schoolmaster, John Trapp and the new royalist vicar collected side by side, as they had done the previous year for the victims of the fire which had ravaged the town centre. But at the same time the legitimate fears aroused by the plight of the 'distressed Protestants' were not allowed to subside by radicals like Lord Brooke, eager to exploit the situation for wider political aims. In a developing war of words there was a new spate of local petitions to Parliament, a major instrument of parliamentary activists like Brooke, Saye and Pym (and one involving, according to Clarendon, widespread fraud and

Spencer Compton, second Earl of Northampton (1601–43).
Courtier and personal friend of Charles I long before the war, he was prominent among the peers declaring loyalty to the king at York and was immediately impeached by Parliament for disobeying its summons to return to London. Appointed the king's chief representative in Warwickshire, he recruited energetically, lodged with Stratford's bailiff, John Woolmer, when organizing the mass royalist rally outside the town on 29 July 1642, and attempted unsuccessfully to wrest the initiative from his arch-rival, Lord Brooke. Present with Prince Rupert in Worcestershire, at Banbury and Edgehill, he died heroically at the minor battle of Hopton Heath, near Stafford, in March 1643.
(The Marquess of Northampton)

intimidation), in order to pressurize public opinion. One typical one, presented at Westminster in February 1642 by a Warwickshire delegation, 'here present in the behalf of themselves and many others of the said county', has all the hallmarks of a Brooke initiative. Skilfully combining sensitive religious and political issues with popular support for 'the speedy Relief of bleeding Ireland', it congratulated Parliament on its intention to abolish bishops, pursue further drastic religious reform, arrest conservative 'delinquents' and make nationwide military preparations. It is unlikely to be a coincidence that, at the same time, Lord Brooke was voted 'to be intrusted with the Militia of the Kingdom' in Warwickshire, to replace the king's ally, the defiant Earl of Northampton, prominent among the group of peers swearing loyalty to Charles at York.[7]

The one single issue which forced the pace more than any other in the spring of 1642 was that of the control of the armed forces. Troops were needed both to suppress the Irish rebels and, no doubt, to guard against local disturbances. But the king was widely distrusted, and Parliament decided to name its own lords lieutenant in the counties, hitherto a main instrument of royal centralized authority and therefore a clearly provocative step. In Warwickshire, Parliament appointed Lord Brooke as lord lieutenant to replace the Earl of Northampton, with Stratford's William Combe as one of his deputies, a move clearly representing a key stage in the developing struggle for power. A contest for supremacy in the county now looked unavoidable. Shortly after, in the king's continued absence from London, Parliament further voted itself the power to raise troops, in the Militia Ordinance of 5 March. When the king was rebuffed, this time in person, at Hull in April, and invited nobles like the Earl of Northampton and Lord Dunsmore to join him at York at a time when Lord Brooke was making the running in Warwickshire, the polarization seemed irreversible. Some commentators already feared the worst. The Norfolk Member of Parliament Thomas Knyvett wrote to his wife in May: ''Tis to be fear'd this thretning storme will not be allay'd without some showers of bloode' – a gloomy prediction soon to be echoed at Stratford. In early June, when Old Stratford and Shottery manors were finally being transferred away from the impoverished Sir Charles Smith to his kinsman John Caryll of Sussex, Charles made a belated attempt to regain the initiative by issuing his own call to arms, delegating military authority in Warwickshire to the Earl of Northampton and Lord Dunsmore in order to reassert his control over local defence forces through the so-called Commissions of Array (see Appendix 4). Although Warwickshire's was the first of these to be issued, on 6 June, there was much delay in finalizing details, and, moreover, a serious misreading of the situation in Warwickshire, when a newsletter from York on 17 June complacently noted the overwhelming loyalty of 'all the Baronets, Knights and Esquires of note' in the county, apart from isolated known troublemakers like William Purefoy, William Combe of Stratford and a few others, 'which are not many'.[8] The result was that before the king's party could act, Parliament on 7 June ordered a series of military rallies in Warwickshire to be organized by the deputy lieutenants, among whom was William Combe, and was soon calling for additional emergency measures to help 'King and Parliament', as the deliberately ambiguous term went. These included principally the raising of troops and the collection of money and plate to be either sold or melted down for ammunition, to which, as before in the Irish emergency, Stratford responded generously as future political rivals in the town joined together in a long-term operation lasting many months. Arms and horses were being rounded up, and further collections made at Stratford, this time to maintain soldiers billeted at Evesham in May or June. It is not always clear on whose authority some of the more local measures were taken, but again Lord Brooke seems the likely instigator. Events were now gathering speed. Attempting to retrieve a situation rapidly escalating out of control, and conscious that, with Lord Brooke's hostile intentions increasingly clear, Warwickshire was likely to be in the forefront of the national struggle for power, the king despatched his devoted ally the Earl of Northampton to lead the group of Warwickshire commissioners entrusted with carrying out the royal mandate there. In an attempt to make Coventry the Royalists' regional capital in opposition to the threat from Warwick Castle, Northampton arrived at the great Midland city on 25 June, as both its recorder and Charles's personal envoy, in order to coerce the city leaders into rallying behind the king. But even though the leading citizens were far from being unanimously hostile to the king, the royalist attempt was bodged and the earl himself was forced to escape ignominiously through the back door of the Black Bull Inn, the whole attempt proving counterproductive. It enabled the leading local Puritan John Barker to alert his friend Lord Brooke, who promptly seized the initiative, took control in Coventry, transferred the county magazine thence to Warwick (where five shillings was paid to the bellringers 'at my Lords comeing downe') and, assisted by local Puritans like William Combe of Stratford and Edward Peyto of Chesterton as his deputies, put the parliamentary Militia Ordinance into effect. The result was that a month before the Royalists could organize any comparable show of force in the county, a series of military rallies was held for Parliament, beginning at Stratford on 30 June, while Lord Brooke exhorted his newly elected captains at the castle 'to fight the good fight for the Lord of hosts, your religion and freedom of your consciences'.[9]

The rival military rallies were broadly similar. Intended as a day of action to mobilize support, they combined an official declaration of policy to satisfy the more thoughtful with the main purpose of recruiting, a process helped by thinly disguised bribes to pressurize the waverers. They were evidently colourful occasions, accompanied by marching, shouting and much feasting. Lord Brooke's accounts include payments of more than £85 for refreshments and even overnight accommodation for these few days of musters, both extremely welcome in the summer to those reportedly travelling many weary miles from outlying parishes. Officers recruited by drum beat, notables parading on horseback, field exercises were held, rusty weapons checked, identifying 'colours' distributed and handsome offers of five shillings per week wages made, irresistible to many a starving country lad – while Stratford's taverns did a brisk trade, particularly the 'Lion' (probably the White Lion), where Lord Brooke himself dined at a separate table with his chiefs of staff. Here alone, on 30 June 1642, large quantities of wine, beer, beef, bread and venison pasties were consumed, and musicians paid to offer ongoing entertainment (*see illustration, page 14*). The chamberlain, Thomas Horne, was required to contribute £1 15s. from the town's funds 'for provitione for the Company at the Lion', while shortly after, further payments were made to John Rutter at the Maidenhead for wine 'for the entertayning of Colonell Fines [Fiennes]'. Volunteers trooped in from all parts to be welcomed at appropriate locations, the Henley-in-Arden contingent, for example, at the Maidenhead, Shakespeare's boyhood home, in Henley Street. In all, £104 15s. 3d. was allocated in the accounts of Joseph Hawksworth, Lord Brooke's steward, for expenses incurred 'in settling the Militia' in the district.[10] It was not until weeks later, when Lord Brooke had returned to London for consultation, that, ignoring a parliamentary order to arrest anyone attempting to enforce the illegal royalist Commission of Array, the Earl of Northampton belatedly issued his own instructions for similar royalist musters, giving village constables a week's notice to summon as many armed men and volunteers as possible to mass meetings, beginning at Southam and continuing, on Friday 29 July, 'in a meadow beyond Stratford' (*see illustration, page 18*). At the Stratford rally, unlike Brooke's earlier one apparently, the earl had the active support of a number of the town's wealthier and more committed citizens. These included Thomas Dighton, the only Stratford inhabitant whose royalist credentials were sufficiently well known for the great local historian Dugdale to include him in his celebrated list of Warwickshire partisans (see Appendix 1), but who soon fled the town; Thomas

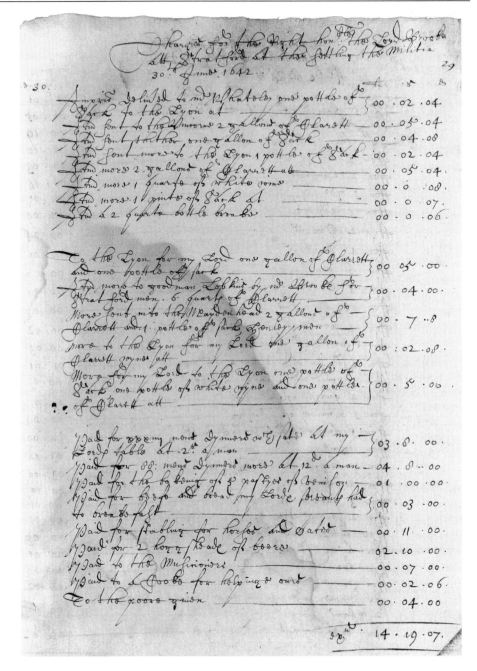

Lord Brooke's Stratford Banquet. *As war approached in the summer of 1642, Lord Brooke took the initiative in organizing parliamentary recruiting campaigns and mass rallies in Warwickshire, the first of these being held at Stratford on 30 June. As Englishmen were traditionally reluctant to engage in military service and political apathy was widespread among ordinary people, both sides offered inducements and bribes to attract recruits, and Lord Brooke laid on banquets and overnight accommodation for volunteers to the parliamentary cause. The document details the entertainment, consisting of a banquet accompanied by music, provided in the White Lion, Unicorn and Maidenhead taverns in Stratford for dinner and breakfast, with Lord Brooke attending in person at the Lion. For a full transcript, see Appendix 6.*

(Warwickshire County Record Office)

*Robert Greville, Lord Brooke. Long conspicuous in his active opposition to Charles I's policies pre-war, Lord Brooke quickly emerged as Parliament's ablest Midlands commander when war finally came. Judging Stratford politically unreliable, he forcibly disarmed the town early in 1643 before routing Royalists attempting to fortify it a few weeks later, but was killed shortly after at the siege of Lichfield. As a formidable parliamentary orator and radical puritan scholar, he was much admired by John Milton, and, had he lived, would undoubtedly have played a major role in national as well as local politics. This near-contemporary engraving reminds us that by no means all 'Roundheads' cropped their hair.
(The Shakespeare Birthplace Trust)*

Hitchcock, also soon reported to have left the town to live in royalist garrison towns; Thomas Greene, the lawyer friend, and possibly cousin, of Shakespeare; William Lindon from the High Street, later to be accused by Parliament of unspecified 'scandalous behaviour'; Nicholas Ryland, a churchwarden, from Sheep Street; William Hiccox, from the prominent family well known to Shakespeare; and Edward Wagstaffe from Bridgetown. At the head of these was the current bailiff or mayor, John Woolmer, at whose substantial house in High Street both the Earl of Northampton and Lord Dunsmore lodged. Not content that day with 'consorting in a Company together in a Warlike posture in a meadow beyond Stratford', some or all of these shortly after rode armed to pay their homage to Charles at Stoneleigh, when he arrived to take personal command, and aided the Earl of Northampton in his subsequent siege of Warwick Castle.[11]

Such open partisanship clearly helped significantly to raise the political temperature in a small town even before the war had begun, as local animosities sharpened and occasional violence erupted. In a court case years after, an ex-Warwick Castle soldier from Stratford, Thomas Sharpe, recalled being attacked by a royalist collarmaker, William Greene, in a Stratford street, 'with a great Clubb in his hand, and unexpectedly and without any provocacon, cryeing Have at you, Parliament Rogue!'. Greene was, he claimed, 'an inveterate Malignant, who hath sevralle tymes raysed the rabble people of the said Towne against the Parliament souldiers' (*see illustration, page 16*). Similarly, the new vicar and bailiff Woolmer were accused of 'betraying the Towne' by approving the billeting of royalist soldiers – a contentious issue in Stratford, as two years previously the town had objected to paying Coat and Conduct money to troops. In view of this, later parliamentary claims that the corporation actually invited the Royalists to occupy Stratford may have

A Stratford Brawl. As everywhere, Stratford's citizens were divided in allegiance, and passions must often have run so high as to boil over into actual violence on the town's streets. In one such incident, Thomas Sharpe, a parliamentary soldier serving under Major Joseph Hawksworth at Warwick Castle, was attacked by William Green, one of Stratford's many collarmakers, 'with a great Clubb in his hand'. Attempting to settle old scores after the war, Sharpe filed a petition against Green in 1649 for unprovoked assault and grievous bodily harm. Green, he claimed, had been a notorious royalist rabble-rouser during the war. The outcome of the suit is not recorded.

(Public Record Office)

some substance. It certainly may have seemed like that. A relentless militarization was taking place throughout the district, and some activists were busily engaged in their own private recruiting. Thomas Tibbott, the head of the Rowington family with relatives in Stratford and Warwick, where one owned an armourer's shop and defied an order from Lord Brooke to surrender its contents, enlisted some twenty Solihull men for the Earl of Northampton, 'and marched before them as their Captaine, and gave them Colours in theire hatts'.[12]

Musters were traditionally unpopular with Englishmen, and it is likely that the two rival rallies at Stratford, with all the conflicting advice and confusion surrounding them, were less effective in recruitment terms than private word-of-mouth persuasion through the peers' network of allies among the local gentry and on their own estates, where they could count on old loyalties and deference. This process certainly brought in many friends, relatives, tenants and servants, along with money, equipment, horses and weapons, to produce the nucleus of a small army. Of the two rallies, the royalist one was clearly the more successful. It is impossible to estimate numbers accurately, since the contemporary reporting is either impressionistic or unashamedly biased and, like most of the so-called petitions, some fulsome parliamentarian reports were clearly propaganda exercises. Even allowing for patriotic fervour and the more lachrymose times, it is difficult, for example, to credit an otherwise sober report of 6 July on the state of the newly-raised Warwickshire militia that 'all men showed themselves very forward and wept for joy', though it concedes, probably accurately, that Lord Brooke's Stratford meeting the previous week had attracted only 200 horses and 300 men and volunteers. In particular, one eye-witness, Thomas Johnson from Alcester, testified to a friend in London that whereas Brooke had been hoping for two thousand, 'very few trained men would come in, because my Lord Brooke's warrants did not give the Country satisfaction' – a lesson he promptly learned in subsequent rallies where he achieved better figures by carefully rewording his text to stress that he was supporting not just Parliament but 'King and Parliament'. The Earl of Middlesex's reliable bailiff at Milcote, Robert Fawdon, wrote to his master in similar terms. Northampton and Dunsmore, he reported:

> with most of the gentrie of Warwickesheire, on Fryday Last, were at Stratford, & as I heere, read the comission of Array, and had many more come in to them then my Lord Brooke Formerly hadd . . . In this cuntrie I veirlie beleave my Lord of Northampton will have the greater partie.

In this relative success, the enthusiasm of the Stratford militants already named must have played its part – not to mention the astonishing wage of 2s. per day which the Earl of Northampton was alleged to have offered to 'certain hundreds of men out of severall Shires' to eclipse Brooke's already generous offer of 4s. 8d. per week. As one civil war historian has written: 'Neither side had much initial difficulty over recruiting, for 1642 was a year of depression, and men enlisted for money as well as excitement.'[13]

The rallies helped not only to recruit and polarise opinion, forcing many to choose between the conflicting orders of king and Parliament, but to militarize

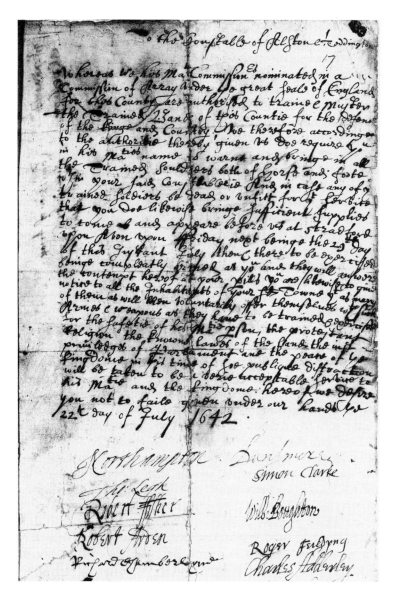

Royalist Muster at Stratford. *After declaring undying loyalty to the king with other peers assembled at York on 5 June 1642, the Earl of Northampton, of Compton Wynyates, was appointed Charles's chief representative in Warwickshire and set about countering the influence of his arch-rival Lord Brooke by organizing a recruiting drive throughout the county. The document is a 'warrant' typical of many sent to village constables, and is signed by the major royalist Commissioners for Warwickshire, headed by the Earl of Northampton and Lord Dunsmore. Addressed to the constable of Alveston and Tiddington, near Stratford, it gives him a week's notice to ensure the attendance of villagers at a mass rally to be held at Stratford (written 'Stradford') on Friday 29 July. The muster was a great success, and was followed by similar ones at Warwick and Coleshill on the following days. For a full transcript, see Appendix 5.*

(Public Record Office)

further a neighbourhood already on the brink of outright conflict, and where force was increasingly beginning to take precedence over civilized custom. One day in mid-July, and coinciding with the Earl of Northampton's unsuccessful attempt to raise Coventry for the king, Judge Edward Reeve was faced with a near-riot at Warwick summer assizes, when Lord Brooke himself with William Purefoy and others were 'about the Hall with swords' as he presided over a provocative action brought by the local Royalist Robert Lee of Billesley against Brooke. It was an explosive situation, and the judge diplomatically deferred judgement pending further consultation. Military matters were beginning to dominate life. In Stratford, ominously, while the corporation allocated money for renewing the grass on the bowling alley, other sums were going to repair the 'Armer howse', to buy and transport barrels of gunpowder, dress old armour, make pins for muskets, and scour steel collanders for casting shot. Soldiers were now a common sight, payments being made 'to goodwife Browne and hir daughter for making cleane the new Hall after the soldiers weare gone'. There was brief consternation in late July when some unauthorized person removed inflammable match for firing guns from Mr Eston's shop, though a majority of the elders eventually decided this was lawful, 'yt beeing for the use and defence of the Corporacon'.[14] Armed men were on the loose everywhere, with random looting being reported. Some theft was evidently officially organized. It was on the orders of the newly appointed governor of Warwick Castle, John Bridges, that Lieutenant Richard Round stole horses from (among others) William Skinner of Shelfield House, Great Alne (including, so desperate was the need, 'one Graye flea-bitten mare'), from Richard Gunn and the vicar, Thomas Green, of Aston Cantlow, and from Mr Ryland of Quinton. Similarly, one of Bridges' scouts, Robert Haines, captured an unnamed person suspected of being a Royalist, at Henley-in-Arden, carrying six pounds, a watch, a pair of silk stockings, books, '& some other Trifles', all of which found their way, no doubt, to Warwick Castle. Lead for bullets was desperately needed, as is evident from the sworn testimony of John Milburn, the constable of Rowington, that on 27 June a Parliamentarian 'came to ye Church at Rowington & tooke of [sic] ye Lead of ye pole whereon ye Wether Cocke stood & carryed it away unto Warwicke'. Often soldiers simply helped themselves to whatever suited their fancy as they wandered expectantly over the countryside awaiting firm orders. John Milward at Henley-in-Arden noted very precisely for 11 August: 'Taken away from me by Lt. Hunt & Lt. Hannaway, one featherbed & all that belonged to it, a buff coat & 2 other coats, a portmanteau of linen, one flagon, one basin, one chamber pot; in all worth £15.' Meanwhile, Lord Brooke was having some success in his local recruiting. According to one account, 300 armed men were now garrisoning Warwick Castle, composed of 'a great Company out of Alcester [his home territory], Stratford & from Brummychum [Birmingham] and all the Country over', installing his trusty former solicitor, John Bridges, as his garrison governor. No wonder that gloomy correspondents in July already saw the Midlands as 'a Cockpit, one [side] spurring against another . . . as if open Wars were already proclaimed betwixt us'.[15]

It was during the Commission of Array rally at Stratford that a dramatic escalation in the local build-up provided the vital spark for the smouldering conflict, fanned by two nearby residents. Parliament had recently ordered reinforcements for Warwick Castle, and a consignment of nine cannons sent from London under escort arrived safely at Lord Saye's stronghold, Banbury Castle, on the same day that the Earl of Northampton was successfully completing the Stratford muster. Lord Brooke collected a 200-strong escort and rode urgently through the night from Warwick to collect them, arriving at Banbury at daybreak on Saturday 30 July. Among his guard, however, was a royalist infiltrator, Thomas Earle of Ailstone, near Stratford, who slipped away in the night halfway between Warwick and Banbury and hurried back to warn the Earl of Northampton at Stratford. Aware that Brooke had so far outmanoeuvred him at every turn and determined at all costs to prevent the further strengthening of Warwick, the earl hastily shelved plans to travel to Coleshill the following day for the next rally, assembled a strong force in the small hours, rode post-haste to Banbury, and confronted Brooke's ponderous convoy of 'greate gunns' shortly after it had left Banbury, at about 9.00 a.m., and was toiling through the hills near Hornton about to enter Warwickshire. Tension was such throughout the district that news of the confrontation spread quickly, and Brooke's force was quickly swelled not only by local labourers and their womenfolk armed with farmyard implements but by reinforcements from Warwick alerted, it was claimed, by another Stratford resident, Thomas Combe of Welcombe, who protested his innocence in the affair when persecuted by the Royalists shortly after. Neither leader was yet prepared to use force, however, and after hours of heated parleying and some scuffling among hotheads, a gentlemen's agreement was reached that the armaments should remain at Banbury until further notice, and the earl returned well-pleased to his lodging at the bailiff's house in Stratford. After a poor summer so far, reported a local resident, August now opened with 'a most happie change of wether' and harvesting was beginning. It must have seemed to the Earl of Northampton, as he attended Holy Trinity Church that Sunday with Lord Dunsmore, overlooked by the new Shakespeare bust in the chancel as he graciously acknowledged acquaintances like the Milcote bailiff among the congregation, that royalist fortunes were at last set fair. The king gave orders from York on 1 August for a combined army to march into Warwickshire to join Northampton's forces. A few days later, on whose instructions is unclear, a sizeable royalist force under the earl's less scrupulous allies broke the recent agreement by storming into Banbury, terrorizing the district, according to some lurid reporting, and threatening the town and Lord Saye's ancestral Broughton Castle with wholesale destruction and fire if the disputed magazine was not surrendered. The cannons were handed over to the Royalists, who promptly transferred them to Warwick and positioned them for an assault on the castle itself. A further fortnight was to elapse before the king gave the official signal marking the opening of the war by raising his standard at Nottingham. But the war in effect had already begun on the banks of the Avon, and two local residents, Thomas Earle of Ailstone and Thomas Combe of Welcombe, had played significant roles in its opening episode.[16]

CHAPTER 3

The Outbreak of War

The king at York had now officially proclaimed both Lord Brooke and the Earl of Essex, the newly appointed parliamentary commander-in-chief of the armed forces, 'traitors', and with Essex setting out from London with a substantial force on 8 August to 'secure' the Midlands by consolidating Brooke's power base, Charles devised a simple three-pronged strategy to defeat them. He would appear in person at Coventry and succeed where the Earl of Northampton had signally failed in winning over the great walled city; reinforce the Earl of Northampton with loyal units assembling in Worcestershire and others in Nottinghamshire and Leicestershire under staunch allies like the Byrons and Hastings, thus enabling him to wrest control of the rebels' stronghold at Warwick Castle; and with these two great fortresses regained he would raise the royal standard in person, perhaps in Warwickshire. In this way the king expected to end the rebellion before it developed into full-scale war, and he accordingly marched south. But Charles was no longer in a position to control events, only react to them, and almost immediately things began to go wrong. The Earl of Northampton's siege of Warwick Castle, at best a desultory, amateurish affair, soon ended in abject failure. In spite of its impressive beginning on 4 August, when the splendidly attired royal herald Sir William Dugdale demanded surrender in the king's name, the castle gates remained closed, the royalist reinforcements failed to materialize, and the few royalist cannon caused only a little random damage to property in the town without making any impact on the impassive medieval walls. When news came of the parliamentary relief army approaching from the south, the Royalists hastily abandoned the project, having achieved nothing. Equally, the eventual royal presence failed to impress Coventry, now securely a parliamentary stronghold, and Charles was forced to withdraw to Sir Thomas Leigh's at Stoneleigh for three days while he reconsidered the situation.

All this fruitless activity provided, nonetheless, a focal point for the developing power struggle. The king was now nearby, at Stoneleigh and Kenilworth, where he installed a garrison, receiving delegations and volunteers, and was ready, it was widely rumoured, to erect his standard on Dunsmore Heath. Forces of both sides were converging on south Warwickshire; the countryside was being scoured by armed groups searching for arms and useful equipment; and soon the puritan preacher Richard Baxter was reporting from Kidderminster how, as the king marched south, the countryside was being emptied of young drunken ne'er-do-wells flocking to join his army. One armed contingent of royalist cavalry under the young Warwickshire gentleman John Smith, brother of Sir Charles Smith of Wootton Wawen, caused fatalities in Northamptonshire on their way to join the Earl of Northampton. At Warwick, against the band of largely unpaid and ill-kept parliamentary soldiers defending the castle under Sir Edward Peyto and including, as we have seen, volunteers from Stratford, Alcester, Henley and elsewhere, were royalist forces also swelled by local volunteers and conscripts, all nominally commanded by the Earl of Northampton who himself lodged for a time, somewhat unprofessionally, at the Swan in Warwick. Some of these besieging Royalists were no doubt less than enthusiastic: the constable of Tanworth-in-Arden, John Court, was summoned on pain of death by the earl to bring in his local trained band, and they duly appeared with their motley array of weapons, not unlike Falstaff's own band of recruits: three muskets with bandoliers, two pikes, some armour and a few swords. But others must have committed themselves voluntarily to both sides, like young John Smith from Stratford, given a horse and a pair of pistols worth £6 7s. 6d. by his father the churchwarden, who watched him ride off proudly one morning from home in Wood Street to join Captain Askew's troop at Warwick. Shortly after, for some unexplained reason, he had to supply his son with a further horse, while yet another one was taken from him by one of the many officers searching the district, so that the father had lost three horses already, even before the war had begun – an ominous foretaste of what the conflict would entail for the civilian population. Throughout the war, of course, many dozens of other Stratford men must have enlisted, particularly from the poorer section of the town's population, but no one thought to record their names. A few are found scattered at random among the archives: George Blancher and Morgan Jones to serve under Sir William Waller, Samson Harris and John Cotton under Captain Essex, Simon Mason with quartermaster John Dalbier, and John Barker (later presumed dead, relief being paid to his widow) with Lord Roberts, and so on. Other Stratford names are no doubt buried among the surviving lists of the Warwick and Coventry garrisons not identified by their home town or village.

As the war crept closer during the summer of 1642, it became increasingly clear that it would not be confined to individual activists or actual soldiers but affect the community as a whole. For in addition to the usual burdens of peacetime taxation of one sort or another, like the Poll Tax of 1641 and the voluntary charitable contributions like those for the victims of the situation in Ireland already referred to, citizens were now confronted with urgent new appeals, or 'Propositions', for purely military ends. At first, war expenses were defrayed by voluntary contributions, many of which, particularly those from the peerage, were extraordinarily generous. In June 1642, publicly admitting for the first time that 'the King intends to make war against his Parliament', Parliament itself made a general public appeal for loans of money and plate, promising eventual repayment at eight per cent interest. In Warwickshire, inevitably, it was Lord Brooke who was authorized to organize and receive the subscriptions, and by September his chaplain at the castle, the late Stratford vicar's friend John Bryan, was producing his first accounts of what had been received to date. As elsewhere, some of Stratford's leading citizens responded generously, with sums

Stratford's War Loans. *In June 1642 when war began to look inevitable, Parliament issued public appeals for loans of money and domestic plate to defray likely expenses. As the appeal was worded ambiguously, on behalf of both King and Parliament, citizens sank political differences and responded generously, the puritan schoolmaster, John Trapp (sixth in the left-hand column) and the royalist vicar, Henry Twitchet (second in the right), each contributing £5. Heading the town's donations by 24 September 1642, a month before the battle of Edgehill, were the corporation's £50 and Shakespeare's grandson-in-law Thomas Nash's lavish £100 – by far the greatest single amount given. Most donations were collected by a local dignitary and taken to Warwick Castle, though some individual donors travelled to Warwick to deliver their gift in person.*

(Public Record Office)

ranging from the extraordinary £100 in plate and money lent by Shakespeare's grandson-in-law Thomas Nash (and understandably, therefore, placed by Dugdale firmly in the parliamentary camp) (see Appendix 1), the £26 lent by William Mills of Wood Street and the more usual £5 each sent in by John Brooks, John Loach, John Woolmer and the new vicar, to the modest few shillings of lesser men. The Quiney family were particularly generous, £20 each being offered by William and Thomas, and £10 by Matthew. Collection was usually through the town constable or one of the aldermen, but some of the inhabitants evidently travelled to Warwick themselves in order to hand their donations directly to either Bryan, the castle governor John Bridges or even, as befitted the dignity of the chief alderman Baldwin Brooks, to Lord Brooke himself. The parliamentary appeal evidently got off to a slow start, since it had to be repeated, and some townsmen specified more than one loan. John Brooks even recorded £21 'upon several propositions' – for which he was careful to stress he had kept receipts. It is tempting to draw conclusions about an individual's allegiance from these loans, to assume that a generous gift to Lord Brooke meant that the donor was a committed Parliamentarian. But there are simply too many unknown factors involved to make such an assumption on this basis alone: the degree of coercion or manipulation exercised by the astute Lord Brooke; the extent of peer pressure in a small community like Stratford; the sheer bewilderment of people in an unprecedented crisis faced with conflicting interests. As already noted, Parliament was constantly invoking 'King and Parliament' in its appeals in order to maximize support, stressing that the quarrel was not against the king but against his evil counsellors. In such circumstances confusion was inevitable, and many were unable to reconcile rival claims. The case of John Fetherston at Packwood is no doubt typical of many. He confessed his dilemma in a touching letter to his brother, explaining how the contradictory demands of the day left him quite unable to act with an easy conscience:

> I am in a great distraction concerninge my armor (beinge all-togeither unable to satisfy my self in point of judgement and conscience what to doe) by reason of the severall commands of the Kinge and parliament. My protestation [oath] putts me in mind that I am bound in conscience to serve both, and yet there seems now a very great difference betweene them, which I humbly desyer allmighty god, if it be his will, may be peaceably & timely composed and settled for the good of this churche and kingdome. I have not yet sent in my armes, eyther to my lord of Northampton or my lord Brooke, because you know I am joyned with Mr Bettom, who is a known profest papist [Walliston Betham of Rowington]; hee is to find the horse & man, and I the armor, pettronells and sadle. If I should deliver my armes to Mr Bettomes man, I should then have done an act contrary both to the Kinge & parliament, who have both declared that papists are to be disarmed. I have therefore left my armor at your house & my pettronells I have sent by my man now, & as for my sadle, I cannot have it from Mr Bettome. I understand that Mr Dugdale lyeth at your howse. I pray you present my respects to him, & tell him my armes are there ready, & I desyer they may be imployed for the safety of the church and kingdome . . .

In the light of such perplexities it is not surprising that the list of Stratford subscribers of money and plate should include, side by side, those who would soon become sworn enemies: the militant cleric John Trapp alongside the conservative vicar, Royalists Edward Wagstaffe and Thomas Dighton next to the Parliamentarian Thomas Nash, and so on.[1]

More important than ideology for most, however, at this stage at least, was natural caution, an instinct towards neutralism, particularly for the affluent who had most to lose through radical change, a clubbing together to defend the status quo. But neutralism, which was to be a feature of the later stages of the war in neighbouring Worcestershire and elsewhere, never stood a real chance in Warwickshire, torn between Lord Brooke's energetic radicalism and his formidable propaganda machine, and the determined, if less well-organized, obstruction of the courtly Earl of Northampton. The Stratford 'Propositions' lists hint occasionally, nevertheless, of protectionist rather than activist thinking on the part of donors. Thus, included alongside the frequent endorsement 'for the Parliament service', are occasionally slightly more ambiguous terms: 'for the State and Parliament', and John Beddom's and Peter Holland's pointed 'lent to the Lord Brooke for the service of the Parliament when many other neighbours lent, *for safety of ye County*' (author's italics). For a common assumption was that the money collected would go to local defence, a hope that, whatever happened elsewhere, the violence and disruption associated with unwelcome intruders must be avoided, if necessary by using the only viable local force, the garrison at Warwick. In Cheshire, Parliament was firmly told that the gentry would not subscribe plate, money and horses until assured that they would be used for local defence. The Warwickshire accounts, clearly headed 'sums of money subscribed for the service of Kinge and Parliament and disbursed for the mayntenance of the Garrison in Warwick Castle', leave little doubt that whatever the intentions of the individual donors, Lord Brooke had once again stolen a march on his opponents, and that the sums collected went directly into Parliament's coffers to be used against the king. The additional £100 voted by the Stratford corporation to Lord Brooke on 29 August 'to be imploied for the use of the Kinge & parlamentt' would have gone to the same destination.

As already indicated, the parliamentary appeals extended to household metalware as well as ready cash, to be instantly weighed, valued and sold, or else melted down for armaments; and a few surviving lists of this 'Plate subscribed & sold for the maintenance of Warwick garrison' record the precise weight and equivalent cash value of individual donations. By 18 September, for example, the wealthy Thomas Nash at New Place had sent in a substantial quantity of plate weighing 364 oz valued at 5s. 4d. per ounce, while a few days later the more modestly placed schoolmaster John Trapp contributed 15½ oz, and even the paltry 4 oz each from such as Thomas Taylor and William Cawdwell were gratefully itemized. The gifts are not usually described, but where they are there is something touching about these homely reminders of domestic life: Francis Ainge's 'peece of plate', or the silver bowl belonging to Shakespeare's Henley Street friend, the glover William Shaw, 'which I delivered to Mr Bryan at Warwicke, and valued by him at £2 4s.'. There follow payments to Job Lord at the castle 'for his paines in weighinge, breakinge & packing plate'. Among the losses to posterity in this rich haul from Stratford and all the surrounding countryside figured, no doubt, not only valuable items inherited from many a Tudor home but a few even more priceless ones. Shakespeare in his will had left all his plate to his only grandchild Elizabeth, now married to Thomas Nash and living with her mother, Shakespeare's daughter Susanna, at New Place. We surely need look no further to explain the fate of much of the Shakespeares' family silver: it was bundled up unceremoniously in the old home, loaded on to a waiting farm wagon and last seen, shortly after, disappearing through the trees along the lane to Warwick one late summer's day of 1642.

The result of this community effort in the face of what was clearly felt to be a national emergency was that by 24 September the citizens of Stratford had contributed some £348 in money and plate, increasing later in further loans raised by the committee at Coventry to nearer £400 and peaking, probably, in October or November. But the subscription was kept open long after, until at least the following summer, and that, together with the discrepancies between John Bryan's accounts and the claims later made by the donors, suggests that further accounts were probably produced but have not survived, making a complete picture impossible. To these voluntary contributions must also be added, of course, the huge quantity of money and plate later stolen indiscriminately by soldiers throughout the district which eluded any accounting system. Interestingly, one whose home was plundered of plate, valued at more than £4 on the occasion recorded, was the vicar of Whitchurch, Thomas Warmstry, who as reported earlier had coveted the Stratford living. Despite his earlier anti-Laudian stance, following information from named local inhabitants in September, he had evidently become politically suspect in these volatile times.[2]

The process of collection 'on the Parliament's Propositions', as the phrase went, did not end there. More than anything the fledgling armies of both sides urgently needed food, horses and equipment, and every community was officially expected – an expectation if necessary reinforced by threats or converted into outright organized theft – to provide these further items. Sums allocated for 'the raising of dragoon horses', initially for Lord Brooke's mounted infantry and soon the Earl of Denbigh's too, became a universal refrain in the accounts submitted later by each village and hamlet across the countryside during the summer of 1642, often coupled with saddles, bridles and 'gears', plus a miscellany of weapons. Unlike the collections of money and plate which affected only the more prosperous, virtually every householder responded to these new appeals. From High Street alone in Stratford, Richard Castle sent 6s., William Walker 12s., Francis Smith 6s. (and also 'a musket, bandileer and sword'), John Beddom the town clerk 7s., Peter Holland 4s., Edward Rogers 6s. 8d., chief alderman Baldwin Brooks 18s., and so on, all towards the raising of dragoon horses. Again, Thomas Nash responded generously, on 13 September, and in the turmoil of these weeks his contribution was at first overlooked: 'Memorand. that £7 was received of Mr Nash of Stratford to buy a dragoone Horse for my Lord, which was forgott to bee sett downe.' Once more, constables, aldermen and local dignitaries like Anthony Stoughton, the parliamentary militiaman of Warwick who accepted Luddington's modest offerings, acted as receivers, with officers on standby at the castle to accept them. Occasionally Lord Brooke would appear in person: 'he received the horses, sadles & bridles himselfe', noted Francis Smith, perhaps with a touch of pride, to which he added: 'a newe musket & sword delivered at Warr Castle unto Mr Brian'. Some individuals, as always, were taking the law into their own hands: Hastings Ingram of Little Wolford was one, Richard Wootton, the militant rector of Warmington was another, both becoming notorious locally for taking horses in the district with little ceremony. Wootton was evidently highly committed to the parliamentary cause and spent little time in the pulpit: on one day, 20 August, his collection of horses included three for Colonel Fiennes, Lord Saye's son, together with 'the furniture for 2 men for the service, 2 sords [sic], 2 musketts, 2 new sadles and 2 bridles'. But Lord Brooke, as usual, tried to ensure that the process was both legal and courteous. William Broad of Bidford-on-Avon, later to be sorely tried by the continual passage of soldiers through his property, sent Brooke one horse 'for service of Kinge and Parlimt' 'upon his lettre', while paying for an extra horse 'for some of his neighbors'. A similar note was appended by the villagers at Great Alne, headed by Edward Greene: 'horses, saddles & bridles required from us by letter from Lord Brooke'. The town clerk at Stratford, Thomas Greene, while himself donating 7s., noted that 'the towne of Stratford delivered to his Lordshipp 20 horses'. Every village contributed, some more than once: Snitterfield a first contribution of £4 then a second instalment of £3 15s. 6d., Alveston at first £1 3s. then a more respectable £6, and so on. Even tiny Temple Grafton was able to send the peer two horses with saddles and bridles valued at £9, and a village collection produced a further 13s., all duly delivered, we are assured, despite the sudden death of the village constable George Biddle and the loss of his accounts.

A continuous trickle of weapons was also handed in to the Warwick authorities during the autumn, among which, from Stratford, were some precisely dated at 10 December: 'Recd from Mr Hunt of Stratford: 2 muskets, 2 pistols, a carbine & a petronel & Belt & a pr of bandeliers.' Unlike the earlier cases discussed above, where political affiliations cannot necessarily be inferred from the subscriptions, these later donations, made at the time of Edgehill or some time after, may indeed indicate clear commitment to Parliament. Additionally, the rounding up of livestock was increasing, though it seems not to have been systematically accounted for: Governor Bridges later testified that from August, following 'warrants' from Lord Brooke, many 'Beeves, Sheepe, Cowes, Oxen and Horses, to a considerable value [were] brought into Warwick Castle for the service of the Parliament . . . from the Enemies Garrisons, others from malignants'.[3]

All these collections, then, directly benefited the parliamentary cause. But it must not be forgotten that similar gifts in cash and kind were also being made to the king's side by committed Royalists. Unlike the parliamentary system, however, this operation was more surreptitious, unplanned and usually unrecorded, without any proper accounts ever being made. But that it existed is beyond doubt; occasional parliamentary sources refer to this royalist effort. Thus at catholic Rowington the merchant William Shakespeare was later to be penalized specifically for contributing £1 10s. for dragoon horses for the Earl of

Northampton (as well as being fined, incidentally, simply 'for bringing up his Children in popery'). Parliamentary lists were later compiled of 'sums of money taken and recd. from Malignants' for such offences and include many local names without the alleged crimes being specified. Among such were, again, William Shakespeare and Thomas Tibbotts of Rowington, fined £1 6s. and William Greene of Stratford, fined a very heavy £15 (presumably reflecting the gravity of the offence).

Now that active units were being formed and deployed in the district, large quantities of provisions were beginning to be demanded to maintain them, the start of a major imposition which was to drain the already meagre resources of many a village for years to come. What must have been one of the very first of these demands, at the beginning of August, was conscientiously if painfully recorded by an anonymous villager of Snitterfield:

> A leavie made by our Constabell of Snitterfelde by a warrante frome my Lord Broocke for Wheate, Backen and Cheese, at three shillinge foure pence a yarde lande, much about the Shege [siege] of Warwicke Castell, which rises to the sume of £9; which provision was bonde & sende to Warwicke Castell.

With all this frenzied activity in and around Stratford during the summer, one thing is certain: no one there could have been unaware of the deteriorating situation. The series of musters in the field outside the town had filled Stratford with armed men, rustic volunteers and curious onlookers flooding in from all parts, with shouts and drum beats in the streets, noisy debate in the taverns and speculation in many a home as to the likely course of events. Those at Warwick, only a few miles away and full of Stratford friends and relatives, had been breathlessly told from eye-witness accounts and confirmed by the ominous booming of the Royalists' cannons heard across the fields. Most homes had by now responded to the crisis in one way or another, many publicly, through Lord Brooke's appeals, but others, no doubt, more furtively, to royalist ones, as family plate, money and old weapons unused for years had been handed over to the collectors. Some who had not contributed had perhaps been looted, others reluctant to do so had been forced to by pressure of one kind or another. The fields had fewer labourers, the yards fewer horses, and the barns smaller stocks of fodder and grain than before. Cartloads of goods and provisions were on the move, and the road to Warwick especially was more heavily used than ever. Relatives of local worthies were among those enlisting, headed by the sons of both the Earl of Northampton and Lord Saye and Sele, all to serve with distinction in the coming conflict. The young Sir Henry Rainsford, lord of Clifford Chambers, had joined the Earl of Northampton as a captain; as had John Smith, brother of Old Stratford's late lord, Sir Charles Smith; Sir Simon Clarke and his son from Bidford; Thomas and Henry, the two eldest sons of Sir Henry Gibbs of Honington; and Henry Hunckes, Viscount Conway's son-in-law from Ragley, soon to be promoted colonel, made governor of Banbury Castle and knighted. Old Sir Thomas Lucy's son Spencer likewise became a royalist colonel, despite his father's puritanism. As Dugdale said: 'many of the trayn'd-Band Souldiers

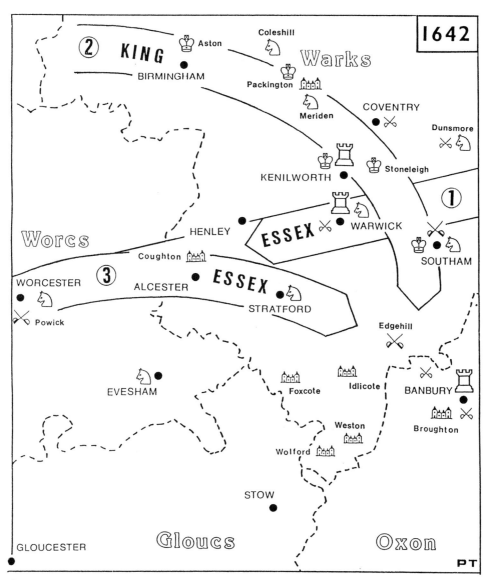

Map 2. Major Events in 1642.

× Major battle

× Siege or skirmish

🏰 Mansion plundered or attacked

👑 King's lodging

🐴 Major military rally

and other loyall persons came with Horse and Armes' to join the Earl of Northampton's growing army. The district was fast becoming militarized, with organized bands of soldiers billeting here and there under orders to report to some local centre. In August, two troops of cavalry under Lord Saye's son Nathaniel Fiennes spent a night at Kineton, perhaps the same who had been entertained at Stratford's Maidenhead, as earlier reported; others, nominally under Lord Brooke, were reported at Charlecote 'severall tymes', and yet more, Royalists this time, under the Earl of Northampton, would be quartering before long at Aston Cantlow.[4] Not surprisingly, apprehension and fear are the keynotes of surviving private correspondence throughout July and August, as villagers pieced together what they could from hearsay or first-hand accounts from their constable, parson, estate officials and neighbours back from market. Confirming fears already expressed in July, the Earl of Middlesex's bailiff, Robert Fawdon, relating events to his absent master from Milcote on 1 August, wrote gloomily: 'this cuntrie is full of feares that Warwickesheire will be the seat of warr, for it is reported that supplyes are cominge to both parties'. Thomas Johnson, writing in similar terms to a London friend from Sambourne, near Alcester, a few days later, was full of the same forebodings: 'here in Warwick Shire wee are like to fall into great calamities and distresses; here is nothing but providing of armes'. He concluded dolefully: 'I am afraid wee shall have a wofull time of it.' 'God knows whether wee shall ever send to you againe', wrote yet another shortly after, 'for we have a mighty distracted Countrey [district]. Here is mighty providing for warres.' Everywhere, he went on, armed gangs were taking the law into their hands, 'and where [citizens] will not deliver their Armes they kill, and take their horses away by force. Ours are taken away this night.' John Fetherston told an identical story from Packwood: 'wee weare lately very much affrighted by reason of a troop of horsemen that cam to some of my neighbours howses and did disarme them & took away what they pleased under color of takinge of their armes'.

Such was the picture of Stratford's summer of 1642 as the countryside drifted into a war which, apart from insignificant hotheads, few wanted. Everywhere there was a dogged reluctance to admit the gravity of the situation; but the correspondents quoted above were not sensationalizing. Even before the rival forces began to converge on south Warwickshire and the king's standard was finally raised at Nottingham on 22 August, the siege at Warwick represented the point of no return. From now on it was the recourse to force which would dominate the political landscape. Speaking for many a jumped-up roadside captain-adventurer like those plundering Rowington, Henley or Packwood, Falstaff's exultant cry was to echo over the Warwickshire landscape for the next few years: 'Let us take any man's horses; the laws of England are at my commandment!'[5]

CHAPTER 4
Edgehill via Stratford

Nothing came to calm the anxieties. On the contrary, the remorseless build-up of armed units continued throughout the district and indiscriminate harassment, pillage and tit-for-tat violence increased as events, still sporadic and confused, began to escalate. Events at Warwick had seemingly unjammed a backlog of bitterness under the studied moderation, apathy and desperate reluctance to become involved. Militarily feeble though it had been, the siege had for the first time since the Wars of the Roses pitted one Englishman against another in the neighbourhood. It had caused damage in a peaceable old market town when amateurishly aimed cannon balls had struck chimneys and the church tower, and had resulted in some deaths – including that of a local butcher carrying a shoulder of lamb down the street taunting the hungry defenders on the castle walls. There was to be no going back. The ending of the siege, the abortive royal attempt on Coventry and the departure of the disconsolate king to Nottingham released throngs of aimless, indisciplined and vengeful Royalists into the surrounding country looking for more trouble. They met it in the form of the large parliamentary relief force from London which finally entered Warwickshire near Priors Marston on 22 August and which, joining with Lord Brooke's contingent which had outpaced it, routed them in the first sizeable encounter of the war in the Midlands, in cornfields between Long Itchington and Southam the following day, a full two months before Edgehill. The surrounding fields were strewn with corpses, many of which were hastily thrown into the nearby River Itchen. The full horror of these events was too distant to affect Stratford, though they were soon known and William Walker in the High Street (possibly Shakespeare's godson, who had received 20s. in gold in the poet's will and who became the town bailiff after the war) later carefully recalled paying 9s. 'for 2 barrels of beere for Lord Brooke at ye fight by Southam'. In a further unpleasant twist the king's nephew, the dashing Prince Rupert who had recently joined Charles at Nottingham, introduced a new element of ruthlessness when in one of his first characteristic initiatives a few days after Southam he made an unprovoked attack on the north Warwickshire manor house of the local Puritans' staunchest ally, William Purefoy, at Caldecote. Almost as though in direct retaliation, some of Lord Brooke's men promptly plundered the homes of John Hunt, Elizabeth Atwood and others at catholic Rowington on 30 August. Minor though they were, such events were becoming commonplace; things were turning ugly. Robert Fawdon, observing for himself from the Milcote estate just outside

Stratford, and learning more, no doubt, from clients met in the Maidenhead in Henley Street, was in no doubt that things were getting worse. He no longer felt inclined to venture abroad: 'Trulie, I doe scarce goe any way from Melcot', he wrote on 16 September just after Stratford fair: 'heere the times are verie dangerous, for this cuntrie is full of scattered troupes which doe pillage in manie places, as also of vagrant persons which waite for mischeife, soe that we are full of feares.'

Some of the pillaging was officially organized: Edward Peyto, one of those in charge at Warwick Castle, sent out a raiding party from there on 14 September to one of the king's most loyal local supporters, Robert Dormer, of Grove Park, outside Warwick, seizing inmates as prisoners, a quantity of gunpowder and armour hidden in a vault disguised as a dovecote. But a sterner test was to come. The Earl of Essex, the supreme parliamentary commander, had already set out for the Midlands with a considerable force from London and, although no one could have known, the countdown to Edgehill had begun.[1]

Understandably, the Edgehill campaign is usually taken as having begun with Essex's departure from Worcester on 19 October to meet the Royalists moving south from Birmingham. But long before the two armies finally met at Edgehill, Essex's forces had twice crossed the full width of Warwickshire, passing through

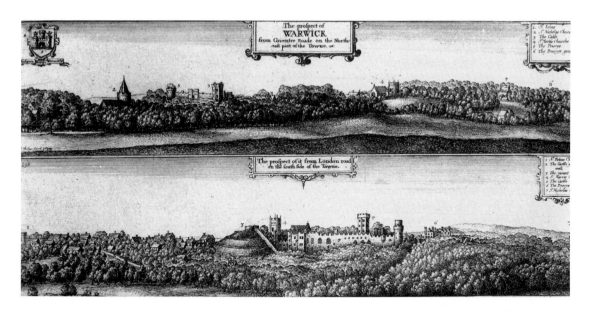

Warwick Castle. The great medieval fortress of John of Gaunt and Henry V played a crucial role throughout the war in the Midlands. Strengthened and provisioned in the months before the outbreak of war by its puritan owner, Lord Brooke, it effortlessly withstood a royalist siege to become the major permanent parliamentarian stronghold in the region. Under its energetic military governor, Major John Bridges, it remained a major garrison and staging-post throughout the war, launching successful military operations over a wide area, including Lord Brooke's defeat of the Stratford Royalists in February 1643. It also served as the main military prison in the district and collection point for local taxes and donations, including those from Stratford and the surrounding villages.

Robert Devereux, third Earl of Essex (1591–1646). Son of Queen Elizabeth's disgraced favourite, Essex was appointed Parliament's supreme commander at the outbreak of war, and marched twice through Stratford in the opening campaign leading to Edgehill. The heroic equestrian portrait quickly became a propaganda stereotype used by both sides, and Essex is seen against a map of England showing a succession of his supposed victories, including Edgehill ('Kenton' for Kineton – in fact, a parliamentary defeat) under the horse's knees. The medal, issued in 1642 as a military honour, depicts him in armour, protected by the sword of divine justice emerging from the clouds of war, with the biblical motto 'The Sword of the lord and of Gideon' (Judges VII, 18, 20). On the reverse are shown the two Houses of Parliament assembled with King and Speaker, and, in pointed criticism of Charles's attempt at personal rule, the message that 'In the multitude of counsellors there is peace'.

(Medal: The British Museum)

or close to Stratford and all the nearby villages on both occasions, while the king's own army had marched by only a few miles away to the north, via Kenilworth. Once the battle was over, too, neither army immediately left the area, as is often implied by writers eager to pass on to the next 'campaign', and the presence of the dismembered parliamentary army in particular was felt in the district almost as acutely in the aftermath of the battle as before it. For the local population, therefore, the experience of what contemporaries called simply 'Kineton field' was more widely felt and more prolonged than has often been recognized, even for communities like Stratford at some distance from the fighting.

The Earl of Essex had left London to a rapturous citizens' send-off on 9 September and as commander-in-chief, immediately joined the Midland forces which had been assembling at Northampton, intending to march straight to Nottingham and capture the king. But Charles had no intention of falling into this trap, and moved west into loyalist Shropshire to continue recruiting before deciding on his next move. This was widely expected to be Worcester, where he could count on considerable support, and Essex was accordingly ordered by Parliament to march west to shadow the king. Another, smaller parliamentary unit under Lord Saye's son, Nathaniel Fiennes, was ordered to join Essex from Banbury. Wisely ignoring an impertinent challenge from Prince Rupert to test his unready troops against the Royalists on Dunsmore Heath, Essex accordingly moved from Northampton into Warwickshire on 19 September. The chaos and widespread resentment felt in the countless villages through which the unruly, ill-nourished and often mutinous soldiers passed as they fanned out across the country through Rugby, Coventry and Warwick are well caught in the surviving parish accounts, and are a foretaste of what Stratford was shortly to experience for itself.

Once arrived at the friendly garrison town of Warwick, Essex's army paused to allow its large convoy of heavy guns to catch up, allowing some soldiers even a short sight-seeing expedition to marvel at Guy's Cliff, while they complained about their officers and the conditions in the villages in which they were desperately seeking board and lodging. Barford was dismissed as 'very poor', since 'many of our soldiers can get neither beds, bread nor water', while Aston Cantlow, already unfortunate enough to have been recently emptied of provisions by the rival Earl of Northampton's soldiers, was no better: 'we could get no quarter, neither bread nor drink'. Although news of their coming had certainly gone on ahead and preparations for war were visible all around, this mass influx into the district preceding the battle of Edgehill was the first, unnerving evidence that the war had finally come. By 23 September one appalled local resident could report: 'Daylie now feares arise, for this cuntrie is likelie to be the seat of warr. My Lord of Essex is heare with great forces, & the other partie, as is reported, [is] at Worster, & neare about as strong.'

Lady Monmouth at Kenilworth, widow of Robert Lord Carey, who had died the previous year, was busy commandeering furniture and goods from local aristocrats so that the king could be properly entertained at the castle, where he was shortly expected. The parliamentary soldiers were everywhere, not in twos and threes but in substantial numbers, swamping tiny villages, interfering, noisy and lice-ridden, in no hurry to move on to engage the enemy at Worcester. For some reason Aston

Cantlow was chosen for a rallying point, and huge numbers must have congregated in the surrounding fields. The prosperous Edward Greene of nearby Great Alne (who, as mentioned earlier, had been busy collecting horses for Lord Brooke), was obliged to send large quantities of hay to these troops, 'carried to the Rendezvouse in Aston feelde', not to mention suffering the theft of further quantities of oats stolen from his barns, costing him £20. Binton too was full, sixty or so of Lord Rochford's men loitering (and therefore pilfering) for a whole week:

> Wee quartered Capteyne Willowby [George Willoughby] and his Company of Foote, beinge under the Comand of the Lord Rochford, when the Earle of Essex went to Worcester, and beinge about sixty in number, a Weeke beinge at the Townes Chardge by the rate of Six pence a day for a man.

Snitterfield likewise had no option but to receive Lord Mandeville's regiment (soon to be disbanded after performing ignominiously at Edgehill), with its chaplain the fiery Puritan Simeon Ashe, many of the villagers noting simply that they had 'suffered by the Earle of Essex in his march toward Worcester and back againe', or 'at the Yearle of Essexe going furste against Wossiter', as one entry has it. A little further north, Henry Parry at the hamlet of Edstone, Wootton Wawen, had somehow to feed twenty of Essex's men 'when hee wentt to Worcester, att diet', half of whom stayed 'and lodged with mee att night'. Times were getting hard in other ways too. One less publicized but equally significant effect of the increasing turmoil was to end any hope that the local economy might revive. George Willis had complained as long ago as April 1640 that the unsettled times were depressing land values, and as the soldiers arrived in the district the bailiff at Milcote took up the same theme. He reported to his master, the Earl of Middlesex, the unwelcome news that tenants no longer able to make ends meet were intent on driving hard bargains, threatening to surrender their leases:

> In these sadd times your tenantts complaine they canott sell any thing to pay their rents, & divers have been att me to speak to your honour to give over their groundes. I mett Mr Brunt [Richard Brent] att Stratford faire, & he wished me to acquaint your honour he could hold no longer.

'I heare of none that will give readie monie', he concluded gloomily. As the war set in, not even great landowners like the Earl of Middlesex were to escape its effects.[2]

Stratford seems to have escaped with minimum disruption – though not for long – as most of the troops passed by some miles to the north. Many of the town's references to the passage of Essex's men are undated, so it is impossible to be sure, but the bulk of them probably relate to the return journey from Worcester a month later. Some quarter is referred to, as in Jane Bumpus's note of having lodged a few foot soldiers 'when they went to Worcester', but the town's contribution seems mainly to have been confined to sending food to the regiments passing nearby. Typical are the 10s. and 6s. worth of unspecified 'provision to ye Earle of Essex when hee went to Worcester' sent from their High Street homes by Richard Castle and William Lindon respectively, and the cheeses sent by Peter Holland and Elizabeth Wheeler. The horse 'taken by Warrant from ye Earl of Essex, with bridle & saddle', worth £5 to John Careless, also probably dates from this time.

As for the soldiers, their lot was even less enviable than that of the harassed villagers as they resumed their march towards Worcester. They were unpopular with the country folk, exhausted and dispirited, and to make matters worse the weather had now deteriorated. The roads were quagmires as they trudged due west, after the rendezvous at Aston Cantlow, on towards Alcester and Bidford: 'this day we had such foul weather that before I had marched one mile I was wet to the skin', reported one subaltern, Nathaniel Wharton, on 23 September. Little wonder that, cold, hungry and drenched, rather than hurrying on to confront the Royalists now joined, it was learnt, by Prince Rupert, one group should burst excitedly into the great palatial mansion of the hated Throckmortons of Gunpowder Plot fame, at Coughton, hastily abandoned by the family, and wreak havoc. The naive pleasure and sheer amazement of these raw recruits, until recently ploughboys, shepherds or poor artisans living in hovels, is well caught in one soldier's excited report:

> We lay at a place called Colfon [Coughton] in Warwickshire, and there lived a great Papist, one Frogmorton [Sir Robert Throckmorton], who hearing of our comming fled away from his house, and his whole Family, which the Souldiers did plunder, and found abundance of Images and Pictures, which they brake and committed to the fire. They likewise burnt many popish Bookes, some of them being almost as big as we could lift with one hand, printed in parchment, and others were throwne into a great moate. In the house we found 3 or 4 Murthering peeces, brasse pots, and a great sheet of lead about 500 weight, which was hidden under ground. The Souldiers dranke up his Perry, Sider and Beere almost all, they did lye on his Fether-beds all night, and in the Morning cut them, emptied out the feathers, carried the tikes away with them, and also silke hangings for Beds.

Like other family seats, Coughton was shortly to suffer the indignity of becoming a garrison, albeit only a minor and occasional one. But although it was looted and damaged it was to escape surprisingly intact. As will be seen, other local mansions were not to be so fortunate. Events at Coughton are a reminder that, at this stage at least, the war was still largely considered by many of the participants as a religious one. The parliamentarian troops marching from London to Northampton and on to Worcester, encouraged by their puritan chaplains' frequent sermons on the theme of a righteous war against spiritual 'delinquants', had already deviated more than once to loot, deface or destroy goods and property of anyone perceived as hostile, and much more was to come. In particular, suspect clergy like George Dale at Walsgrave-on-Sowe, described insultingly as 'an old base priest', or Francis Holyoak at Southam, 'very evil and of dissolute conversation', were harassed, abused and pillaged. Shortly, many local clerics would be similarly victimized, and the Royalists in their turn would mete out the same treatment to known puritan clergy. Looting became increasingly indiscriminate, but it was always given a particular self-righteous thrill when directed against a known religious enemy. Meanwhile, braving the atrocious weather and the appalling news of the routing of Fiennes's unit intending to join them by an opportunist Prince Rupert at nearby Powick Bridge, the bedraggled Parliamentarians finally trudged into Worcester on 24 September. Maintaining their crusading spirit by singing hymns, they relieved their long pent-up frustrations in a vicious three-week stay in what they saw as a hostile and treacherous land, arresting the city's mayor, plundering the Royalist Sir William Russell's house at Strensham 'unto the bare walls' and, in C.V. Wedgwood's eloquent summary, 'sacked the cathedral and tore down the sweet-toned organ that had been the joy and pride of the region'. Confirming the general anarchy, the Earl of Middlesex's bailiff wrote again to his absent master deploring events: 'neither can I promise safetie of anything in any place heere, in these uncertaine times'.[3]

It was mid-October before the king's intentions became clear, when it was learnt that he had left Shrewsbury and Bridgnorth and was marching not, after all, for Worcester but south-east into Staffordshire and Warwickshire, making eventually for London. The Earl of Essex accordingly turned about and ordered his army back eastwards in the hope of intercepting the royalist advance and protecting the parliamentary garrison at Banbury now threatened by the king's approach. Other far-flung units were ordered to converge on the Banbury area, Lord Brooke's from Droitwich and Lord Grey of Groby's from Leicestershire. The march through the sodden countryside was anything but dynamic, hampered by local obstructiveness, uncertainty over royalist movements, lack of horses, cumbersome baggage and artillery trains and sheer amateurism, with the result that the various units straggled over a wide area and loitered seemingly aimlessly in remote districts far from any central control, allowing ample opportunity for more plundering. The convenient arrows beloved of military historians of the civil war are often clearly misleading, and the precise dating of the commanders' whereabouts bears little relation to their widely dispersed regiments. The army in this autumn of 1642 consisted mostly, it is well to remember, of half-hearted amateurs, and was a cumbersome, ill-disciplined force whose ramshackle progress in any given direction bore little resemblance to arrows. Strategy was rudimentary, professionalism patchy, logistics unsophisticated and the lure of plunder imperative. There were virtually no maps or signposts, roads were rutted tracks or quagmires, local information was unreliable. None of the soldiers, of course – including their commanders – knew that they were marching to the battle of Edgehill, or even where they would find shelter for the night. In a telling comment to Prince Rupert, one royalist commander complained that 'troops are sent out without any manner of forecast or design, or care to preserve or quarter them when they are abroad', while Nathaniel Fiennes later confessed that he and his men rode to Edgehill 'little dreaming of a battle the next day'.[4]

As they re-entered Warwickshire after an absence of barely a few weeks, the Parliamentarians' scattered forces extended from at least Alcester and Great Alne in the north, with John Fiennes billeted even as far as Studley for three days and nights, to Ilmington, some fifteen miles to the south, with Stratford and its neighbouring villages in between. In flagrant disregard of their chief's recent gentlemanly proclamation that 'no soldier should plunder either church or private house, upon pain of death',[5] pillage was an almost automatic accompaniment to the forced quartering, particularly where local informers told of wealthy catholic homes nearby. One such victim was Margaret Sheldon, related to the great family of Weston, Long Compton, who suffered losses at her Temple Grafton mansion totalling £60 on this occasion alone, besides having to quarter the soldiers 'when they were in ye country', and having horses stolen by them 'for his [Essex's] carriage to Kineton Feeld'; while to the south, at Foxcote, Ilmington, the wealthy Richard Canning was another victim, when 'I had my house broke a little before the battle at Edge Hill'. Teams of horses were urgently needed for transporting Essex's guns and equipment and were repeatedly commandeered, and once a villager was deprived of them there was little likelihood of recovering them quickly, if at all. Thomas Townsend at Alveston noted not only losing 'my Teame of horses to Keinton' for the battle itself but also 'from thence to Warwick with the Earle of Essex' in the aftermath and later for the much longer journey back to Northampton when Essex finally left the district in November. Snitterfield was another village lending horses for this later journey, while Leamington Priors complained of having provided horses for the whole of this protracted campaign, from its beginning in Northamptonshire to Worcester and all the way back again. Even for the wealthy the loss of horses so indispensable in a rural economy must have been intolerable, but the soldiers spared no one, not even Widow Adams at Alderminster, who reported that Essex's men 'toocke away from mee a horse to drawe his Carridge away. My horse was worthe £4.'

Virtually every village received its unwelcome consignment of soldiers and their officers, including many, like Snitterfield, Bishops Tachbrook, Studley, Great Alne and Henley, which had already suffered them on the recent outward journey to Worcester, and sometimes in substantial numbers, as before. Drayton and Luddington specified forty-six men and horses of Lord Mandeville's regiment quartering on 21 October, two days before the battle; John Cole alone at Bishops Tachbrook lodged twenty foot officers 'a little before Kington fight' [Edgehill]; while Morton Bagot likewise noted 'a little before Keynton fight, a party of ye Lord St. John his Regymt'. At Snitterfield, Sir Arthur Haselrig shared out his men between Joan Webb, Mr Goodrich, Nathaniel Cooke and the vicar, Edward Nicholls, while William Harbage, Goodrich and Cooke also had men under a Captain Hunt, 'an Oxfordsheire man'. Parsonages usually offered more comfortable accommodation than most and were popular, and Giles Ryland at Morton Bagot and Edward Nicholls at Snitterfield were among local vicars complaining of having to billet soldiers. Leamington's claims offer a particularly interesting insight into the insecurity in the district, when the residents pointed out that a mass invasion by thieving Royalists and subsequent outrages by them might all have been prevented by proper protection from the parliamentary forces of nearby Warwick:

Lost, by the Kings armie for Want of protection: For quartering an hundred men and a hundred and Ten horses three days before Kingston fight, one day and one night. And also, Besides these aforesayd accounts, neere as much

Contribucon payd unto the Kings Army at the Garrison of Banbury as unto the Parliament, our horses taken from us [and] our houses plundered for want of Protection.

Known Catholics could expect particularly harsh treatment. At Rowington, the affluent merchant William Shakespeare was ordered by Essex to accompany the army to Kineton with his horse and cart for three days and nights and apparently did so, as well as being forced later as a penance to spend three days digging on the fortifications at Kenilworth. Most villages reported thefts, often identifying culprits by name or regiment. The seizure of sheep was particularly common. Milcote's report is typical: 'Taken away by ye souldiers under ye Command of the right honble. ye Earle of Essex in their march from Worcester, xi sheepe worth £8.' Similar complaints came from Charlecote, where Thomas Boddington lost 'Ten Fatt sheepe' and John Tew nine, all 'taken away by the Parliament souldiers a little before Kyneton fight', and from Alveston's vicar, who lost three more. At Snitterfield the vicar Edward Nicholls noted very precisely the loss of 'Halfe a ricke of Hay by the Earl of Essex Armie the Friday before Kinton fight', underlining his anger with the comment: 'All this I will affirme uppon Oath.' All told, these were eventful days in the Stratford countryside. Whether singly, in small groups or *en masse*, for a day or for much longer, the passage of this first major force through the district was seldom less than memorable to the individual, as testified by the careful submission of Ann Canning at Morton Bagot, near Henley-in-Arden:

Att the first comeinge downe of the Earle of Essex there lay att my house my Lord St. Johns, Lt. Coll. Essex & major Andrewes, with most part of theire Regimt, they payinge for nothinge but 2 sheepe . . . This Regimt left behind them a lame souldier att my house, which stayed wth me 8 or 9 weekes, & when he went away hee tooke a brasse pistoll, a new paire of bootes & a new shirt, with many other odd thinges.

At the heart of all this frenzied activity lay Stratford itself, no longer on the fringe, as when Essex's army had largely by-passed it a few weeks previously, but finally in the thick of things, for months to come. Its comfortable yeomens' houses, convivial inns and air of prosperity would have made it a magnet even without its strategic position halfway between Worcester and Banbury, for which Essex was making. Not surprisingly, therefore, virtually every one of the 130–odd householders whose compensation claims have survived record the quartering of troops throughout the town centre on this fateful journey. These records are highly informative, even though they are incomplete and were compiled almost four years after the event from 'what hee can well remember', or 'soe neere as I cann for the present', as two residents, Francis Smith and Thomas Nash, put it. It is clear that the town, already forewarned by the local musters, hectic recruiting and collections, was now hit by a mass influx during the week preceding Edgehill, probably peaking on the Friday and Saturday, 21 and 22 October. Nothing in the Tudor musters of Shakespeare's day or even the panic over the Armada was comparable to the excitement of this military build-up. Streets, taverns and houses were full of armed men, the sound and smell of their horses everywhere, and yards, barns, market hall and perhaps even church served as temporary dormitories for the common soldiers while lordly commanders banqueted off oak tables in the yeomens' houses and slept in four-posters in gabled chambers. And once they were there, some remained for many long weeks, not always – whatever the precise dating by military historians of the commanders' movements – for a brief overnight stay, before quickly moving on. Periods of quarter lasting several days and even a week or more are commonly reported. Robert Fitzhughes specified 'for about 12 daies' and George Gale reported a whole month. It is also likely that many missed the battle altogether, or managed to do very little indeed there: the cautious Essex left a defensive unit in Stratford before continuing to Kineton, some of the men manning control posts or 'courts of guard', while Robert Fitzhughes lodged '16 men, most of them officers, on Saturday & Sunday, the same day yt Kinton fight was'. Others found their quarters so congenial as to return there within a few days, Thomas Greene, for example, having to entertain Captain Meldrum under Sir William Balfour 'at 2 severall times, in free quarter'.

To have to quarter soldiers was in itself bad enough, but the householder's liabilities seldom rested there, as any random selection from their complaints reveals. Thus although Richard Morrell in the High Street was for some reason let off lightly as regards actual billeting, this did not prevent his 'Bill of Losse' for this particular phase of the campaign from becoming a fairly heavy one. It included the disappearance of two mares, two bridles, two saddles and a stirrup, a 'pannell' (a kind of saddle), a green coat, four sucking pigs, a pillowcase and a napkin, besides the further expenses incurred by lodging two 'boys' and six horses, and caring for a sick soldier who then died in his house; plus a gentleman of Lord Grey's Leicestershire company 'who lay sicke & lame 20 weekes' – until well into the spring of the following year. Such a catalogue is repeated, with variations, for almost all the inhabitants. Nicholas Ryland in Sheep Street lodged thirty dragoons, eight other soldiers with their horses for a night ('and breakfast in the morning', he added pointedly), and for a further couple of days nine more men and horses under Captain Hymans, eight more under Sir William Balfour and eight under the Earl of Bedford, and not forgetting a 12s. debt left unpaid by some of Colonel Fiennes's men. Edward Wells in Sheep Street lodged thirty-seven of Essex's soldiers 'for a night and breakfast', and eight more of Bedford's for four days and nights. Richard Smart in Wood Street had thirty-four of his sheep and one cow killed, as well as having to billet and feed 'a Capt, officers & soldiers, Friday before Kinton fight'. Thomas Cleaver lost seventeen loads of his hay and had five soldiers staying with him in Wood Street a whole week at his expense. Mrs Alice Halford nearby billeted as many as fifty men with their horses, who used up seven loads of hay and corn and paid for only a fraction. Thomas Walker in Henley Street lost an entire hayrick and seven sheep, his neighbour Richard Sturley a saddle 'and other wares out of his Shopp'. Richard Ingram in Bridge Street complained of 'damage in his corne, haie and fewell when the Earl of Essex was in towne, by his cariages & soldiers horses', while, the late October weather turning very cold, the churchwarden John Smith recorded that 'the Earle of Essex his soldiers Burnt me 4 loades of lath & hurdles & other timber & firewood' worth £6. Pewter and linen were stolen from the chamberlain Thomas Horne, four lanterns from Francis Smith, and others, like William Lindon and John Barton, told of having to provide teams of horses for several days' service on the battlefield and of losing equipment there. Elizabeth Wheeler lost a pig and a bag; horses were requisitioned, like Francis Ainge's gelding 'prest for ye service'; horsemeat was provided by Thomas Horne for Lord Saye's carriages, as, he stressed, 'the Master of the Wagons knoweth'; and quantities of other provisions, usually bread and cheese where specified, were furnished. Few escaped such multiple commitments.

Of all the bills for compensation later submitted to the parliamentary authorities, the most detailed is that of Thomas Nash, son of Shakespeare's old friend, Anthony Nash of Welcombe, and now married to the poet's granddaughter and living in New Place with Shakespeare's widowed daughter Susanna. It is unlikely that Nash, a captain in the pre-war town militia but now nearing fifty, took any active role in the war itself, though he was, with William Combe, a member of the parliamentary sub-committee which met regularly at Warwick and liaised with the county committee at Coventry. This, his generosity in the charity collections for the Irish refugees and, especially, in supporting the various appeals already mentioned confirm that Dugdale was right to list him in the parliamentarian camp. As we shall see, he was indeed to be later specifically targeted by the Royalists for reprisals. As the largest and most impressive house in the town centre and the home of a known and wealthy sympathizer, New Place clearly recommended itself to the chief parliamentary commanders, and Nash entertained most of them there during this campaign. Having already sent provision to the two Fiennes brothers and to Essex himself on their outward journey to Worcester, he now received into his home not only the Fiennes, 'divers times, with their horses and servants', but 'from tewsday to munday following' Lord Brooke himself, together with all three major commanders of the parliamentary horse at Edgehill, Sir Philip Stapleton and the two Scots, Sir William Balfour and Sir James Ramsey, 'with divers others', as well as Lord Willoughby of Parham for one day and night. Willoughby, fresh from an encounter with Prince Rupert near Kings Norton on 17 October, had come with his eight hundred horse and foot via Henley-in-Arden, marking their passage down the High Street there by taking what they liked, including, from John Horsley's (unspecified) premises, his 'Case of Instruments belonginge to my profession'. Willoughby later paid 'Mr Nash of Stratford' 10s. for lodging him. All this was a signal honour for Thomas Nash, though he could not avoid noting that once the august company had gone a silver spoon was missing. A dung cart and a gate were also burned for firewood by other passing soldiers, and (an interesting insight into the life of the common soldier) 'two loades of straw for litter beds for soldiers' were taken from his barns. Curiously, Essex himself is absent from the list of guests in Stratford. He could have lodged with the conspicuous local Puritan William Combe at the College, just outside the town, who did not submit any claims for compensation; but it is likely that Lord Brooke had offered his commanding officer sumptuous accommodation in Warwick

The King at Edgehill. Though technically Edgehill was a drawn battle, the Royalists could justifiably claim victory in having foiled the Earl of Essex's attempt to block their route to London and dispersed his demoralised troops throughout the Stratford countryside. Probably designed by the king's chief engraver, Thomas Rawlins, at Oxford, the medal depicts Charles dressed in the richly decorated Garter robes, and, on the reverse, as military commander on horseback, in armour and wearing a plumed hat, under a victorious palm and wreath, and accompanied by the famous motto of the Order of the Garter.

(The British Museum)

Castle in which to supervise the logistics of the campaign. As for New Place, the grand old house, which had perhaps heard the poet speak of Hotspur and Harry in English battles long ago, became itself, for a brief moment, the unofficial military headquarters of a new generation of commanders, engaged in the first real battle of the English Civil War.

The long-suffering inhabitants of Stratford were mistaken if they imagined they had seen the last of the soldiers as they finally moved off towards Banbury. In the first place, as already said, not all left town. Whatever was to happen in the following days there was Essex's defensive contingent still loitering in case the Royalists should unexpectedly appear. No one knew that the confrontation would eventually take place at Edgehill, and although Lord Brooke reported correctly from Warwick that the king had arrived at Southam on 22 October making for Banbury,[6] the Royalists had recently been in quick succession at Birmingham,

Kings Norton, Meriden, Packington and Kenilworth, and there was no saying what, for example, the mercurial Rupert might decide to do next, particularly in an area like that to the north and west of Stratford full of royalist sympathizers. The guard posts or 'courts of guard' supplied with fuel on several occasions by the town's chamberlain Thomas Horne are therefore likely to have been permanently manned after Essex's army had left, and this must explain why some Stratford residents complained of his soldiers lingering for weeks on end. The actual battle does not concern us here, though the sounds of it, carried clearly the ten miles on the still air of that frosty autumn Sunday, must have caused consternation among Stratford's churchgoers, as they did even farther away, at Alcester, where Richard Baxter's Sunday afternoon sermon was punctuated by the distant sound of gunfire.[7] But Edgehill had a messy sequel, about which the standard military histories tell almost nothing, as hordes of Essex's defeated soldiers scattered throughout the countryside in all directions, making for unknown destinations, many deserting. Richard Baxter reported many fleeing through Alcester at about sunset on the day of the battle, and sent a messenger to Stratford for news, who returned at 4 o'clock. the next morning. His report must have been graphic and emotional, as few of the nearby villages can have been without their share of dispirited soldiers, many wounded, and 'charges with a maymed souldier after Kineton fight' was a recurrent entry in many a parish account. Long after, memories remained vivid, like Hester Whyte's in 1646, as she appealed to Parliament for relief in a moving human document:

> [She] did ymediatly after Kineton fight take upon her ye care of 2 of ye Parlyamts souldiers there maymed whoe contynued at her house in great misery (by reason of theire woundes) for ye space of three months at ye least, she being constrayned many tymes to be up night & day with them, wch was not only a greate trouble to her but, in respect of her tendernes to ye Parlyamts freinds in that case, a great charge alsoe, she laying out her owne moneys to supply their prsent necessytyes. And further . . . her husband [Daniel] was kylled in the Parlyamt service at ye seige of Banbury Castle: Anno dni 1644, wherby she is left destitue [sic] and comfortles. Your poore petitioner therefore humbly prayeth . . . your help to releeve her whoe in ye tyme of her abylytie willingly afforded both her paines & cost for ye help of such distressed.[8]

Some soldiers reached Newbold Pacey and stayed there bewildered three days and nights, one, desperately wounded, collapsing. The parish register recorded: 'A Souldier wounded in that great battell betwene ye King and the parliament Oct. 23 was buried Oct. 29.' Bishops Tachbrook also received an influx, some remaining a week or more, during which forty-three sheep disappeared from William Elliott's pastures, while Offchurch was another village full of wounded, receiving relief, a drain on the churchwarden's already meagre funds. Many, including the chief royalist prisoners and those unable to fend for themselves, were dragged off to rudimentary surgery in Warwick Castle, and a year later hundreds were still being cared for in Warwick and Coventry. Many others lingered in the villages, dependent on cottagers' wives. Some commanders managed somehow to maintain part of their units intact: typical of other villages, Alderminster was able to send 5s. worth of 'provision and provender for the Releife of the souldiers under Capt. Vines [Fiennes] at Kinton fight'.

There had already been a few sick and lame soldiers being cared for in Stratford homes before the battle, and these were now joined by serious casualties whose condition meant either long convalescence or non-survival, at the homes of such as Thomas Scriven, George Cale and Richard Morrell. Typical entries are those of John Hunt, who recorded: 'Charges with a maymd soldier after Kineton fight, [for] diet & lodging, 11 weeks at 3s. a week', and for a further guest who left without paying for '15 weeks lodging, fire, diet & one to keepe him'; and the similar record of Francis Ainge for 'Charges in keeping one John Staples, a maymd soldier at Kinton fight under Capt. Wing, who lay 6 weeks under the Chirurgeons hands, & a maid to keepe him.' The picture is further confirmed by entries in the chamberlain's own accounts under the heading 'Mr Bayliffes Bill', recording 'monyes disbursed & given unto the Parlimt souldiers which weare wounded & died in the Towne after Kinton Batell' for individual Stratford men who had enlisted. There follow various additional payments: 1s. to '1 Souldier which was wounded', 5s. 4d. to a war widow, 1s. 6d. to '3 severall men that were hurte', 1s. 6d. to John Mason 'for dressinge to Souldiers', 13s. to Edward Palmer for carrying some of them to Warwick and Evesham, perhaps for more expert attention, and a poignant, evocative entry: 2s. 9d. 'for a [metal] sheete for Eggs & for a pann to burne coales in for the wounded Souldiers'. Finally, there is a more sombre note: 'Paid for 3 shrouds for 3 Souldiers, 6s. 6d.', followed by a further 8s. 10d. for four more shrouds. Unfortunately, the Stratford burial register contains no entries for the war years, almost certainly a reflection of the turmoil of the time, when registers were often interrupted or disappeared altogether.[9]

None of this, of course, was happening in isolation. Just as Richard Baxter had reported villages near Kidderminster being depleted after the passage of the king's army, so after Edgehill the Stratford district was full of new recruits passing to join the royal army on its advance to Banbury and Oxford. From Milcote on 30 October the bailiff again wrote to the Earl of Middlesex about his fears for the safety of property and goods, since 'all our parts [are] full of soldiers marching to wards the Kings armie, & makeing use of any mens sheep & provisions where they come'. A long tale of woe follows, giving a graphic illustration of the insecurity of the times. He has just returned to Milcote, he continues, to find that eight sheep have already gone, and now, in the aftermath of 'that bloudie Incounter neare Edghill', the arrival of parliamentary soldiers was causing him equal alarm, 'the Armie after the battell being unrulie':

> . . . the parliament forces returning to Warwick, Stratford & their abouts, their came a Troupe of horsse to be quartered at Melcott, under the comaund of Sr Samuell Luke, & of my Lord Feildings Regiment. Noe meanes I could use would preveile wth them to change their quarter. The Captaine came late in the night, to whom I appeald, but he told me he was quartered their by the Quarter maister generall, & hoped to doe your honr a favour, to keep others from coming who would have plundered your house.

The anxious bailiff finally persuaded the officer to send half of his troop elsewhere, leaving the remainder, still numbering about forty men with their horses, to remain on free quarter at Milcote. He sought out Lord Feilding at Stratford the next day and mollified him by inviting him to dine at Milcote that evening off a piece of mutton and a chicken the day after. The troops eventually left, after three days, but on departure took with them more animals and quantities of timber for fuel, promising airily to pay later. Others were threatening to take the earl's hay for their quarters at Stratford, where it was evidently in short supply. The town was clearly still being occupied by Parliamentarians into November.

These revealing and human documents vividly evoke the disruption that the war was causing in a district where, as we have seen, tenants could no longer afford their rents and were surrendering their plots to landlords, themselves unable to sell their produce, and where 'provisions are verie much wasted', as the Milcote agent put it. Villagers were still having to scrape together to send food and provender to units loitering in the district awaiting instructions: much was sent to Barford, for example.[10] Those carts remaining in the villages, as at Milverton, Snitterfield and Stratford, were being requisitioned to transport Essex's surviving goods and equipment away to Warwick, Daventry and eventually even farther off. William Lindon in Stratford was one who noted despairingly 'following his Cart to Northampton and mending one, being broken, taken by [Essex's] army after Kineton fight'. Letters were being intercepted on the roads and messengers were liable to be seized and imprisoned; traders were being hit; and carters were reluctant to operate. Armed men were roaming everywhere, and nothing was safe; certainly not the horses and pigs in the yards, nor the cattle and sheep under the elms or the crops in the fields, nor the wood and grain stacked in the barns; and neither Thomas Walker's carefully stored corn at Bridgetown nor even Robert Simcock's apples in his burgled loft at Luddington.

Above all, finally, plundering and violence were now a way of life, almost routine. Raiding parties were no longer simply opportunistic but highly organized. In one expedition, typical of other less ambitious ones, the mansion of the great catholic landowner William Sheldon, at Weston, Long Compton, was pillaged shortly after Edgehill by a parliamentary troop of horse from Warwick, while colleagues from Kenilworth, now in parliamentary hands after the king had withdrawn the royalist garrison and being fortified by local forced labour, even had the leisure to drive an entire herd of Sheldon's cattle well over twenty miles back to their garrison to replenish their stock. Deserters, stragglers and vagabonds, often indistinguishable, wandered the countryside, mingling with fugitives from the battle, so numerous that Essex was obliged to write wheedling letters to call back to duty those he tactfully described as having 'gone to visit friends', and local supporters were engaged to round them up and send them back to duty while scavenging for arms at the same time. William Loggins of Butlers Marston was entrusted with the task of collecting booty and useful salvage from the field at Edgehill for the Royalists, while Hastings Ingram, an active Parliamentarian from Little Wolford, performed a similar task for Essex.

The duty was not always without danger, as Ingram found. In charge of an armed patrol on about 25 October, he came across a group of parliamentary deserters loitering at an alehouse at Long Compton, and persuaded them via a good meal to return to their unit. A week or so later, Ingram's manor – whether coincidence or not is unclear – was attacked by a sudden incursion of 140 Royalists, 'untill all his barnes, stables and outhouses, 400 pounds worth of corne, 120 loads of hay and five bayes of his said dwelling house were burned downe by the souldiers'. The Royalists duly plundered the house before setting it on fire, causing £2,000 worth of damage. Less than a year later the Royalists returned to complete the task, setting Ingram's house ablaze a second time. As we shall see, such houses, stoutly built, conspicuous and invariably alleged by the other side to be garrisoned and fortified by the enemy, were increasingly to come under attack as the war developed.

Such was the first phase of the war in the district, where soldiers associated with Edgehill remained scattered in and around Stratford and Warwick until mid-November, when a more cheerful Milcote bailiff could report: 'this cuntrie now is well relieved of Soldiers'. But by 19 November he had already retracted:

> I thought now we should have been safe & quyett heere. But their is some Troupes of horse about Warwicke castell that have been at dyvers places in this cuntrie & plunder howsses & take mens horsses as they ryde on the high way whome they please not to affect, wch puts many in great feares. I had word sent me they threaten to be heere.

His fears were to be amply justified. The neighbourhood could not so easily return to its former peaceful state, for permanent royalist garrisons were now established at Banbury and Oxford to challenge the parliamentary ones at Warwick, Coventry and Kenilworth, while great mansions like Compton Wynyates, Broughton and Milcote, and any available manor house, like Beoley, Chipping Campden, Baddesley Clinton, Lark Stoke and Little Wolford, were liable at any time to be invaded, taken over and converted into a minor fortress by one side or the other and attract more violence. Stratford's own autumnal peace was simply a temporary lull.[11]

CHAPTER 5

Stratford's Own Battle

Edgehill seems to us now a clear watershed. Before it, war might always have been avoided; after it, both sides were aware that no quick, painless solution was available, and settled down to a long, bitter struggle. Although the battle had in effect been a parliamentary defeat, it was only marginally a royalist victory, and the heavy casualties that each side inflicted on the other enabled both to imagine themselves victors. Few, therefore, thought of compromise or moderation. During the summer and autumn there was indeed occasional talk of negotiation. But Lord Brooke himself led the hawks in opposing any idea of 'accommodation' with the king except on terms so humiliating as to be deliberately unrealistic, and summed up his position with the utmost clarity in a speech in Parliament on 19 December: 'I am with all my heart against this Accommodation, against any whisper or thought of Accommodation, till his Majesty shall submit to our Nineteen Propositions.' When he went on to urge members to 'proceed to shed the blood of the ungodlie' if the king did not accept terms, it was clearly an ultimatum. For the civilian population the war had finally come, stark and clear. In many Midland counties local administration was now breaking down as anarchy spread to the civil courts. On 4 October the Warwick Quarter Sessions started late when the two long-serving, elderly Justices of the Peace, Sir Thomas Holt and John Lisle, were delayed from arriving at Shire Hall, only to have the proceedings then violently disrupted within the hour, when:

> . . . the Lord Rochford entered Warwick with 800 [parliamentary] soldiers, and the noise of the drums and trumpets which came with him so disturbed the court that [it] was instantly adjourned to the Swan, which was so filled with his Lordship and his soldiers that nothing could be done there.

The court would not resume for three whole years.[1]

In the autumn of 1642 the main focus of the conflict gradually shifted away from the area, but with the king establishing his court at Oxford and the parliamentary garrison at Warwick now counterbalanced by a new aggressive one when Charles seized Banbury Castle in the wake of Edgehill, violence was likely to recur at any time. This was the situation, requiring vigilance 'both within doore & abroad', which Robert Fawdon at Milcote described in mid-November on a day when he had consulted with John Ryland about some Stratford rents: 'This cuntrie now is well relieved of Soldiers, yet their forces remaine'. Although

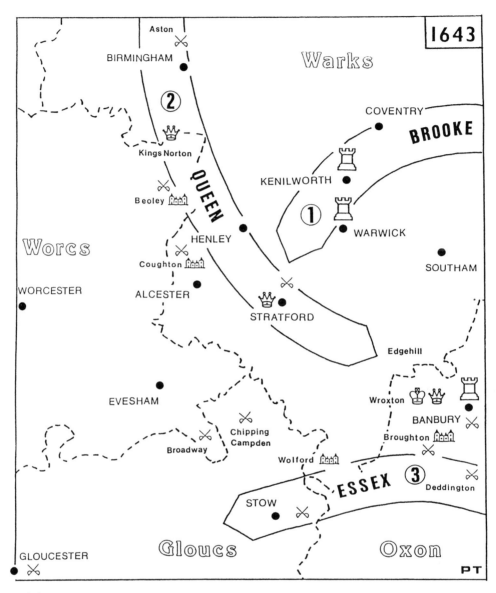

Siege or skirmish

Mansion plundered or attacked

King's lodging

Queen's lodging

Map 3. Major Events in 1643.

their inhabitants were as divided as any, both Warwick and Banbury were now under virtual martial law, with minor outrages being constantly reported, and the occupying forces only too prepared to interfere with the ordinary life of the citizen. Stratford was not occupied as such, but was near enough to both not to be left alone for long. The success of Lord Brooke's various initiatives, together with the newly formed parliamentary committee at Coventry, has led some historians to claim that Warwickshire was 'held for Parliament'. But this neat formula does not bear much examination. Brooke himself was more often at Westminster than Warwick, organizing the wider political struggle, and depended locally on the initiative and energies of loyal deputies like his governor and chaplain at Warwick, John Bridges and John Bryan, his radical ally William Purefoy, who dominated the Coventry committee, and other staunch allies, like Edward Peyto of Chesterton, Anthony Stoughton of Warwick and William Combe of Stratford. But against this group was the equally determined opposition of the Royalists under the direction of the Earl of Northampton, given increasing powers by the king in the area, and who began by fortifying the castle at Banbury and placing it under the governorship of his son William Compton. Neither the earl nor his sons can have spent many nights at the family seat at Compton Wynyates during the autumn of 1642. In addition, whole districts, especially those west and south of Stratford stretching into the adjacent counties, were very far from being under parliamentary control. There, the king could count on the fierce loyalties of Sir William Russell in Worcestershire, Lords Chandos and Molineux in Gloucestershire, Sir Thomas Pope in Oxfordshire and a host of influential gentry, besides the great catholic families already referred to. The region was, in effect, therefore, a frontier zone between the two opposing factions in which neither side held undisputed sway, crossed by routes passing through or near Stratford which each desperately needed to keep open. Neither side was prepared to allow the other to establish a further presence in the district. It was this scenario which was to lead directly to Stratford's own battle.

Meanwhile, both sides continued to scavenge to equip and maintain their needy garrisons and targeted each other's homes with vicious raids. On 25 November the king issued a warrant to the Earl of Northampton to seize plate, money and ammunition, and the earl was also busy plundering local carters of their wares. As already reported, quartermaster Richard Round was engaged in similar activities for the Warwick governor, while in early December parliamentary forces reportedly ransacked the Earl of Northampton's home – whether Compton Wynyates or Castle Ashby is unclear – 'mangling and cutting into pieces rich chairs, beds, stools and hangings, drinking as much and as long as they were able, then letting the rest run out upon the floor', while Royalists were similarly accused of 'most shamefully pillaging my Lord Saye's house' following its capture after Edgehill. While such relatively trivial events were now almost routine, more serious raiding was also continuing throughout the region and was always likely to attract forces from outside and escalate into something even more serious. For example, the two great Leicestershire rivals, the young Lord Grey of Groby and Henry Hastings, were both active in the area, Hastings liaising with his ally Northampton and capturing much ammunition near Coventry in late December, Grey at Daventry threatening a strike against Banbury. Much skirmishing was also reported from the opposite direction, in Worcestershire, where Sir William Russell's Royalists were reportedly tyrannizing the land, and there were clashes between the Royalist Sir Lewis Dyve and the Parliamentarian Earl of Stamford. The Banbury district was particularly dangerous. The new royalist garrison was despatching raiding parties over a wide area in order to maintain itself and keep up morale, and to supplement the precarious royal finances. The Earl of Northampton complained to the king that the district allotted to him for the collection of the dreaded 'contributions' was inadequate to support the four regiments needed to police the Banbury area satisfactorily, while the king at Oxford had to make a personal plea to his assembled lords to fill the royal coffers and so prevent mutiny in an army whose condition even he described as deplorable. The climax came over Christmas and well into the New Year, when at one point Prince Rupert and further reinforcements had to rush out from Oxford in answer to urgent appeals from Banbury, under threat from Northamptonshire Parliamentarians aided by peasants brandishing pitchforks. In one engagement, a much-publicized incident on 5 January, Colonel Joseph Wagstaffe, a senior parliamentary commander under Colonel John Hampden, was captured by the Royalists, and when he sued for pardon on the somewhat implausible grounds of 'being not sensible of the niceties of the distinction betwixt King and Parliament', was pardoned and promptly joined the Royalists. As often with these cases of suspiciously sudden conversions, of which there were many in the civil war, it is impossible to be totally sure of the facts in their now remote context. But Wagstaffe, a local man who had served the French king as a major on the continent and was, as he blandly pointed out, 'now more perfectly informed of his owne misdoings' in serving Parliament, was being economical with the truth. The supposed convert was shortly to be engaged in the violence at Stratford, and as an inveterate royalist adventurer was still in the Stratford district plotting an armed coup after the war.[2]

Such was the confused and tense situation throughout the region when, for reasons which are far from clear, the Royalists turned their attention to Stratford. It may be that they intended garrisoning the town, where it was known they could count on considerable support from the many leading citizens already named. But Stratford was hardly defensible and the plan, if there was one, could never have been viable. Unlike Coventry or Banbury it had no ancient walls which could be hastily restored, and although the Avon provided a useful barrier to the east, the town lay open to the fields on all other sides, including the north-east looking towards Warwick, from which any serious parliamentary attack might have been expected. It was also, like Banbury, surrounded by low hills facilitating attacker rather than defender. There is no evidence that the Royalists devised any serious plans to offset these natural disadvantages, although a later parliamentary report claimed that the Royalists had begun 'fortifying and entrenching the Towne', and the 'quantity of wood lying upon ye River of Avon neare Stratford' belonging to Sir Edward Peyto which the king ordered the Earl of Northampton to seize on 2 January may well have been earmarked for just such a purpose.[3] If so, such activities must have been followed with the keenest interest by the ever-alert governor at Warwick, John Bridges, as a small force of about a hundred of his cavalry suddenly arrived one day to neutralize a town clearly considered politically suspect. The Parliamentarians, however, were met by a hostile reception committee 'upon Saturday last, being the 7 January':

> The Towne did oppose their entrance. Uppon which, comming to a parley, they demanded all the Armes in the Towne; which, when the Bayliffe and Aldermen had refused to deliver up, they went away in discontent, threatning to come againe with a greater number, not onely to disarme the Towne but to plunder it also.

It is, in fact, far from obvious how a group of ageing aldermen could physically obstruct a determined force of cavalry, so the reporting may be unreliable in detail; but the Warwick governor was clearly seriously alarmed, and the unexplained visit of John Lewis of Warwick to Stratford's bailiff recorded in treasurer John Bryan's accounts the following week may well relate to the tense situation building up between the two towns. In early January the Earl of Northampton was reported to be 'raising money upon that Towne [Stratford] and in the Countie, to the great impoverishment of the Inhabitants', stealing horses, and clashing with Bridges' soldiers several times in the process. Occasionally Bridges was able to win a small victory:

> I haveing notice of great sadles [being] sent to Stratford uppon Avon by George Wincoate, a sadler in Warwick, to be sould to a partie of the Kings Armie that were there or expected to come there the same day, I sent a partie of souldiers after them, and tooke them upon the roade.[4]

Unsure how long he could continue without reinforcements, however, Bridges appealed to Lord Brooke in London in mid-January to 'haste downe with all speed, lest more forces should come against him, and so confine him within the walls of the Castle'.[5] Bridges' anxieties were in fact perfectly justified by the ominous situation in the district. Farmers were increasingly unable to subsist, or avoid being sucked into the conflict. One of the Earl of Middlesex's tenants, Thomas Combe of Welcombe provides an interesting and no doubt fairly typical illustration of someone probably guilty of nothing worse than weakness or attempting to steer a middle course and ending up being condemned by each camp for helping the other. He had unwisely, though perfectly understandably, hesitated to lend the king the enormous sum of £1,000, claiming, no doubt correctly, 'how unprovided he was to satisfie his Majesties desire', while protesting his loyalty. But the Earl of Northampton pointedly asked him to think again, and before long, though protesting his innocence, he was condemned by the Royalists as an enemy informer and collaborator, harassed, had his servants seized on the road at Shotteswell and his crops stolen and sold at Banbury. He also had a large cargo of woad seized as it was being taken by barge down the Avon into Worcestershire along with large quantities of Edward Peyto's, though he was adamant that his own bags were quite separate. Shortly after, to add insult to injury, he was imprisoned at Coventry by the Parliamentarians and when released 'suffered much dammage by the plundering of souldiers and ame still persecuted by those under the Earle of Northampton'. Not surprisingly, he was one of those named as unable to pay his rent.[6] Other local dignitaries had no compunction about taking sides and were beginning to convert their manor houses into mini-garrisons, like Richard Brent at Lark Stoke, near Ilmington – later to pay heavily for his royalism. To add to the general anarchy, at the end of a snowy January Prince Rupert dashed across 'the hithermost part of Warwickshire' through Kineton, first hijacking sixty cartloads of goods near Daventry and selling them profitably at Southam Fair, then pillaging Peyto's home at Chesterton and careering through Butlers Marston, Shipston-on-Stour and Darlingscote, before going on to storm Cirencester.[7] Two of the many dramatic rumours rife in mid-January are of particular interest in illustrating the mood of hysteria: a royalist plot to assault Warwick Castle to rescue prisoners, 'considerable persons [who] can carry many after them'; and a highly provocative plan by the Royalists to hold the county assizes at either Warwick or Stratford under Robert Arden, lately one of the king's Commissioners of Array and an officer under Northampton – provoking an anonymous urgent memorandum addressed to the Coventry commissioner John Barker, on about 14 January:

> I, beinge informed that the quarter sessions are intended to be kept either at Warwick or Stratford on tuesdaie next, wch is comanded by Mr Arden the newe Sherriffe . . . thought good to advise wth you touching the same, entreateinge you to enquire out their Intentions the neere as you can & let me know what course we may take wch may in any wise hinder their proceedings & conduce to the publike service.[8]

It is against such a turbulent backdrop that Stratford's troubles came to a head in February 1643. The Warwick delegation, rebuffed by the town elders on 7 January, had promised to return with reinforcements. The threat was no idle one. A month later Captain John Needham, recently engaged, on his own later admission, in plundering Robert Lee's house at Billesley and Sir Thomas Leigh's at Stoneleigh, was given the task by John Bridges of disarming the town. Arriving purposefully with a strong force on about 10 February he evidently carried out his mission thoroughly: 'By order from ye Lord Brooke I went to Stratford, disarmed ye towne, tooke awaye theyr Ammunition (all of which did amount to ye value of two Cart loades) and delivered them at War. Castle, to be disposed of by Col. Bridges.' Recorded payments included in the Warwick treasurer's accounts to soldiers who 'went to disarme Stratford', and a few details in Stratford's own compensation claims, corroborate the event: from alderman Richard Castle in High Street a musket and a case of pistols taken worth £2 4s., from John Whiteland a carbine 'when they disarmed the towne', together with a slightly richer haul from the corporation's own stock: ten muskets and seven calivers, four pikes, four corslets, ten helmets, ten swords and belts, and six bandoliers. Needham's own claim of two cartloads seems therefore somewhat exaggerated. No other details of the exercise have emerged, but there seems to have been some token opposition, since some citizens, like Edward Wagstaffe of Bridgetown, John Woolmer and William Lindon were later accused of 'raising the townsemen against Col. Needham', and Woolmer, then bailiff, of having the church bells rung to mobilize the citizens against the Parliamentarians. It is unclear how long the operation took, but some of Needham's soldiers were reported quartering at Thomas Walton's at Alveston for as many as six days, and this may well have been on this occasion. Shortly after, Needham was promoted to colonel and became governor of Kenilworth garrison, where he was soon engaged in decimating ancient coppices 'in the Kings wood lying betwixt Kenellworth and Stonley' to fortify the castle.[9]

One unexpected and dramatic development directly linked to these events was the flight of Stratford's vicar, Henry Twitchet, doubtless fearful for his young family and unwilling to contemplate living under an autocratic parliamentary regime in the district. He and Thomas Dighton were reported by 10 February to be already 'much out of towne', and some other leading citizens like Nathaniel Duppa (and probably, from the opposite camp, William Combe), whose names are suspiciously absent from subsequent records, probably left the area at about the same time. Of these, some, no doubt, were indeed political activists. Dighton, for example, later confessed to 'delinquency' in leaving home to join the king's forces at Oxford, as did Thomas Hitchcock, while John Stew had probably left some time before, having sent money, horses and arms to the king. Others, as already noted, tried to organize opposition to Needham. But whether Stratford's vicar can be placed quite so firmly in the same category as these is more doubtful. Certainly he had already been accused the previous summer of approving the billeting of (royalist) soldiers in town, and he was later roundly condemned by the parliamentary authorities as a delinquent who 'was at ye beginning of theise warres in Armes at such tyme as Captayne Needham came to disarme Stratford, & did leave his usuall place of abode and cure at Stratford & betake himselfe to ye Enemyes Quarters & Garrisons'. Having thus 'wholly neglected & absented himself from the said cure for the space of three years', he was duly punished in the usual way by having his living and estate 'sequestered to ye use of ye state', pending the appointment of a more politically acceptable incumbent. But unless the charge that he was actually 'in arms' was true, none of this proves real political commitment – though he may indeed have lacked the stomach for a fight that his formidable predecessor clearly had. It seems more likely that when Stratford was becoming dangerous in January 1643 he took temporary refuge elsewhere, in what Parliamentarians considered enemy quarters, before resorting to the calmer environment of his other parish in rural Huntingdon, in June 1643, where he remained for the duration of the war. But he evidently kept his interest in Stratford, still paying rent for the chapel orchard and churchyard in 1645, as though he had not quite abandoned the hope of returning there one day, in quieter times. Stratford was fortunate in avoiding the fate of many parishes, left without an incumbent when their parson was ousted by political pressures. It possessed in William Hawling, Twitchet's curate, a ready substitute who evidently won the respect and affection of the community during the war years when he conscientiously deputized as minister.[10]

The news from the Midlands was now such as to increase Parliament's fears, and Lord Brooke could no longer afford to remain in London, however valued his political skills were there. His arrival in the Midlands was indeed overdue. Recognizing that the war effort was being seriously hampered by petty local thinking, personal jealousies and inefficient organization, Parliament had instructed him in December to organize Warwickshire and Staffordshire into a joint 'association', and at the same time had told the Lords Lieutenant and committees of both counties to summon all inhabitants able to bear arms. In January, quartermaster-general John Hunt was made responsible as provost marshal for local recruiting 'for his [Lord Brooke's] Army raysed or to be raised in ye Countyes of Warrwicke & Stafford'. Moreover, the rumoured royalist plot to storm Warwick Castle and release their prisoners was taken seriously, and the Earl of Essex instructed Brooke to prevent this.[11] By February the situation in both counties was further deteriorating, as though the Royalists were deliberately attempting to forestall Parliament's plans. The Yorkshire Catholic Sir Francis Wortley, a fierce divine-right Royalist who had done much for the king's cause in the north at the outset, had been plundering in Staffordshire in November, and his soldiers were reported there again in February, 'at Stafford, and the Town would gladly be shott of them', as one exasperated journalist put it. In Warwickshire, as we have seen, the situation was regarded by John Bridges as so perilous as to justify an urgent appeal to Brooke for immediate action, and a similar plea came from Northamptonshire on 28 January. The appeals were evidently heeded, since throughout February there are hints of an impressive military build-up in the 'cannons, musketts & frames', other 'engines' and carriages to draw them 'to the Lord Brooks house', saddles, and even 'things belonginge to Chyrurgery' appearing in the accounts of Rowland Wilson, Lord Brooke's treasurer at Coventry, for what was described on 10 February as Brooke's 'presente expedicon'. A convoy of ordnance was similarly reported to be on its way from the parliamentary high command at St Albans – where, incidentally, a rising officer named Oliver Cromwell had recently broken up a pro-royalist meeting in the market-place. Lord Brooke finally set out from London in mid-February on what was to be his last fateful journey; he was not to return south. He took what was by now the usual route for Parliamentarians travelling to the Midlands or the north, via their great safe havens at Northampton and Coventry, and where he could receive the latest reports from trusted commanders on the spot. At Northampton he was joined by more volunteers and given much ammunition before moving on to Coventry, on about 22 February, where the bulk of his equipment, ammunition and army was being assembled and where, according to a probably truthful parliamentary report, he was 'joyfully entertained' for a brief day or so of what must have been a hectic round of consultations, briefings and last-minute planning. While at Coventry he summoned more local volunteers to join him 'in this present expedition'.[12]

Coventry's strategic position gave Brooke the option of either continuing north via Coleshill (the old road supposedly taken by Falstaff in *Henry IV*) into Staffordshire or concentrating on matters nearer home. But the news from the north was more reassuring: an uprising of local people had attacked Sir Francis Wortley's 'papists and malevolents' at Stafford, forcing them to flee with many casualties. Much more disturbing was the local news: Stratford was reported to have invited Royalists to occupy the town ('Wee have some reason to believe they invited the Enemy', reported one news-sheet). Also, the hated renegade Wagstaffe and his unsavoury ally Colonel Gerard Croker were there organizing resistance: Wagstaffe, 'the run away who was from the beginning false' and

> most perfidiously fled away from his Colours, . . . is now in Warwickshire with such ragged forces as he hath since gotten together, being in all three hundred, and it is reported he hath entered Stratford upon Avon, where he doth yet continue.

One scaremongering account inflated Wagstaffe's force to nearer eight hundred, but a more sober one from the reliable information service organized by Sir Samuel Luke confirms the general picture through a parliamentarian spy, William Tudman, who at Stratford on Friday 24 February 'sawe Collonell Croker and Lieftenent Wagstaffe with 400 men whoe intended to have fortified the towne, and chargd all the towne to aid and assist him if any of the Parliament forces came'.[13]

It looks, therefore, as though little or no progress had been made in the earlier plans for the defence of the town, and an interesting sidelight on the whole episode was given later in an aside by the authoritative Sir Edward Nicholas, the king's secretary at Oxford. He attributed the dismal royalist performance at Stratford, a town 'too long neglected through an unreasonable desire of command in some', to the military indiscipline and petty jealousies to which the great civil war historian Clarendon referred more than once. It would have called for rare skills indeed to blend into a disciplined and effective fighting unit the egos of the mercenary Wagstaffe and the blustering Croker (whose own main contribution to the war so far had been to accompany Prince Rupert on his recent vicious assault on Cirencester, and who was soon busy bullying friendly south Warwickshire villages into paying exorbitant taxes by methods so unscrupulous that the Earl of Northampton complained to Rupert about him). Moreover, an additional complication may have been provided by the extremist Sir Francis Wortley and the city merchant Sir Nicholas Crisp, adept at intrigue, both of whom were also reported interfering at Stratford. The much-absent Earl of Northampton clearly had other pressing concerns than those at Stratford. The benefit to the town of royalist incompetence was, however, real, since it meant it was spared the major disruption suffered by Warwick's inhabitants during the fortification of their town. But Stratford was now having to pay substantial sums of money to the Earl of Northampton; and there were at least five visits in February alone by leading citizens of Stratford to consult with the Warwick governor, John Bridges, on business whose nature is not disclosed but which must have related directly to the approaching crisis.[14]

By the time Lord Brooke finally moved from Coventry to Warwick, on Friday 24 February, he had decided to act.[15] Clearly he could not countenance a royalist garrison at Stratford, additional to that already proving a major irritant at Banbury, and he now had at his disposal a sizable army – though probably not the 10,000 claimed in one parliamentary report, since he was still calling for volunteers. He was accompanied by a regiment under the formidable veteran William Purefoy, now about to be promoted to colonel of horse. Having first sent out an armed patrol towards Stratford 'to give them an Alarum' and prevent the enemy from having a good night's sleep, Brooke spent barely a few hours in Warwick, working furiously to overcome last-minute hitches over the supply of horses. He was obliged to go 'into Towne, and from house to house call up the Cartars to goe away with his Cariages', but somehow still found the time to make the humane gesture of visiting one of the royalist prisoners, the young Earl of Lindsey, in bed in the second chamber in Guy's Tower. He then set out in the small hours of Saturday 25 February with a strong force estimated by one sober royalist report as four troops of horse and dragoons, four thousand foot and four guns, easily outnumbering the resident Royalists which sources gave as about three hundred horse. Strict disciplinarian though he was, even Lord Brooke could not prevent some disorder among his men; a few were reported miles off course, stealing from William Evitts at Butlers Marston, who complained of losing over £2 'taken from me by ye Lord Brookes Army in money etc as they went to Stratford'. Unlike the Royalists who were most probably left to fend for themselves, Lord Brooke saw that his men were reasonably fed, Major James Castle paying out 10s. from the castle funds 'for victualls given to the soldiers when they marched to Stratford', and some local inhabitants sending their own contributions, like William Hopper at Alveston, who despatched a load of bacon, cheese and barley to Stratford 'before the fight'. Marching through the night, 'hoping covertly to surprise the enemy early next morning', Brooke sent ahead a patrol to cut off the retreat of any local inhabitant likely to alert the Royalists, but slowed down by their guns it was daybreak before the Parliamentarians were near Snitterfield, where they were sighted by an anonymous royalist sympathizer at about 8.00 a.m., who 'espying us 2 miles on this side crossed the Fields and gave the enemy advertisement'. The Royalists hastily assembled forces and 'drew out of the Towne to encounter [Lord Brooke] upon a Heath distant about a mile from thence' – or 'under a Hill' in another version – presumably one of the low hills near Welcombe. Brooke pushed forward his artillery but fanned out units to the rear also, in case the Royalists should attempt to wheel round, so that 'we stood tryangle upon three hills in full view of each other'. Brooke then fired his cannons 'through the midst of them', and 'we played so hot upon them that with the losse of 40 men they were forced to retire into the Towne', and 'we hasted after them so fast as our Carriages and the plowd Lands well softened with the raine would permit us'. The royalist retreat turned into headlong flight along the undulating slopes of the Welcombe Hills, probably between Snitterfield and Ingon, across land rich in Shakespeare associations, 'some flying one way and some another, in great distraction', with a number making for Clopton Bridge ready to escape back to Banbury. Nothing is heard of any royalist stand, let alone a counter-attack, nor of any street fighting when 'the Lord Brookes horsemen entered pell mell with them', and one parliamentarian version states, probably truthfully, that 'our enemies hast was such that we could not come within musquet shot of them'. It must have been all over in a few hours, as is suggested not only by the consistent parliamentary reports that Brooke went to Stratford and simply 'beate them out of the towne & took away their arms', but also by the people's own uncomplicated recollections of the day when, according to Nicholas Ryland, 'ye Lo. Brooke was in towne & drove away ye Kings force'.

Jam: calth:

A TRVE
RELATION
Of the death of the Lord BROOKS, who was flaine
by a bullet difcharged againft him as he ftood in a window aginft the Minfter at LICHFIELD;

VVith the defcription of a bloody confpiracy prevented
by Gods providence, from deftroying the Councell of warre
at Stratford upon Avon, wherein is a true relation
of thefe particulers following.

    1. *Of the ~~~~~~~~ of the* Lord Brooks *his Army.*

    2. The Parliament forces that went to Stratford.

The Lord *Brooks.*   Captaine *Gardner* and his Re-
Colonell *Purifoys.*   giment.
Captaine *Bridges.*   A Regiment of Dragooners.
Ceptaine *Hunt.*   A Regiment of Foot.

    3. The Cavaliers Commanders.

Colonell *Wagftaffe.*   Captaine *Trifke.*
L. *Robert.*
Ser. Ma. *Ruffel.*   L. *Sallington,* &c.

    4. *The manner of the fight at Stratford.*
    5. *The manner of the contriving of the Plot.*
    6. *The blowing up of the Town-hall, and the hurt it did.*
    7. *The Lord* Brooks *his valour before his death.*
    8. *The relation of his death.*
    9. *Advertifement to the City of London.*

LONDON,
Printed for *Tho. Bates,* and are to be fold at his fhop
in the old Baily, *Anno. Dom.* 1643.

The Battle of Stratford. *The title-page of one of several contemporary newsletters printed in London shortly after the events related. The account gives the parliamentarian version of the short battle at Stratford on 25 February 1643 when Lord Brooke marched from Warwick and easily routed Royalists, nominally under the Earl of Northampton, who were attempting to garrison and fortify the town. There is no equivalent royalist version of events, but the account given here, though biased, appears substantially accurate, compiled at least partially from first-hand eye-witnesses.*

(The Shakespeare Birthplace Trust)

Old Market Hall, Stratford. Apart from Clopton bridge, Stratford's ancient Market Hall is the town's only building known to have suffered serious damage in the war. Completed less than ten years previously in smart Cotswold stone, it was partially wrecked by an explosion on 25 February 1643 as Lord Brooke's parliamentary soldiers pursued fleeing Royalists through the town. It had recently been used to store gunpowder, so the explosion may well have been an accident rather than the vile royalist plot to assassinate Lord Brooke that propagandists immediately claimed. It long remained derelict before being repaired and modernized, but was eventually demolished in 1767 to make way for the present Town Hall. The sketch is eighteenth-century, but likely to have been based on an earlier one.
(The Shakespeare Birthplace Trust)

The Royalists made an unconvincing attempt to play down the encounter, claiming that they 'made the bridge good for a while' before making

> . . . a safe retreat, and left the Towne unto the Enemy, who fearing there might be some stratagem, or hearing that the Country rose to come in upon them, returned againe in hast towards Warwicke, not doing so much spoile as might give satisfaction for their paines in comming thither.

Probably of more consequence to the townspeople than the skirmish was a dramatic sequel, when a mysterious explosion partially wrecked their new Market Hall, a stone's throw from Shakespeare's New Place:

His Lordship having gotten possession of the Towne, he called his Commanders into the new Towne Hall to consult of what was to be done. In the interim a false Alarme of the enemies re-advancing upon them made them leave their Councell and runne out to stand to their Armes, and they were no sooner departed out but the Hall was blowne up by a Mine and traine of Gunpowder laid by the Cavaliers, without hurt to any of them.

Each side in the civil war was always quick to accuse the other of atrocities, often with justice, and the Parliamentarians searched for superlatives to express their outrage at this 'treacherously laid' plot: 'a bloody conspiracy prevented by Gods providence', or even 'an hellish designe by bloody-minded Papists' which, using '5 Barrells of powder designed to have surprized my Lord and all his chiefs, presuming they would have sate in councelle there', reawakened the horrors of the Gunpowder Plot. But it is just as likely to have been one of the many accidents in a war in which unreliable ballistics and amateur bungling bedevilled both sides and caused many fatalities. The hall had been used to store the town's armoury in the past, and the Royalists may have been stockpiling ammunition there again to replace that recently taken by John Needham. Significantly, even one parliamentarian account admits that while the building was indeed wrecked, 'by which side is uncertain'. Whatever the truth, the incident was instantly known to the townspeople who, according to one lurid report, set up 'a most lamentable and pitiful cry'. Only recently completed in Cotswold stone fresh from the Westington quarries outside Chipping Campden, after two years of ill-tempered wrangling over building and design costs, the 'faire Market Hall' now remained derelict and roofless for years as a long reminder of that wet February when the war came to Stratford.

Lord Brooke had repeated his usual strict order 'that none of the army should pillage, or take away any thing from any inhabitants of the towne'.[16] But it was hardly to be expected that his soldiers' visit should be quite as painless as that described in the parliamentarian reports which admit to a single theft of an old cloak taken by a soldier 'to watch in' on the cold February nights and which anyway, it was claimed, was promptly returned. Some of the town's people tell a different story: of the theft of a sword and pistols from Thomas Lucas (evidently overlooked in Needham's cleansing operation a few weeks previously), of the drinking of William Lane's beer, of the theft of clothes and linen from Nicholas Ryland, of shoes from Peter Holland, a coat from John Bellamy, ready cash here, a few more horses and saddles there. Again, teams of horses were taken to transport Lord Brooke's goods back to Warwick, this time from Richard Smart and John Bellamy, the latter for 'an evening & 2 daies'. A few soldiers even managed to stray as far as Henley, where they took two hides from John Holmes on the day 'when Stratford hall was blown up'. But Stratford's citizens escaped lightly on this occasion, almost certainly owing to Brooke's haste to leave for Staffordshire. There are, however, two intriguing exceptions to this. Money, goods, a horse and a saddle, totalling a considerable £70, were stolen from John Woolmer in the High Street in what looks like a deliberately calculated punishment of the bailiff for having recently entertained the Earl of Northampton and Lord Dunsmore during the July rally, and more recently, no doubt, for having led the group of elders obstructing the parliamentary delegation from Warwick. But perhaps the most evocative entry in the litany of homely items taken from Stratford homes by the soldiers is one with strong Shakespearian connections: domestic objects from the Maidenhead inn, the eastern part of the Henley Street house now known as Shakespeare's birthplace. This property, used recently, as we have seen, by soldiers and also by Robert Fawdon when collecting the Earl of Middlesex's Stratford rents, had been kept for several years by widow Jane Hiccox (a friend of Shakespeare's widowed sister Joan Hart, who lived next door, in the western house, until her death in 1646) with her two orphaned children, Annie and Thomas, as tenants of the poet's daughter Susanna Hall. Picked out in bold lettering on the original manuscript, as if to draw attention to a particularly shameful deed, the widow's losses 'from the howse called the Maidenhead' include items probably once, if not still, belonging to the Shakespeares:

> Tooke away by the Lord Brooks soldiers when hee came to Stratford and drove away the Kings forces there, as followeth:

> 17 silver spoones, 2 silver boles (a bigger & a lesser), a double silver salt in old money £3. 7s., & divers other things in a trunke, to the value of £20 0s.[17]

One more interesting Shakespearian link to the civil war, of a different nature, relates to Lord Brooke's 'surgeon', James Cooke of Warwick, and probably dates from this time. Attending a detachment of parliamentary soldiers left to guard the strategically important entrance to the town over the ancient Clopton Bridge, Cooke was invited to New Place by a colleague who had formerly been an assistant to Shakespeare's son-in-law, the physician John Hall. There, the poet's daughter Susanna showed Cooke her husband's medical notebooks, from which he was later to publish a selection of unique case-histories compiled by a seventeenth-century doctor going about his daily business.[18]

With his Stratford mission successfully completed, Lord Brooke returned to Warwick the same night and prepared to resume the original task assigned to him, that of securing Staffordshire against the Royalists. He lost no time in setting out, some of his men helping themselves to free footwear from John Thomas's shoemaker's shop in Warwick as they did so, and William Greene at Stratford noting an unexplained extra payment of 1s. (this looks suspiciously like a personal punishment as he is the only resident to have mentioned such an imposition) 'charged by Order of the Lo. Brooke at his going against Liechfield'.[19]

A few days later, in one of those grotesque ironies of war, the leader who had given so much to his cause and dominated Midland politics for so long was killed at Lichfield by a stray shot through the eye as he sat in an open window in the Close, fired by a boy perched on one of the cathedral's towers. Lord Brooke's military power, his discipline and his haste to fulfill his duties elsewhere had spared Stratford serious disruption; the town's next invasion by parliamentary soldiers would prove more painful and protracted.

CHAPTER 6

Queen and Country

The period immediately following the battle at Stratford was momentous for the course of the civil war, for within days first Lord Brooke, and then, less than three weeks later, his arch-enemy the Earl of Northampton, were both dead, Brooke killed, as we have seen, by a sniper's bullet in Lichfield Close, Northampton, when successfully routing Parliamentarians nearby at Hopton Heath. Ironically, two closely-related incidents within a short space of time and separated by only a few miles robbed each side of the leader who more than any other had brought the war to Warwickshire, initiating and directing every major action. Brooke in particular had been such a driving force in the religious and political struggle

James Compton, third Earl of Northampton (1622–81). Barely twenty when succeeding to the title on the death of his father Spencer Compton near Stafford, in March 1643, he successfully assumed his father's role as the king's most energetic supporter in the Midlands. A friend of Prince Rupert, he waged an aggressive, sometimes ruthless campaign of harrying enemy forces and collecting taxes, and along with his brothers dominated the Stratford-Banbury district throughout the war. Continuously active in the field, he was with the queen and Prince Rupert in Stratford in July 1643, fought at Cropredy and Naseby, and raised the first siege of Banbury in 1644, though he was unable to prevent the Parliamentarians from seizing the family seat at Compton Wynyates and destroying the church. After the war, Compton Wynyates was eventually restored to him, looted, damaged but substantially intact, on payment of a fine of over £20,000 (later reduced to £14,000).

(Private Collection; photograph: Courtauld Institute of Art)

since the 1630s that it is difficult to imagine that he was still in his mid-thirties; and Northampton too was barely forty. 'Great was the Contention about that time in Warwickshire', summed up an historian writing immediately after the war, 'between the earl of Northampton for the King and the Lord Brooke for the Parliament, not without sharp encounters and slaughter on either side.' The local war had at times appeared indeed rather like the baronial wars of the Middle Ages, a personalized conflict between two powerful rivals. For the Royalists, Northampton was instantly succeeded by his son James, who continued to conduct the war as vigorously as ever from his military base at Banbury; but the loss to the parliamentary cause was even greater, since there was no Midlander remotely possessing the prestige, intellect and energy of their lost leader. After a hesitant interim period of shared command among which Edward Peyto and William Purefoy were prominent, the Earl of Essex eventually replaced Brooke in June with the far less impressive, more controversial Warwickshire figure of Basil Feilding, Earl of Denbigh, of Newnham Paddox, head of one of the most tragically divided of local families. When her royalist husband was killed in April during Prince Rupert's storming of Birmingham, a distraught Lady Denbigh had prayed that her son might abandon his wrong-headed attachment to the opposite side: 'O my dear Jesus, put it into my dear son's heart to leave their merciless company that was the death of his father!' To no avail: a few months later her son was appointed the new Midland parliamentarian commander-in-chief.[1]

The reaction of Stratford's inhabitants to these crucial developments is not recorded. Those of Thomas Nash and John Woolmer, who had recently entertained Lord Brooke and the Earl of Northampton respectively in their homes, would be particularly fascinating to have. Fulsome tributes were paid to Brooke in the national parliamentarian press, but at Stratford the days of heavy puritan sermons from visiting star preachers were long past, and if the absent vicar's curate moralized from the pulpit of Holy Trinity on the twin disaster, no one thought to record the event or publish the contribution. Ingrained habits of local rather than national thinking, poor communications and sheer parochialism prevented much awareness of wider perspectives, and would have relegated such events below pressing local concerns. And these were as onerous as ever. Once again it is the estate agent at Milcote, writing only a fortnight after Lord Brooke's soldiers had gone from Stratford, who conveys the insecurity of the times in his alarm over the mounting taxes exacted by the two sides simultaneously, 'both threatning', and the spread of anarchy in 'these lawles times' where former friends were taking each other's goods: 'everie where they steale wood by authoritie, saying, the soldiers burne theirs, & they must have Fyreing [fuel]'. 'These times will make any man dishonest', an appalled neighbour confessed. Everyone knew that although the soldiers had gone they could always return, and as spring advanced such fears were justified. Before the month was out that had seen Brooke's soldiers march off – a month of rumours that the humiliated Royalists were planning to seize Warwick Castle – more soldiers were back, Prince Rupert's this time, on their way north to recapture Lichfield. Charles's queen, Henrietta Maria, had left England a year ago for the Netherlands, where she had spent busy months recruiting, raising funds and collecting arms; she had

Queen Henrietta Maria's Arrival in Holland. When Parliament accused the Queen of fomenting rebellion in Ireland and civil war seemed increasingly likely, Charles decided to send his wife abroad, partly to accompany the Princess Mary to safety in Holland with her new husband but above all to buy arms and military supplies for the coming war. The young queen is shown on this Dutch medal, with ringlets, necklace and jewelled brooch, arriving in Holland in February 1642. The reverse, depicting a stately ship in rough seas, proudly proclaims her to be 'unmoved amidst storms'. It was on the return journey over a year later, via Bridlington, York and Stratford, that the further medal was struck commemorating her reunion with the king at Kineton (see page 76).

(The British Museum)

now returned and was at York, eager to deliver her valuable cargo to the royal headquarters at Oxford and be reunited with her husband. Yorkshire and the north Midlands were unsafe territory for the queen to cross, however, with the Fairfaxes, Brereton and Lord Grey of Groby posing ever-present threats, and with Lichfield now also in parliamentary hands following Lord Brooke's expedition. As desultory peace negotiations dragged on between the two sides, Prince Rupert set out from Oxford at the end of March to clear such 'obstructions' from the queen's intended path and so escort her triumphantly to the king. He moved north briskly but in easy stages, quartering successively at Chipping Norton, Shipston-on-Stour, Stratford and Henley, marching rapidly enough to reduce the opportunities for widespread plundering but not eliminate it, and parliamentary reports were quick to claim extensive looting in all these towns supposedly royalist in sympathy. In a desperate attempt to denigrate the charismatic Rupert's reputation as a military leader – though not necessarily inaccurate for that – a mischievous parliamentary reporter described Rupert's halt at the little royalist town of Shipston, long associated with the bishopric of Worcester and surrounded by royalist estates:

Prince Rupert came hither with 7 Colours, and upon the Green at the Towns end kept his Randevow [rendezvous] . . . There attended him two Lords, the one supposed to be the Lord Digby, the other the Lord Denby; with foure small field-pieces and some horse, most of which had Cases for Pistols yet but one Pistoll a peece. His Dragoones were double armed all most all, with a Musket before; and behind him, an Irish-Whoore (which seems rediculous, but is a truth) furnished with a strong-water bottle. His foot men [were] thus armed: with Pikes, halfe Pikes, Pike-staves, Holbeards, Brown-Bills, Hedge-bils, Welch Hookes, Clubbs, Pitch-Forks, Cowl-staves, with Choping-Knifes and pieces of Sithes fastened into them. Thus this ragged Regiment marched halfe clad with miserable poore ragges. This Towne being formerly visited with Prince Ro: [Rupert] and part of his matchlesse Regiment before his Last passage to Cicester [Cirencester], were known to bee true Malignants, and therefore favoured each other at that time. But now, the Prince Ro: pleased their Malignancie and Plunderd most, if not all of them.

If this picture is at all accurate it can have done little to reassure the people of Stratford as Rupert approached on 31 March with his sizable force, reportedly 'pillaging extreamly'. It is well to remember this portrait. Although it is blatant character assassination by an enemy, it serves as a useful corrective to the glamorous image of Rupert created later, largely by Victorian poets and painters. To half the population he was simply 'that bloudy prince' or 'the prince Robber'.[2]

Rupert's regiment was far from being the only one in the district. Several other royalist units were reported operating across the region throughout April and May: one stayed at Stratford one night at the beginning of April *en route* from Oxford, supposedly to deal with a threat from Sir William Waller in Gloucestershire; another belonged to Prince Maurice's Evesham forces quartering at Alcester, where there was skirmishing and plunder of 'every house in the Towne of what ever was portable'; and in May others, unruly and marauding, were lording it at Little Wolford under Lord Chandos and at Sezincote under Colonel Gerard. The Warwick governor John Bridges sent out several successful raiding parties against these forces, resulting in violent clashes and casualties, and, as always, foraging parties were a law unto themselves. In one typical raid from Warwick, a widow at Hillborough, Ann Kempson, of the catholic family of nearby Temple Grafton, lost not only a horse but also money, plate, rings, jewellery and linen, all stolen by a light-fingered trumpeter, Thomas Boovy, in about May.[3] A particularly vicious confrontation took place at Middleton Cheney, near Banbury, on 6 May, when the new young Earl of Northampton routed Parliamentarians, leaving many dead. But it is difficult to tie such events together into any meaningful pattern: they were almost chance encounters in a conflict which, following the deaths of the two leaders, had seemingly degenerated into a chaos of local feuding and indiscriminate pillaging. The entire district was in this ferment of aimless violence, the constant sorties, militarily insignificant though they were, keeping the local population in a state of bewilderment, tension and outright fear, as one wretched local resident lamented:

Prince Rupert *(1619–82). Nephew of Charles I, whom he joined at Nottingham on the raising of the king's standard in August 1642, Rupert was the leading royalist commander throughout the war. Charismatic and feared as a brilliant if sometimes reckless cavalry tactician, he fought, usually with great distinction, in all the major battles of the war before being eventually forced to surrender at the fall of Oxford to Fairfax in June 1646 and banished from England by Parliament. He passed through Stratford several times on campaigns, besides accompanying* Queen Henrietta Maria *on her visit in July 1643.*

The soldiers will have quarteringe, and dayly their Comaunders send warrants for provision to be brought to their quarters . . . and trulie, I can see no hope of amends, but dalie new feares. God of his Mercie amend it, or the Soldiers will have all, for they are Maisters of all . . . for between the one side & the other, none is safe. One day they pillage on the one side, & where they misse the other takes.[4]

From all parts individual cases of harassment or worse confirm this testimony. Thomas Combe at Welcombe complained of persecution by the Earl of Northampton's men; William Croft at Todenham of losing eight sheep taken by Royalists comfortably encamped in the Earl of Middlesex's houses at Bourton-on-the-Hill and Longborough; the wealthy Francis Clarke of Tysoe of being plundered by troops from parliamentary Kenilworth. Welford-on-Avon was looted by more Parliamentarians from Warwick, Drayton, outside Stratford, and catholic Rowington (again) by more, from Colonel John Fox's Edgbaston garrison. Yet more parliamentary troops were at Edward Ferrers' great mansion at Baddesley Clinton, on 12 May, under Lieutenant Creed, of Joseph Hawksworth's troop. These stole horses, guns, armour, gunpowder, money, spurs, a silver spoon, a Geneva Bible, and 'many linnens' from the drying chamber; and on a return visit by Captain Otway's men three weeks later, two yoke of oxen and eight milk cows were added to the booty. The anger and distress such thefts caused the victims on such occasions are apparent in the care lavished on the description of what were clearly much-loved personal belongings: 'One rich plush saddle, trimmed round aboute the skirts with a gold lace and a gold fringe, with the cloth cover belonginge to itt, and other furniture.'⁵ As the parliamentary garrison at Warwick became a permanent feature the local people began to suffer from a presence almost as oppressive as the rival royalist one at Banbury, and John Bridges, like his counterpart William Compton at Banbury, found a highly lucrative pastime in the hijacking of goods on the highway and the arbitrary imprisonment of innocent wayfarers for ransom. Several inhabitants of Tysoe suffered this outrage travelling to market at Stratford in May (still evidently functioning, in spite of everything), like Rose Mister's servant and Henry Middleton's son:

> His sonne, going towards Stratford Market with two horses and a quarter of barley, was taken by Collonel Bridges his souldiers to Warwick Castle and Imprisoned, where he payd too Coll Bridges for his liberty six pounds, and for his horses and barley eight pounds.

Occasionally, tragedy struck. When a parliamentarian messenger, William Needle, set out from Banbury to warn a local regiment that a Dutch captain fighting for the Royalists, injured and captured at the Stratford battle, had broken the parole given him by Lord Brooke, he was caught by royalist scouts, dragged back to Banbury and promptly hanged in the market-place. Perhaps the worst incident of all from the immediate Stratford district was one involving the wealthy catholic Thomas Peers of Alveston, in February. Although the reporting is far from impartial, the details suggest a fairly accurate account of the ruthlessness of the extortion procedures now being adopted by both sides:

> One Thomas Pierce [Peers] of Alveston in the County of Warwick, Esquire, a Gentleman of very good life, etc., of about £500 per annum Estate, about a Moneth or five weekes since, refusing to pay £100, was first plundered of all his Cattel and portable stuffe (for he had conveied away his Plate & Monies), and then haled away by Ingram (the prisoner that ran away from Oxford) to Warwick Castle. There he remained some time, during which, to toll him on to a fuller ransome, he had some freedome, as of walking abroad in the Castle and Towne, which neverthelesse cost him deare, the market of his deliverance rising from one to two hundred, & so to five hundred pounds, . . . as constantly refused as the little sum at first . . . He was about the end of the last week threatnd with the Dungeon, and was accordingly cast into it, . . . where in few daies, what with want of sustenance and the noisomenesse of the stinking vault, he died a true patient of those cruelties.⁶

Peers had already been repeatedly plundered (the same trumpeter, Thomas Boovy, being a culprit on one of these occasions), and at one point a £100 ransom was paid. And so it continued throughout the spring, from late April when Prince Rupert again passed through Stratford, triumphant after reconquering Lichfield, and where the town paid for beer for his men, to late May when Ilmington, 'the poore Towne who medled not with either Party was indamaged by [the Royalists] at least three hundred pound, and no distinction made between either friend or foe'; and so into June, when Sir Thomas Aston's cavalry rampaged through the district and emptied Tredington of '40 of our best horses', beating and abusing those who had the temerity to offer to buy them back, and deliberately trampling the villagers' crops as they stormed off 'in a body of 7 or 8 score horse'. None of these incidents was important in itself in any wider, national context, but, taken together, they convey something of the insecurity and lurking horror that increasingly stalked ordinary people during these troubled months.[7]

The rural economy was suffering too. By now, the ancient water-mill a little downstream from Clopton Bridge, leased to John Rogers of Shottery and already beset with legal wrangling over leases and rents, was no longer working, the corn-grinding and fulling processes halted when 'part of the water works were distroyed' some time before July 1643. It is not clear what had happened, but as the mill's commercial profitability had also been linked with the tolls paid for using sluices 'for the benifit of the navigacon upon the River of Avon & for the passing by Boats upon the said River', the impact on the local economy must have been equally serious for those used to transporting woad down-river to Worcestershire dyers, like Edward Peyto, Thomas Combe of Welcombe and the Earl of Middlesex; for local dyers like Richard Bartlett, who leased the now silent fulling mill; and for owner and occupier alike, who instead of making a profit made 'much losse in regard of the troublesome tymes of War, by Plundring, Payments & contribucons'.[8] In addition, estate managers were having to travel many miles to plead with haughty garrison commanders to discipline their men and reduce their extortion in taxes and produce. Tenants likewise pleaded for leniency, for the landowner 'to take these desperat tymes into your consideracon and allowe me somethinge towards my losses', as William Croft at Todenham petitioned. One simple, telling indicator of the state of things was the decline of Stow Fair, 'soe miserable are these times', as Robert Fawdon grumbled: 'I was on May Day at Stow Faire, that usuall great Faire for Sheepe, where thousands used to be sold, and I am assured their was not 100 sold that day.'[9]

More than anything for the population at large, however, was the burden of taxation which was now acute. It had quickly become clear that neither voluntary contributions nor usual peacetime methods of taxation were adequate for financing a war which was likely to be long and costly, and far-reaching and draconian legislation had passed through Parliament in February, masterminded by Lord Brooke's great radical ally John Pym. The measures, which instantly affected virtually everyone, comprised a scheme of compulsory taxation for all counties through local committees that would assess communities and individuals on their estimated wealth. Collection was to be through the constables or, if necessary, the soldiers themselves, with massive penalties for non-compliance, though with safeguards for the very poor. The money thus collected would go to maintain the field armies and, especially, the local garrisons, and was popularly referred to as 'the weekly assessment'. Prominent on the committee at Coventry deciding these things were the leading Puritans whose names were becoming all too familiar to Warwickshire people: the two inseparable zealots, both now colonels of horse, William Purefoy and John Barker, Godfrey Bosevile of Wroxall and Thomas Basnet, their treasurer. The assessments themselves and the erratic and high-handed manner of collection were instantly resented, particularly as they could be seemingly arbitrarily increased at a moment's notice by a diktat from the committee. Nor were the collectors too particular in their methods: 'and now the burthen is growen intollerable,' wailed the Milcote bailiff in April as a collecting party arrived with the bad news, 'for they have dubled the monthlie payments'. The Warwickshire committee came under heavy criticism for over-taxing the county relative to neighbouring ones – a direct reflection, no doubt, of the degree of puritan zeal on the part of its members.[10] But the committee also tried to be fair, and reductions were not uncommon. Thus from May 1643 Stratford was at first required to pay £20 per week to John Bridges at Warwick, but this sum was progressively reduced and by December had been halved. Following the earlier visits made by leading members of the corporation to Warwick in February, already reported, Thomas Horne, accompanied by Job Dighton, made several more unexplained visits to see Bridges during April, when the level of assessment must have been known, and some of these were evidently lengthy, since Horne specified maintenance charges 'while wee tarryed there'. More items of expenditure included the hire of horses for Richard Castle to go there also, and even a deputation of four citizens to travel to Coventry to confer with William Purefoy. Recalling earlier appeals over Ship Money, these visits are likely to have been to negotiate the new tax levels, and if that is so, the appeals seem to have been successful. Nevertheless, by the end of January 1646 Stratford had paid a total of £1,528 for the thirty-three months from May 1643. Assessment of individuals reflected their estimated wealth based on ready cash, property, goods and estate, and ranged from the 5s. per week initially paid by the more affluent, like William Walker, John Woolmer, Nicholas Ryland, and William Lindon, to the modest 2d. per week from John Hunt, Richard Whittle and Richard Gray. Those owning land outside Stratford were naturally taxed on that too: thus William Greene and William Hiccox paid extra for their land in Old Stratford, William Shaw for his in Clopton and Welcombe, and Francis Ainge for his interests at Halford. Thomas Nash, who had tenants at Haselor and also across the county border at Welford and Sudeley, found himself paying sums to the Gloucestershire as well as the Warwickshire committee. The 'out' towns were naturally assessed separately from Stratford: in June, Milcote was paying £5 per week, Shottery with Old Stratford £12 per week, and so on. The committee men missed little: a sardonic note by one official representing the corporation noted the sum of almost £60 paid to Warwick garrison 'out of the tythes given to pious uses' in happier times. Perhaps the puritan committee was not satisfied that the tithes were being spent as they were supposed to be, or decided that in a crisis, charitable giving must be suspended in favour of more pressing concerns.[11]

As though this were not enough, the Royalists had by now devised their own almost identical scheme, so that by the spring of 1643, and without taking into account all other 'contributions' – not to mention the widespread theft – both sides had arrogated to themselves the right to collect large sums of money from whatever districts they decided they had a right to control. As we know, Stratford was nominally under parliamentarian control and regularly paid its taxes to Warwick. This in itself was not without its problems, for both sides could and did punish with vicious reprisals any communities paying to the enemy. Thus although Milcote was thought by Robert Fawdon to be fairly safe from paying royalist taxes, 'considering their is noe garrison of the Kings soldiers kept in the Countie', he could not be sure and promised to 'looke after it with all vigillance'. In the event, he was soon disillusioned and complained bitterly about paying taxes to both sides simultaneously, not only to Gloucester as well as Warwick for Parliament, but also to various royalist commanders just outside the county borders. Nearby Alderminster took the bold, if risky, decision not to pay the royalist taxes 'for feare of being ploundered by Warwick Castell', and Robert Fawdon told Lord Chandos that this kind of retaliation had already occurred at Welford and elsewhere.[12] The eventual compensation claims submitted by Stratford's inhabitants naturally specify only those relating to parliamentary impositions, but there is occasional evidence that some individuals did indeed pay forced contributions to the Royalists as well. Unlike the Royalists, however, whose scheme was ramshackle and increasingly unenforceable in Warwickshire as the war dragged on, whatever the complications and universal resentment, the weekly assessments assured to Parliament a steady flow of funds into their coffers. And at the same time, not content with these draconian measures, Parliament introduced a second package of legislation, providing for the sequestration or taking over of the estates and revenues of all Royalists and Catholics, and this affected very many in the Stratford district. The far-reaching repercussions of these particular measures took longer to materialize; but, all told, the parliamentary legislation of the spring of 1643 was to have a major impact on the eventual outcome of the war.

None of these matters, of such vital consequence to so many lives, would have been of much concern to the queen, still at York and now finalizing plans to journey south to rejoin the king. Still in her early thirties, daughter of the ancient kings of France and undeterred by squabbling Englishmen, she was in buoyant, girlish mood at the prospect of the forthcoming adventure of the long march south: '*Il y a fort longtemps que je n'ay été si gaye et si satisfaite que je suis,*' she enthused to the king in mid-May. Following Edgehill and the recent death of Lord Brooke, Parliament was in some disarray with the Earl of Essex still retained in London, unable as yet to reassemble an army to replace the one which had disintegrated at Kineton. With Rupert's vicious taming of rebellious Birmingham and his recapture of Lichfield in early April, and with the Banbury–Daventry approaches to Oxford patrolled by the dependable Henry Hastings and the Earl of Northampton, the way seemed open for the queen to venture south without incurring undue danger, so long as the obvious direct way via enemy Leicester, Coventry, Warwick and Northampton was avoided. Secrecy was needed over her precise route: 'she does not say which way she will come, hoping that secrecy and speed will constitute her surest escort,' commented one adviser. Her precise route was naturally the subject of intense debate on both sides. Even before she left York, a long westward detour was being advised, 'there being no question but that the Queene must for many reasons come by Worcester, to avoid those forces at Coventree, Northampton and Warwick'. It is equally clear that she herself was the effective decision-maker, informing Charles unambiguously that only once one stage of her journey was completed would she determine the next: '*nous prendrons une résolution sur le chemin à suivre*'. She finally left York on 4 June, riding at the head of a substantial army and picknicking in the open air with her young officers (and, according to mischievous rumours spread by parliamentary news sheets, entertaining a scandalous affection for one of them: 'What Relation Master Jermin hath to the Queen is well known to the world'). She entered the Midlands via Newark, Nottingham and Ashby, her undisciplined troops then sacking Burton, with tensions rising on both sides as parliamentary scouts began reporting her movements.[13] In the meantime, Royalists under Rupert were preparing to meet her in the Daventry area, while in the opposite direction others were patrolling the northern Cotswolds and interfering with goods along the highways to Cirencester. As she approached, Warwickshire's own awareness of the danger posed by an army reported by Cromwell to be composed of 1,200 horse and 3,000 foot was fuelled by panicky and sometimes fanciful reporting from both sides. A parliamentary newsletter claimed implausibly that 'all the inhabitants in Warwickshire from the age of sixteene to sixty are up in Armes and have encamped themselves on Dunsmore-heath to stop their march that way', while a royalist one claiming that Lord Grey of Groby and Cromwell had fled at news of Rupert's approach sounds hardly more likely. But there was clearly major concern. The warrants issued from Coventry on 10 June to high constables throughout south Warwickshire to summon men for military service at Warwick 'for the present defence of the County' were likely to have been directly prompted by the queen's impending arrival, as were also Purefoy's moves to have instructions read in local churches for a mass rally on Dunsmore Heath 'to oppose that accursed Popish Army of the Queenes' (it was no secret that she was a practising catholic). Furthermore, John Smith and William Lindon at Stratford cannot have been alone in sending 5s. each in response to a 'Warrant from Colonell Purefoy for men & maintenance to Dunsmore', or 'when hee was at Dunsmore heath'. As usual, too, the state of general alert gave an opportunity for some to resort to plunder, one inhabitant of Kenilworth complaining of losing a mare 'taken by a soldier when ye Randesvous was at Dunsmore when ye Queene came by'. But as the queen's march was assumed to be along Watling Street, far to the east, and as most of the parliamentary soldiers charged with going to intercept her left from Coventry and Warwick, Stratford was not yet implicated.[14] Purefoy's own commitment to the cause took an even more dramatic form, however, for it was while the queen was approaching that there occurred the most serious incident of church vandalism which Warwickshire was to suffer in the war, and one directly attributed to him. He had already been charged with directing the attack on a Buckinghamshire church in August of the previous year, and his regiment is also likely to have been involved in the two major acts of desecration in the Midlands, at the cathedrals of Worcester and Lichfield. The events at Warwick on 14 June 1643 were later described in one of those lurid, tabloid-style accounts beloved of both sides:

In St. Maries Church in Warwick and the Chappell (commonly called the Earles Chappell) adjoyning to the Quire of that Church are diverse faire Monuments of the Beauchamps, anciently Earles of that place, which Family long flourishing there had been great Benefactors & beautifiers of that Church . . . But such is the barbarousnesse of the pretenders to Reformation, that upon Wednesday the 14th of this instant June, the Souldiers, by the appointment and encouragement of one . . . called Colonel Purefoy . . . did beat downe and deface those Monuments of Antiquity; and not content with this, by the same Command they break down the Crosse in the Market-place, not leaving one stone upon another, Purefoy all the while standing by, animating and encouraging them until they had finished their so barbarous Work.

Naturally, such reports were written to extract maximum propaganda value, and there is no attempt here at objective reporting by the outraged Royalist. But the restrained and civilized Dugdale accepted the account without question, and its substance, significantly, was never denied by the Parliamentarians. While there is no evidence of a clear link between this shameful vandalism and the queen's arrival and Purefoy's attempts to mobilize the neighbourhood, the whole desperate deed must surely take its place in the general fear and frustration felt by the Parliamentarians at this time at the consort's unimpeded march towards them.[15]

Eliminating a threat from the Earl of Essex near Oxford in which the great parliamentary stalwart John Hampden was mortally wounded at Chalgrove Field, Prince Rupert now turned to the pressing matter of the queen's arrival. As she continued due south through Lichfield to Walsall at the beginning of July, he was given overall command by the king to guarantee her safety through the last, potentially most dangerous, stage of her journey to Oxford. Marching swiftly north into Leicestershire, Rupert was evidently unaware that the queen was travelling south on a roughly parallel track almost forty miles west. Only at Lutterworth was he informed of the decision, evidently taken by the queen herself, to continue south to Kings Norton, relayed to him by letter from Lord Falkland on 10 July, that the consort 'will be this night at Kings-Norton in Worcestershire'. At this stage, with the queen lodging (though this is not recorded) either, according to one tradition, at the manor house identified as the later Saracen's Head inn, or with the catholic Middlemores at Hawkesley House, the safer route via loyal Worcestershire was still the king's preferred option, his secretary informing Rupert of Charles's anxiety over a more direct route:

. . . and therefore layes it to your Highnes consideracon whether you will not advise ye Queene to come by Worcester, least if she come by Stratford upon Avon the Earl of Essex may force her to fight before it be possible that his Majestie can come up to her.

Essex was, in fact, so far away, in farthest Buckinghamshire, as to pose no threat at all, but the anxious king was taking no chances and repeated his view in an urgent postscript in his own hand:

. . . the best way for my Wyfe will bee Woster, for otherwais it will bee impossible for her forces to eschew fyghting, & that before I can come up, & certainely our game is so faire that it is not fitt to hazard a Battayle except our forces wer joyned.

As a further precaution to guard against every eventuality, Rupert ordered Lord Capel to march to Chipping Campden. Telling evidence that the risks were all too real was provided by yet another lightning exploit of Colonel John Bridges, who was able to pounce from Warwick on part of the queen's convoy of provisions and arms on the way between Burton-on-Trent and Banbury, the Royalists being laden with so much recent plunder, as the queen herself told Charles, that they could hardly march effectively, let alone defend themselves against a resolute attack: '*ils ont tant pillé, qu'ils ne sauraient marcher avec leurs paquets et ne les veulent point quitter*'. It seems likely, in the absence of further surviving letters which would clarify the situation, that it was the intrepid queen who decided to ignore good advice and march directly from Kings Norton to Stratford on 11 July. There was little enough secrecy: as she approached, property at Edgbaston was plundered 'by the Queens Army' (undated, but probably on this occasion), and the Warwick garrison was put on alert and efforts redoubled to block up the town's entrances against the possibility of a surprise attack from her Cavaliers, one Robert Morrell requesting payment 'for beare for Laborers that blockt up the towne when the Queene lay in Stratford . . . the 11th of July 1643'.[16]

Once again, therefore, the district was militarized, a commentator shortly after confirming 'all the Townes about us being full of soldiers' belonging to the queen's 'verie great Armie'. Justifiably anxious, the conscientious Milcote bailiff rode many miles on his master's behalf to ask for a guarantee of Prince Rupert's protection for the Milcote house and estates. This was granted but proved useless, since 'before I could returne, the soldiers from Clifford [Chambers], Ludington & Welford had gott ten lambs & 4 sheep, and at my coming backe [were] busie in the grounds', evidently looking for further spoils. Some entered the house and stole some of his personal belongings from a ground-floor room.[17] Other royalist soldiers (or perhaps the same, acting on specific orders) captured the Stratford schoolmaster John Trapp who, as a conspicuous puritan activist, could not be allowed to sour the royal visit: 'I was taken prisoner, lost my horse, & had my house pillaged. But God of his infinite goodnesse so provided that the next morning I was delivered by an exchange [of prisoners] from Warwicke-Castle . . . that was July 11, 1643.'

Although he in fact escaped lightly, the self-righteous academic never forgot this indignity, recalling many years after the outrage of 'being carried prisoner by the enemies'.[18]

Of the unique occasion of Henrietta Maria's visit to Stratford, tantalizingly little record survives. Only a curious tradition – though a firm and venerable one dating from at least 1733 which has been widely accepted – lodges her at New Place with Shakespeare's granddaughter Elizabeth, still only in her thirties and married to Thomas Nash, the wealthy son of one of Shakespeare's friends. It is plausible to suppose that the theatre-loving queen pointedly ignored the Puritan

William Combe, owner of the largest house in Stratford, The College, preferring its second largest house, the old home of a dramatist whose plays she had often enjoyed at court performances at St James's and Hampton Court in happier times, and a copy of whose second folio was in her husband's possession. Living at New Place, too, was the poet's daughter Susanna, 'good Mistress Hall', 'witty above her sex', whose husband, the eminent physician Dr John Hall, had once cured the Earl of Northampton, a personal friend of the queen since the days he had accompanied Charles to Spain to promote the royal marriage.[19] It was at Stratford, evidently long vacated by the parliamentary forces, that Prince Rupert finally joined the queen, having doubled back through the night from Lutterworth across Dunsmore Heath again via Southam and lodging in Stratford, according to tradition, in Bridge Street. Much conjecture has naturally been lavished upon the romantic Stratford interlude, one aristocratic biographer of the queen evoking a scene of unparalleled splendour, with the town streets thronged with welcoming, good-humoured citizens as Cavaliers (dismissed malevolently by one Parliamentarian as 'a most filthy, wicked crew') strewed flowers before her cavalcade. Why should it not have been like that? This was, after all, a royal visit unlike any other, a brief interval in the war, a sumptuous tableau in an age which relished spectacle. Stratford had witnessed grim scenes recently, and would see more. But for the moment it must have poured out its citizens in hundreds to greet the young queen who, they said, had crossed hundreds of miles through enemy territory and who now rode accompanied by Prince Rupert and the young Earl of Northampton at the head of a procession of Cavaliers amid plumes and jingling harnesses to be welcomed by the awed dignitaries. The surviving evidence is disappointingly sparse, but the accounts of the chamberlain, traditionally responsible for organizing the town's official feasts, nevertheless evoke a lavish celebration, with peals of bells being rung, fanfares from Rupert's trumpeters and a banquet whose highlight was a huge presentation of cakes:

Moneys disbursed and payd when the Queene Majestye laye in the Towne:

Payd to 6 foote men for their fee	£1	10s.	0d.
Pd to the Cochmen and porters for their fee	£1	10s.	0d.
Pd for 4 Quayles	£0	04s.	0d.
Pd for 3 heens, 1 Coke, 8 chickins	£0	05s.	4d.
Pd for Cakes presented to the Queene	£5	00s.	0d.
Pd for 6 malt shives for them	£0	06s.	0d.
Payd to the Buchers for meate	£3	18s.	6d.
Pd to Wm Hopkins for Beare	£0	15s.	8d.
Pd for 1 quarter of Oates and 6 strike of Beanes	£1	02s.	0d.
Pd to Mr Bayliffe of Warwicke for their fortifications	£3	00s.	2d.
Pd to John Copland for Bread, cheese and Beare	£0	12s.	6d.
Pd to the Bellringers	£0	02s.	0d.
Total	£28	02s.	11d.

After spending two nights in Stratford, during which time Prince Rupert was able to take time off from his official duties to make a short excursion across the river with a coachful of ladies to pick fruit in the gardens of the virtually abandoned Milcote House, 'and walk in to the two Parlers & hall, but did not stay', the queen left on 13 July, the royal party being observed, according to a Lucy family tradition, from Charlecote's turret windows as it passed towards Kineton on that summer afternoon.[20] Parliamentary scouts assumed, inaccurately but understandably, that the queen was 'expected at Banbury eyther this or tomorrow night':

> All the Kings-forces which lay quartered at Adderbury and Deddington are advant to Banbury . . . It is certainly reported that the King is at Banbury, and if the Queene come not this night the King intends to goe to Stratford upon Avon to her, and that the greatest parte of the Kings forces are there.

The king had in fact planned what he considered to be a pleasant surprise for Henrietta Maria, and the reunion finally took place near Kineton that same afternoon, on the site of the battle of Edgehill whose great cavalry charge Rupert must have recalled with particular pride. Curiously, although commemorative medals were struck (*see illustration, page 76*) and fulsome verses composed for the occasion, there survives little record of what must have been a spectacular and highly emotional ceremony, even though a parliamentary commander had noted the previous week that there was 'much preparacion for [the queen's] entertaynment' and the event must indeed, as the royalist account boasts, have been witnessed by 'great multitudes' of country people from the surrounding district. It is not even certain precisely where in the 'Vale of Kineton' the reunion took place. The parliamentary account is terse, and notes tartly that 'the common Souldiers [were] very unruly': 'On Thursday, July 13, the King came to Banbury, where he made no long stay, but went and met the Queene below Edgehill, neere unto the place where Keinton battle was fought'.

The royalist reporter is not prepared to leave it at that, but is more rhapsodical than informative. After stressing the obvious, that the royal family met each other 'with most chearfull countenances', he becomes relentlessly unctuous:

> The place made happy by the meeting of these excellent Personages, whom the unplacable malice of seditious men had so long divorced, was Edge-hill, a place before sufficiently famous for the good successe which God there gave His Majestie, . . . but farre more gratefull to posterity in being the place designed for this blessed enterview. A sight so acceptable to all sort of people, great multitudes whereof attended to behold the meeting, that with their loud and joyfull acclamations they added much to the solemnities of this happy day, and made it little lesse triumphant than their day of marriage.

From Kineton the royal couple and the young princes, still accompanied by Prince Rupert, rode the short distance to spend the night at Wroxton Abbey as guests of Sir Thomas Pope, already specially honoured in November 1642 by

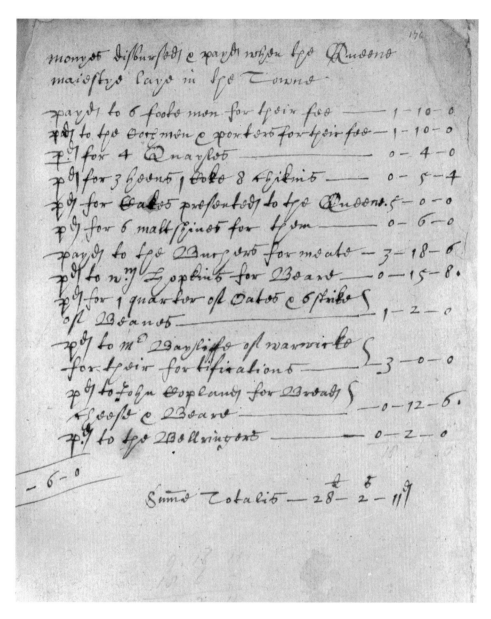

The Queen's Stratford Banquet. Queen Henrietta Maria stayed two nights in Stratford in July 1643 at the head of a large army bringing military supplies from Holland for the King at Oxford. Accompanied by Prince Rupert, the Earl of Northampton and many other dignitaries, the soldiers comprised 'a very great army, all the towns about being full of soldiers', and the event would clearly have been a major one for the small town. Although there is no precise evidence to support the tradition that the young queen lodged at Shakespeare's old home, New Place, the Corporation accounts do confirm that she was entertained at a lavish banquet, the costliest item of which was the presentation of a large supply of cakes costing £5. For a full transcript, see page 73.

The Kineton Medal. Immediately after leaving Stratford for Oxford on 13 July 1643, Queen Henrietta Maria was finally reunited with the king on the battlefield of Edgehill after an enforced separation of over a year. Coinciding exactly with their victory over Sir William Waller at Roundway Down, outside Bath, the two events were seen by the Royalists as such a good augury that this commemorative silver medal was struck to celebrate them jointly. Designed by the king's chief engraver Thomas Rawlins at the Royal Mint at Oxford, it portrays the King and Queen as representative of Apollo and Diana, united under their symbols of sun, moon, and Pleiades, crushing the monster Rebellion, with the inscription 'When united they will more certainly destroy the dragon'. The reverse proclaims 'the auspicious meeting of Charles and Maria, King and Queen of Great Britain, France and Ireland, in Kineton Vale, and the defeat of the rebels in the West, 13 July', as 'an omen of victory and peace'. The crude workmanship, below Rawlins's usual standard, suggests that the medal may have been hastily produced to provide an instant propaganda coup.

(The Shakespeare Birthplace Trust)

receiving the king's protection. Pope had recently been appointed the king's receiver for the Banbury–Bloxham district in order to maintain Prince Rupert's forces, who were now charged with guarding the eminent visitors from look-out posts on Warmington Hill. The next day the king and queen continued to Woodstock, where they paused briefly to await news of Oxford's most recent outbreak of plague. Shortly after, reassured that the danger was past, they allowed the prepared bonfires to be lit for their final triumphant entry into the city, on Friday 14 July. As the celebrations and revelry got under way the royal couple were greeted by news of the resounding royalist victory over Sir William Waller on Roundway Down, which had taken place exactly at the time of their Kineton reunion; it must indeed have seemed to them a providential conjunction. That the completion of these last stages of the royal journey should have passed without enemy interference was due essentially, however, to parliamentary ineptitude and the virtual occupation of the south Midlands by royalist units. Even villages not obviously on the road to anywhere, like Tysoe, are mentioned, as the parliamentary commander Sir Samuel Luke sums up the situation as it seemed to his scouts on about 17 July: 'Divers of the Kings forces lye at Tizur [Tysoe] in Warwickshire, and a troope of horse at Adderbury, and 300 in Banbury, and 4 drakes, and all the townes betweene Banbury and Stratford upon Avon are full of the Kings soldiers.'[21]

If no major battle was fought in the Midlands in the summer of 1643 this was little short of a miracle. With the bellicose queen journeying south, the king's protective army dispersing north to meet her, Parliament's supreme commander approaching to within a few miles of Oxford to intervene and, above all, with the two ablest commanders, Cromwell and Rupert, loitering in the wings spoiling for a decisive fight, the converging forces presented all the ingredients for a spectacular showdown. That such an explosive combination produced nothing more than the picturesque midsummer cameos of the queen partaking of cakes and ale at Shakespeare's table or embracing the king under the brow of Edgehill is indeed one of the quirks of England's history.

CHAPTER 7

The Convoys for Gloucester

The emotions released by the queen's visit had hardly subsided when a very different alarm was raised as remnants of Sir William Waller's defeated army approached over the Cotswolds on their way to Warwick after suffering an ignominious defeat at Roundway Down, in Wiltshire, on 13 July. The details of Waller's passage remain obscure, and there is little trace of his march through Warwickshire, but after allegedly intercepting a troop of the queen's horse, which had strayed into the Cotswolds (though this was denied by the Royalists) and passing through Evesham, some of his men quartered at Exhall, near Alcester, on 'the retreat from the West', with others at Temple Grafton, before reaching Stratford, on about 20 July, probably following the old Bishopton–Warwick road. As the soldiers moved through the district, some seized a horse from Francis Smith 'as they past by Snitterfield grounds', while others quartered at Francis Billings' and elsewhere in Stratford before arriving at Warwick. Other isolated incidents of pillaging were reported, Margaret Sheldon at Temple Grafton being victim once again and losing four more horses, this time together with household goods and provisions valued at £30 'when Sr Wm Waller came out of ye West'. But in the main, Stratford was spared disruption, and Robert Fawdon at Milcote could breathe a sigh of relief at the beginning of August that in the immediate area, at least, 'all is safe, I blesse God'. As usual, however, his confidence was short-lived, for only a few weeks later, with more 'multitudes of Soldiers now in these partes', a uniformly pessimistic account followed of conditions throughout the district: commercial transport to London was suspended, messengers were unable to transmit mail, a usually profitable sheep fair held at Milcote had been disastrous, since he had not sold a single beast, and, as usual, it was impossible to collect rents. A particularly alarming rumour that Prince Rupert or one of his regiments was returning to garrison Milcote house as their headquarters proved unfounded, Fawdon went on, 'yet it hath been in agitation' and nothing was certain. Trade was severely depressed: 'Heer is no selling of wool now, nor indeed of any thing else neare the vallew of other times, nor like to be, untill it please God of his great mercie to put an end to these sad times'.[1]

One reason for this new upsurge of activity was the struggle to control the crucial parliamentary stronghold of Gloucester, coupled with the king's growing

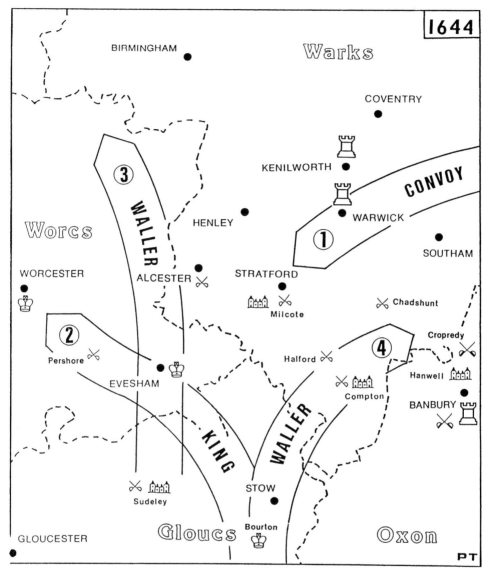

⚔ Major battle

⚔ Siege or skirmish

🏰 Mansion plundered or attacked

♔ King's lodging

Map 4. Major Events in 1644.

confidence. Once reunited with his wife, Charles turned his attention to this important port and bridgehead, and Prince Rupert seized Bristol on 26 July as a prelude to a general offensive in the south-west. The Royalists were now in control of large parts of the country, even some Parliamentarians like John Corbet, the chaplain at Gloucester, conceding gloomily that the king was dominant 'from the utmost Cornwall to the borders of Scotland'. Justifiably, Charles felt he could now add further conquests by gaining the great prize of Gloucester since, as he put it succinctly, 'Waller is extinct and Essex cannot come'. His subsequent siege of the city, begun on 10 August, turned out to be a costly mistake, but it was preceded by a long royalist build-up throughout the summer across the Cotswolds. The Cavaliers then dispersed once the siege was finally abandoned, as news came of the approach of a strong relief force under the Earl of Essex. This is the situation referred to precisely by another detailed report from the ever-watchful estate manager at Milcote in late September. He had hoped for more settled times, but

> . . . not thre daies passed But a verie great Army came downe, And the King drawing all his Forces in these parts together (This whole Cuntry being full of Soldiers) hath made it more miserable than ever, and Likelie more to be, eating up all where they come, without respecting either Persons or protection . . . It is not your honors case alone but every ones else where they come, besides great quantities of provisions comaunded & sent to them dayly . . . some part of them [are] very neere, to our continuall feares, soe that without [it] please God to remove these Armies this cuntry is likely to be left very miserable . . . Noe cattell of any sort will sell, And I have both of great cattell and sheep very good, and whereof I am every houre affeard, neither can I thinke of any safetie in removeing them. And in this straight I know not what to doe, But to Comitt all to Gods protection . . . I cannot receive one pennie of any bodie.

One Welford tenant, Richard Trimell, was forced to yield up his land owing directly to losses 'sustained by soldiers' at this time, and there must have been many more.

During this period a regular information service linked Colonel Edward Massey, the beleaguered Gloucester governor, to Essex's reliable scoutmaster Sir Samuel Luke at Newport Pagnell, via John Bridges at Warwick, and messengers must have passed many times through Stratford on these top-secret missions. Equally, convoys of parliamentary ammunition must already have been in the vicinity for some time, awaiting transport to Gloucester: one large cavalry escort was reported 'by the space of 11 weekes together' at Milverton during the summer, while other isolated parliamentary units were scattered here and there fulfilling no very obvious role, like that quartering at Snitterfield in July under the disreputable former vicar of Warmington, Richard Wootton, who had abandoned his parish at the beginning of the war to roam the countryside as a cavalry captain and horse thief. Essex's own relief expedition from London eventually crossed the region too far to the south to be of immediate concern to Stratford, though many villages throughout south Warwickshire suffered from the attentions of these troops as they progressed towards Gloucester. At Stow-on-the-Wold, Rupert was for once unsuccessful in challenging the Parliamentarians, and was unable to prevent Essex from eventually raising the siege of Gloucester – an event considered by many historians as the turning-point of the war – on 5 September.[2]

Ironically, it was not until now, when Gloucester was no longer in immediate danger from the Royalists, that south Warwickshire was most affected by the city's plight. Gloucester had suffered much during the long siege, and desperately needed large quantities of supplies to survive and above all to re-arm its heroic defenders against the possibility of renewed attack. In answer to urgent appeals from Essex and Massey, Parliament in London acted with uncharacteristic swiftness, voting immediately to dispatch a substantial cargo to the city via the usual dependable Northampton–Warwick route which avoided royalist-controlled Oxfordshire. Unpredictably, this expedition to re-equip Gloucester via a series of armed convoys developed into an extraordinary saga lasting many months and affecting countless small communities on the way, including Stratford, and concentrating the minds of the major commanders on both sides. Yet it has been virtually ignored by civil war historians, simply because it produced no major engagement and few casualties. The impact of the war cannot simply be equated with battles and fatalities, however, and certainly no one in the Stratford district could have foreseen the extent of disruption that the convoys were to cause there.

The supplies themselves, many assembled from the magazine in the Tower of London, amounted even initially to a considerable consignment: 100 barrels of powder and an equivalent quantity of inflammable match, 600 muskets, swords, bandoliers and belts, 100 cases of pistols and 100 carbines, with further large quantities being added shortly after. The whole convoy, with wagons, horses newly 'pressed' for the occasion and considerable numbers of newly raised recruits as an armed escort, as well as other companies joining along the route, must have comprised one of the most impressive military processions to snake its way across the English shires for many a long year. It must equally have been a logistical nightmare for the commanders, as will be seen, but it eventually completed its first stage intact, reaching Northampton by early December. As news of the parliamentary efforts leaked out the Royalists began devising their own plans to intercept the convoy, and there were sporadic attacks throughout the autumn by Prince Rupert and the Earl of Northampton in the Banbury–Towcester sector and also in the opposite direction, in the Warwickshire–Worcestershire border country through which the convoy would eventually have to pass.[3] There, John Bridges established a secondary garrison at Coughton Court in November, already abandoned by its catholic owner Robert Throckmorton, to pre-empt its use by the waiting Royalists or, as one report put it, 'a company of ragged Welsh-men [who] were come into Worcestershire and intended to fortifie themselves in Coughton house'. The Parliamentarians were at Coughton less than two months, but in that short time evidently became a considerable nuisance to the local community. Under two of John Bridges' locally recruited henchmen, John Smith and John Cheshire, shortly to be active at Alcester, they patrolled aggressively a district which they must have considered a haunt of despised catholic 'malignants', assaulting any suspicious traveller, as a Studley resident, William Petford, found to his cost:

In Januarii, Rydinge peaceably on ye way, [he] was suddenly opposed & wounded by one Smith, which was of Colton [Coughton] Garrison under ye Comand of Col. Bridges, ye which wounde was so farre tedious yt hee Lay under ye Surgeons hands some 20 weeks or more, in all which time hee was Carried to bed, beinge not able to dresse himselfe or any way able to helpe himselfe.

A far more substantial initiative took place at the end of December when the Coughton Parliamentarians joined their Warwick colleagues in mounting a concerted and vicious assault on Beoley House, near Redditch, one of the ancestral homes of the great catholic landowner William Sheldon, of Weston, near Long Compton, massacring its inmates, according to one report, burning the house down, emptying the district of cattle and invading and plundering villages like Henley, Rowington, Tanworth, Studley and Wootton Wawen in the process. Shortly after, however, learning of the approach of a determined royalist force, the Parliamentarians surprisingly evacuated Coughton, but not before setting fire to it in three places, having, according to Throckmorton, destroyed the gatehouse and 'quite ruined' the house, and emptied it of '5 Cart loads of bedding, Hangings, Carpets, Stooles, Chaires, brasse, pewter & other houshold stuffe'. The convoy meanwhile made a long halt at Northampton, caused by a lack of adequate support troops to guarantee its safety as far as Warwick and Coventry, and Warwick forces under Colonels Purefoy, Barker and their new colleague, the Dutch mercenary Hans Behr, were called upon to march east to collect it at some undisclosed point near the Leicestershire–Warwickshire border and escort it back to Warwick. It seems nevertheless to have remained stationary outside Warwickshire during most of January; but shortly afterwards, parts of it were reported on the move again, passing through east Warwickshire villages, and by 15 February, at least twenty-eight cartloads had safely completed the second stage and 'lay at Warwicke under a convoy of 1,000 horse and foote', with much more on the way. At this stage, more reminders of the consequences for local farming of the high level of military activity come from the Milcote bailiff. In January, royalist soldiers had stolen livestock and he had travelled to Oxford to protest. During his absence, parliamentarian soldiers from Warwick had seized nineteen more of the best cattle, 'dryven to Warwick for [unpaid] taxes', and costing him £35 before they could be released. He had then journeyed to Coventry, to plead fruitlessly for leniency over taxation, and also to see Lord Chandos (probably at Sudeley). His conclusion is pessimistic: 'For my part I can see noe possibillitie of safe passage for your wooll . . . for this cuntry is full of soldiers all ye way.'[4]

By now a dangerous and volatile situation confronted Parliament in the Midlands generally, and another long halt was made by the convoy at Warwick while Westminster and the local commanders wrangled over how best to deal with it. On the one hand, Staffordshire was threatened by Royalists invading simultaneously from Shropshire and Leicestershire, while the very stronghold of Coventry was considered to be 'in imminent danger' to the extent that an urgent population census was taken in order to share out rations in the event of a prolonged siege, like the one at Gloucester. On the other hand, the forthcoming last stage for the convoy, that from Warwick to Gloucester, promised to be the most hazardous of all, for the Royalists had by now arrayed an impressive force throughout the Cotswolds and Severn valley awaiting the next parliamentary move. Although estimates of numbers are notoriously unreliable there is wide general agreement in this instance of roughly six thousand men, reported on 1 March by the parliamentary chief intelligence officer, Sir Samuel Luke, to comprise the following companies: the Earl of Northampton at Stow; Sir Gilbert Gerard, Colonel Washington and Colonel Sandys at Evesham (the town reportedly 'verie strongly fortified'); Sir William Vavasour at Tewkesbury; Colonel Veale at Painswick; Sir Walter Pye at Pershore; Lord Chandos at Sudeley; and Lord Molyneux at Chipping Campden; plus some smaller garrisons. Massey gave Essex a similar picture ten days later. As though this was not enough, the king ordered Prince Rupert to march with all speed towards Worcestershire on 2 March (though this never materialized), Lord Wilmot was sent to Chipping Norton and the Earl of Forth, nominally the supreme royalist commander, was also ordered into Gloucestershire on 4 March to take overall charge of the campaign. The Royalists were evidently intent at all costs on preventing the convoy from getting through. In December there had been much debate over which of the Avon's bridges the Parliamentarians might use, and although Stratford's (surprisingly) was not mentioned on this occasion, the Royalists were busy in February breaking down those along the Stour, at a safer distance from the ever-alert John Bridges at Warwick, Halford's, on the ancient Fosse Way, being a prime target. The level of royalist activity was certainly enough to alarm the new Midlands commander-in-chief the Earl of Denbigh, who reported his anxieties to London over 'the great forces drawn towards these confines and about Gloucester purposely to intercept this convoy; a number too considerable and much superior to our forces intended for this expedition'.[5] One immediate result was that the Earl of Manchester's eastern forces were instructed to send substantial reinforcements for the convoy, many of them duly taking up positions as far south as Bidford and maintaining a strong guard at Broom Mill there. By now, Colonel Hans Behr's men, many of them reportedly Dutchmen (though probably a mixture of foreign nationalities), were scattered through the Stratford district, incorporating contingents from far afield: not only local forces but also others from Leicestershire, Northamptonshire, East Anglia and even Buckinghamshire – all awaiting orders for escort duty and guarding against royalist attack. A report a little later confirmed that the garrisons of Warwick, Northampton, Coventry and Leicester 'have made up a very considerable Convoy to guard the same [provisions] to Gloucester'. By 19 March these amounted to 3,300 horse and 4,000 foot, with artillery, at Warwick. The peak period for what was in effect a parliamentarian occupation of the neighbourhood was probably a week or so in mid-February, many villages echoing Luddington's claim of 14 February of quartering Behr's men five days 'at ye time of his being at Stratford upon Avon'. Although many of these references in the parish accounts are undated, their details match precisely those that are, as in the cases of Drayton and Luddington, so that it can be fairly safely assumed that they refer to the same events. Thus Binton quartered a large troop of over a hundred cavalry under two of Behr's officers, Major Moore and Captain Goddard, while other villages reported units of Behr's colleagues-in-arms. Drayton sent provisions to Sir Samuel Luke's company at Stratford on 14 February while quartering Behr's own, under Colonel Thomas Archer, for four days 'at the same time'; Alveston's Thomas Walton billed '13 of Warwick men [who] kept Court of gard att my house 2 nights att the first Convoy to Glocester'; Alderminster's Thomas Bolton gave sums of money to Behr's quartermaster-general; and Wasperton's Thomas Toone, interestingly, lodged not only 'Dutch men' but also 'a Dutch man & woman'. Soldiers from other counties were at Charlecote, Alveston and Edstone, where Henry Parry noted ruefully losing 'a bagg of otes to Northamptonshire souldiers & other provisions when they weare to goe to Glocester with the Convoye'. Plundering was again rife. One victim, William Kempson of Ardens Grafton, of the conspicuous local catholic family, lost household goods valued at £30 to Behr's men in addition to those losses suffered recently at the hands of Sir William Waller's. As before, too, the catholic widow Margaret Sheldon of Temple Grafton was singled out for particularly vicious treatment. She had already suffered during the Edgehill campaign and again, more recently, from Waller's soldiers. She now lost a further fourteen of her horses, valued at £80, to Behr's men, and not content with that,

> lost all the houshold goodes within her house, togeather with all her Corne, plate, apparell, money and provision within doores and without, to her totall ruine, plundred by Collonell Beares souldiers, which said goodes amounted to the sum of £400.[6]

This time, Stratford itself was the centre of activity. Following the precedent set by the Edgehill commanders noted earlier, Behr chose to lodge as comfortably as possible, with Thomas Nash at New Place, for a leisurely six days. Militarily, this first of Behr's two visits to Stratford, in mid-February, would merit only a minor footnote in the history of the civil war in Warwickshire were it not for the unique interest of its Shakespeare connections. As already noted, Nash was married to the poet's grand-daughter Elizabeth Hall, who had inherited the old family home, New Place, in which Susanna, Shakespeare's daughter, still lived, as Nash obligingly recorded for posterity in his civil war accounts which include reference to 'my mother in law Mrs Hall, who lives with me'. Behr's reactions to lodging in a house which had, according to tradition, recently entertained the queen of England are not recorded, but whatever they were, Nash carefully noted the losses incurred by the visit. He claimed £10 in compensation for having lodged Behr, his servants and horses, which had meant 'keeping a Constant table, with extraordinary fireinge', for the week; and as Shakespeare in his will had bequeathed all his plate to his grand-daughter, Behr and his officers may well have dined at Shakespeare's own table off any of the poet's tableware which had escaped the earlier collections. As usual, thefts were not confined to objects directly related to the conflict: Nash recorded the loss not only of three sheep and a calf but of 'a scarlet Peticoat of my wifes with two faire laces, taken by his men', two cloaks and a suit of unspecified clothes, losses totalling another £9 or so. Nash's parliamentary sympathies must have been sorely tried that week.

In addition to Nash, nearly every other inhabitant billeted Behr's men at this time, usually for four to five days, though a number of residents record a longer period: like Nash, Thomas Greene, Edwin Godwin and Richard Tyler specified six days, Thomas Lucas seven and John Bellamy '7 or 8 daies together'. Usually the soldiers were fairly evenly placed in small groups of fewer than ten men per house, though occasionally more, Peter Molineau having noted twenty and William Abbott as many as thirty-six on his property in either Church Street or Chapel Street – a heavy imposition. Some residents were specific in their submissions, Francis Ainge noting 'a Captain, 5 Comon soldiers & 7 horses under Colonell Beare, in provision for the men, 30s. in hay for their horses, 12s. for 3 quarter of ots, & tooke away a mare worth 40s.' The soldiers were thirsty, too: William Lane's uninvited guests drank three hogsheads of his beer, and Robert Washbrook's four of his (two hundred gallons). The widespread pilfering referred mostly to trivial domestic items or unspecified 'goodes': John Woolmer and Francis Smith lost a large quantity of horseshoes and nails, John Baxter some linen, Henry Pratt clothing, Francis Smith 'a newe Coate', Jane Smith her hat and several people pairs of boots; while Edmund Hathaway introduced a note of anger into his record: 'Charged in free quarter by Colonell Beares souldiers and by money which they forced from mee at 2 severall times.' Robert Fitzhughes complained of his grass being devoured by the men's horses, while Thomas Davies did not hesitate to use the word 'plunder' – a new one given common currency by the civil war[7] – in reporting his own case. Edwin Godwin's consignment not only stole from him but left him an injured colleague to care for over the next fortnight when they left. Abraham Tibbott had the distinction of supplying oats 'for Colonell Beares owne horse'. Thomas Walker in Henley Street found that more than £5 worth of his stored corn had been stolen from his barns at Bridgetown, and Richard Sturley was forced to do unspecified manual work for the soldiers, claiming for 'his labour & stuffe which ye parliament soldiers paid not'. Occasionally the precise culprits are identified. John Davies's pair of boots worth 8s. were 'tooke away by a Trumpeter of Major Beares' (perhaps the same Thomas Boovy as before), while John Baxter's linen was taken by Captain Carmichael. More substantial than most, however, were the losses incurred by the Stratford chamberlain, Thomas Horne, from his house in Henley Street. Horne, used to keeping the borough accounts meticulously in his official capacity, carefully listed every item of a bill totalling almost £50 for this single week:

They dranke 5 hogsheads of beere at 16s. the hogshead; bread 10s; meate 33s; had from the butchers beside bacon, foure porke, butter & cheese 29s.; fire xxs; fresh fishe, salt, tobacco & pipes.   £9 3s. 6d.

In horsemeate for 57 horse 4 daies & 4 nights at 6d. day & night £5 4s. 0d.; eight strike of beanes; 20 strike of ots at 18d. a strike; candles in the howse & Stable.   £8 0s. 0d.

Two hogsheads of beere £1 12s. 0d.; bread 10s. 0d.; meate for them from the butcher 15s. 8d.; other houshold meate for them, bacon, porke & Sowce 6s. 8d; butter, Cheese & eggs 6s. 8d.; fire 6s. 8d.; 64 horses day & night at

6d. £1 12s. 0d.; candles in the howse & Stables 2s. 6d.; a strike of beanes & ots 2s. 0d.   £23 4s. 6d.

Horne, who, judging from these details, may have been an innkeeper, also appended a note requesting sympathetic consideration in respect of 'a soldier dangerously wounded, left without meanes', and another similar casualty, 'gone away nowe, sound & whole', whom he had lodged. The testimony of Richard Tyler at Shottery or Old Stratford was also circumstantial: he quartered an officer colleague of Behr's for six nights, 'the said [colonel] having Generall Beheare and divers Comaunders att his house att Dinner, and also the Court of Guard was kept att his house'.

For the local community, all of this activity amounted to considerable interference with daily life, and evidently provoked much resentment; militarily it achieved precisely nothing. The Royalists, bickering among themselves, did not attack, but neither did the convoy advance. At the end of February several newsletters reported that 'the Carriages of Ammunition that are going to Glocester are not yet past Warwicke'. Behr must have felt considerable frustration, and evidently left the comforts of New Place on about 20 February, though his subsequent movements are not clear. But this period coincided with his appointment by the Earl of Essex as commander-in-chief of the Gloucester operation, and he is likely to have returned to Warwick to confer with colleagues. At this point, things looked likely to come to a head, as reports openly circulated 'of what distresse that Valiant Commander Colonell Massey is in for want of Ammunition at Gloucester'.[8] In direct response a rendezvous at Warwick was set for 27 February for contingents from 'all the Garrisons betweene Newarke & Warwick', presumably for imminent departure. Massey wrote to Bridges at Warwick on 28 February, 'at nine of ye clock in ye evening', asking to know 'yor resolution of march, and the word signall, and way by wch you meane to march', and adding pessimistically, 'yor ptie will be too slender, I am afraid' to confront the enemy 'verie stronge about Stowe, Broadway, Cambden, Evesham, Upton and Teuxbury'. Nevertheless, he concluded in good heart: 'Yet if I have yor tymelie and certaine notice, I shall endeavoure to divert the enemy in these parts, and keepe them on the other side of ye river.' The following day Colonel William Purefoy was ordered to report to Warwick to take command of the Warwickshire forces under Behr, Denbigh confirming to Essex that 'Col. Purefoy is this day gone to Warwick to command the forces of this county in this present expedition.' By the beginning of March, lords Grey, Manchester and Willoughby had all brought in further reinforcements to assist the convoy 'as yet at Warwick', and by 4 March Behr felt confident enough to announce; 'I entend to morrowe (god willing) by breake of day to advance to Stratford upon Avon wth my whole troope.' The convoy – or part of it – finally left Warwick on 5 March:

... it was advertised by divers who came from Warwicke Fryday March 8 that the Earl of Manchesters Forces and the rest which were designed for that service went thence with the Ammunition for Gloucester on the Tuesday night before, about ten of the clock at night, and that they carried a great part of it upon horses, and some the Troopers carried behind them, in case they should have beene met withall by the Cavaliers.[9]

By 5 or 6 March, therefore, Behr was back again at Stratford, for what was destined to be a shorter visit lasting only two or three days. Many of his men evidently returned to the same homes which they had only recently left, residents specifying their presence on each occasion separately, or simply condensing both visits into a single entry, endorsed 'at twice'. In general, numbers quartering in Stratford on this occasion seem somewhat fewer than on the first, though in a few cases, like those of Richard Smart, Alexander Price, John Ryland and Edward Wells, they were actually more, and the thoughts of these unfortunate individuals as the soldiers clattered up to their front door for the second time within weeks can well be imagined. The chamberlain, in particular, must have felt outrage as he recited his further losses, from more than sixty cavalrymen this time: two more hogsheads of beer (more than a hundred gallons), bread, meat (he submitted the butcher's bill, though this has not survived), including bacon and pork, butter, cheese, eggs, fuel, 'candles in the howse & stable', and beans and oats for the horses. The Milcote estate across the river – evidently known to the Parliamentarians as a soft target – was again raided, about 7 or 8 March, by Behr's men anxious to supplement their diet at Stratford, stealing rams, pigs, fodder and hay, besides extorting money from the bailiff by threatening to take the remaining sheep.[10]

Behr now wrote again to Luke in confident tone, on 6 March, an almost identical letter to the previous, that he was at Stratford, 'where I lie to take my opportunity. I intend to march tomorrow morning'.[11] Whether he actually did so immediately is far from clear. He was an experienced soldier, and it is likely that, as Dugdale suggested, he 'sent out partyes towards [Chipping] Cambden' to reconnoitre before committing the convoys to the road. If so, he was misinformed that the Royalists had withdrawn to Winchcombe, as he reported to Luke. He accordingly set off, but was soon forced to retreat back towards Warwick by a determined royalist assault shortly after leaving Stratford, probably on about 10 March, presumably somewhere approaching Chipping Campden, on the edge of the area under royalist control. The setback is denied in some wild parliamentary reporting (one account even having Rupert, in reality in Shropshire or Cheshire, 'forced to swim over a river'),[12] but was admitted by more sober reports:

> Coll. Beare went out in a silent way from Warwick with about 200 horse load of Ammunition, and being come to Stratford, sent before a party to discover, who before they were aware, fell into an ambush of the enemies, and had hard work to get off. They lost fourty men. We fear they went not forward.

The result was that on 11 March the ammunition had still not left the district, even though 'there are about 2,000 horse bilited in the town and country adjacent to Warwick, and have been these ten dayes', with Behr still somewhere nearby. Two days later a further report repeated that the ammunition was still 'not as yet further then Warwick', while ten days after that, when Gloucester's desperate plight was again stressed, 1,000 horse and dragoons were still reported in and around Stratford, waiting 'to carry in their knapsacks and on spare horses powder and provisions into Glos'. There was clearly considerable confusion, and although, curiously, there was to be no major showdown, with the Cotswolds and

Vale of Evesham seething with soldiers vicious skirmishing took place throughout the district, provoked, directly or indirectly, by the state of alert over the convoy. On one occasion, at the beginning of March 1644, the Warwick garrison forces decided to profit from the Earl of Northampton's absence near Stanway awaiting the convoy and the departure of other Banbury Royalists for Newark, and attacked Royalists recruiting and collecting contributions in the Banbury district. A small cavalry force under Major Abraham Pont and Captain Joseph Hawksworth dashed through the night from Warwick to break into the royalist camp at Adderbury, surprised the sleeping Cavaliers 'before they were drest' at about 4.00 a.m. on this Sunday morning, and 'took them Dormant', as one Parliamentarian mocked. Many prisoners were taken back to Warwick, but about a hundred of Sir William Compton's cavalry from Banbury, alerted by an escapee from Adderbury, caught up with the convoy halfway to Warwick, 'goinge downe Edgehill and in Radway field'. While half of the Parliamentarians with the prisoners hurried on to Warwick to alert their garrison, Hawksworth's rearguard 'faced about neere Keynton [Kineton]', engaged the Royalists 'at the end of a lane' and lost twelve killed, before being forced to retreat and barricade themselves in Chadshunt church. Baulked of their prey and not wishing to linger and confront the inevitable parliamentary reinforcements from Warwick, the Royalists set fire to the hamlet before riding off to Banbury. Fortunately, the parliamentary account concludes, 'by Gods mercy, with little helpe the fire was stayed; two or three houses was [sic] burnt, and some rickes of Corne and Hay, and the rest preserved.' Shortly after, Hawksworth received a substantial pay rise, from 39s. per day to 51s., and promotion to major, probably as recognition of his courage in this incident.

Not long after these events, on about 19 March, Colonel William Purefoy, presumably intent on clearing a way forward, sent out an assault party against the Earl of Northampton's company quartering near Chipping Campden, 'to beat upon their quarters'. Large numbers of Cavaliers were reported to have been taken prisoner, including officers, a victory confirmed by Daniel O'Neale, one of Rupert's cavalry commanders patrolling near Broadway, who promptly promised retaliation near Stratford:

> Puphery iss quartered att Camden this night [with] 5 troopes [and] 2 of Dragoones. This morning he came from Warwyck. [Colonel] Sands & Collonell Westons regiments are drawn between him and Warwyck, [and] I am now going towards him on this siyd . . . I hope wee shall make him pay for our losse.

Occasionally, an honorable act offsets the generally sombre picture. On 27 March one of Behr's captains, James Burkin, wrote to the constable of Wasperton, halfway between Stratford and Warwick, admitting that 'divers of our horses have miscarried in our march', and instructing reimbursement of £4 to Adam Hanks for the theft of one of his horses by the soldiers.[13]

Although the long and complex epic of the convoy did not end here, there is no further record of Stratford's direct involvement with it from this date, and the reason for this otherwise curious fact may lie in the lessons Behr learned from the setback outside Stratford. For the rebuff encouraged a re-think, resulting in important modifications to the project. The supplies had probably never been intended to travel in a single convoy the whole length of the route, clearly vulnerable to concerted attack, and they were now increasingly split up and were to continue by pack-horse rather than wagon, a speedier and above all more flexible mode allowing smaller, more manageable quantities to travel at different times and, if need be, by different routes. It is impossible to pin down the actual routes taken, which must have been decided *ad hoc* in the light of local information, and as a pack-horse is not limited to main thoroughfares the Parliamentarians are likely to have avoided obvious centres like Stratford as a matter of course. Orders accordingly went out for a very large number of horses, complete with saddles and paniers, to be requisitioned, for which the owners were to be compensated; many were found locally, from Gloucestershire and Warwickshire, but many others came from farther afield, even from Newport Pagnell and St Albans. From now on, therefore, it is no longer possible to describe the convoy as a single entity – a point made clear by Stratford residents like Richard Smart in Wood Street who noted 'charges 3 times with Col. Purefoys men going with the Convoys'. By these means, and also because, immediately after, the Royalists suffered a major disaster at Cheriton in Hampshire on 29 March which resulted in the king withdrawing the bulk of his forces from the Cotswolds towards Oxford, the supplies eventually reached Gloucester during March and April, Dugdale noting laconically: 'the Kings forces being drawne away from those parts'.[14]

For Stratford and its neighbourhood the matter did not quite end there, however, since once their mission was completed many of the escorting troops eventually retraced their steps to Warwick, Coventry, Northampton and beyond along the same well-trodden route, so that, as in the Edgehill campaign, many local inhabitants recorded the soldiers on both the outward and the homeward journeys. By 16 April, John Bridges at Warwick could report that Behr and the Northampton troops 'are now returned from Gloucester'.[15] Alveston and Wasperton were two villages that confirmed billeting soldiers 'att the Convoy to Gloucester & 1 night theire returne', while John Ainge in Sheep Street similarly had to provide 'ots & other provision for Major Beares soldiers at their returne from Gloucester'. Colonel William Purefoy remained with his Warwickshire cavalry at Gloucester for a while to lend support to Massey, but his men too, as we shall see, were eventually to return via Stratford. Gloucester's new-found security also meant that, with Massey and Bridges keeping in close contact with each other, further convoys periodically passed through Stratford in both directions, and some of the townspeople, like Thomas Cleaver and Thomas Horne, could from now on add the occasional passage of Gloucester soldiers to their tally of many others. Alexander Hornby suffered a disadvantageous exchange of a horse by them, John Barton lost a mare from his stable to them, and Thomas Nash complained that Gloucester troops left their horses and 'beeff' in his meadows on several occasions. The procession of convoys to relieve the city of Gloucester may have produced no battle and few casualties, but for countless people throughout the Stratford countryside, whose villages and homes the escorting soldiers disturbed for so long, the saga was not easily forgotten.

CHAPTER 8

Summer Alarms

As we have seen, the Gloucester convoys continued to disturb the district well into the spring of 1644, but even before Parliament finally succeeded in getting the supplies through the Cotswolds, priorities were changing on both sides. The royalist defeat at Cheriton in Hampshire at the end of March, according to Clarendon, 'altered the whole scheme of the King's counsels', and although Charles sent Lord Chandos to cover the north Cotswolds in April, most of the royalist forces in the south and west were withdrawn towards Oxford. Recalling Prince Rupert too, from North Wales, the king began slowly reassembling his army in April as he prepared to march north. At the same time, Parliament set about planning to take advantage of the royalist disarray before the king could recover, and for once devised something like a grand strategy to trap him in Oxford by a three-pronged movement. The Earl of Essex would take the initiative by advancing from the south-east, along the Thames valley; Sir William Waller, buoyed by his recent success in Hampshire, would approach from the south-west; while the new Midlands commander, the relatively inexperienced Earl of Denbigh, although in fact already in difficulties in Staffordshire, would march south into Worcestershire and Warwickshire. It was an excellent plan, and might have succeeded; but almost at once things began to go wrong. The king was advised, very sensibly, that he ought not to confront the combined danger and that 'all great engagements should be shunned for a while'. Accordingly, as the enemy approached from the south he eluded Essex and Waller by slipping out of Oxford under their noses on 3 June, making over the Cotswolds for Evesham and Worcester. Essex in pursuit reached Chipping Norton, but then, seriously at odds with Waller and his superiors in London, astonished everyone by deciding that the south-west was his priority, and, leaving Waller to pursue the king on his own, marched off for Dorset. Hoping to 'make the work short' by 'a universal conjunction' of his own forces and those of Denbigh, Massey, Sir William Brereton and even, eventually, Essex, Waller dutifully followed Charles north along the Worcestershire border only to be outpaced at every stage by the king, who caught everyone by surprise by turning back at Bewdley and was soon retracing his steps through Oxfordshire again. Stopping briefly to confer with Denbigh and Brereton at Stourbridge, Waller too turned south again, eventually crossed Warwickshire and finally caught up with the Royalists at Banbury, where he was defeated by the king at Cropredy Bridge at the end of June.[1] The Earl of Denbigh's efforts met with no greater success, though through no fault of his own. His new authority was constantly undermined by suspicion, jealousy and localist thinking, especially by the parliamentary committee at Coventry who systematically starved him of the necessary resources to equip, and even feed and clothe, his men. Above all, he was seriously over-extended in Shropshire and Staffordshire, so that he was quite unable to intervene effectively against local royalist aggression let alone challenge the elusive king when the royalist army arrived on the scene nearby. Locally there were isolated parliamentarian successes, but following Cropredy, the king was able to recross the Cotswolds, in triumph this time, to arrive in Evesham again at the beginning of July. As one loyal supporter enthused, 'his Majestie, with all his army, drums beating, colors flying and trumpets sounding, marched over the Cotswold Hills'. Parliament's grand three-point strategy was in tatters.[2]

None of this dramatic marching and counter-marching affected Stratford and its neighbourhood as much as the repercussions from the convoy already described, but violence was always near. Once the city of Gloucester was out of immediate danger a great deal of frenzied but uncoordinated activity took place in the south Midlands. As Robert Fawdon had already pointed out from Milcote, the withdrawal of the field armies simply meant that the initiative passed back to the wilful local garrison commanders eager to keep their men occupied. Many Royalists were still scattered haphazardly across the north Cotswolds near enough to threaten Stratford's peace, doing nothing very constructive except raiding, plundering and collecting taxes. There was siege and counter-siege in Staffordshire, skirmishing in Worcestershire and Gloucestershire, the unwelcome addition of new garrisons here and there, as at Edgbaston and Hawkesley, Kings Norton, under the unscrupulous Colonel John ('Tinker') Fox, and constant raiding, with the Banbury Royalists, in particular, as active as ever. As spring merged into summer the uneasy calm in Stratford continued; the soldiers were never far away, though rarely, it seems, actually in town. May was a particularly fraught month for the district. Prince Rupert left Oxford for Worcester and the north, and a strong cavalry unit had moved through Warwickshire not far from Stratford on its way to join him, while a royalist attack from Compton Wynyates (in the last weeks of its occupancy by the Royalists) intercepted a parliamentary convoy of cloth only a few miles away, at Wellesbourne. Perhaps associated with these events, parliamentary soldiers reoccupied Leycester's hospital in Warwick, taking over the chapel, situated at a vantage point dominating the countryside towards Wellesbourne, and disrupting life for the elderly pensioners, 'to the fear & trouble of the poor old men', while by July the hospital's conscientious warden, Rice Jem, was fearful that tax demands for the institution could no longer be met and 'must needs fall short, and the poore Hospitall soe nobly founded quite fall to the ground'.[3] As usual, too, although the main armies were at some distance, straggling detachments from them were often uncomfortably close. When Waller passed through Evesham in pursuit of the king, his men were reported successively at Wolford, Studley and Lapworth, and on his march to Cropredy a fortnight later all of the villages between Long Compton, Shipston and Tysoe were heavily invaded. Reinforcements for Waller from Warwick and Coventry marched south to join him at Oxhill, passing by not far from Stratford, and there was skirmishing on the Worcestershire border, not far away in the opposite direction, when Worcestershire Royalists intercepted a party of Fox's men from Edgbaston also hoping to join Waller. Finally, after Cropredy, many wounded parliamentary soldiers straggled back across the countryside, adding to the general unrest and gloom.

But as already pointed out, direct military action was only one of many effects of the war for the civilian population: as the bailiff at Milcote observed gloomily in May, although no armies had crossed the immediate district recently there were only too many 'Garison soldiers, who daly of the one side or the other fetch in their Taxes, which is verie great'. In the first half of 1644, indeed, at least two new financial burdens struck a local community already being exorbitantly milked by both sides. The first of these, imposed from April to compensate belatedly the pitifully under-resourced Earl of Denbigh, was a collection designed to equip his fledgling army, particularly with dragoon horses, together with a major recruitment drive. The former was evidently more successful than the latter, for recruitment was seriously hampered by the appalling conduct of existing parliamentary troops in the district, particularly Behr's, about which Denbigh lodged several complaints with the London authorities. The collections for dragoon horses (inferior to those for cavalry units and therefore cheaper and more readily available) seem to have been more effective and were even more widespread and burdensome than the earlier ones for Lord Brooke already described. This operation was clearly a county-wide, house-to-house affair, extending to the southernmost tip of Warwickshire, and must often have caused considerable hardship to individual yeomen like Thomas Ward of Allesley, evidently far from rich but affluent enough to possess a few horses, a small estate and perhaps two or three tenants. With the renewed search for horses his plight was desperate enough for him to plead for Denbigh's protection, and permission to keep 'a couple of nags or mares of small value for my selfe and man to ride about my occasions'. His distress is voiced in an account all the more eloquent for being sober and unsensational:

> I have not received any rent this three quarters of this yeare, and I am not able to subsist. I have allowed fifty pounds a yeare out of a hundred for the weekly tax, and now my land is throne up into my owne hand, and noe body will take it of mee. I must be forced to stocke it my selfe, which land lieth seaven miles beyond Warwicke, and I must goe very often thither my selfe, which I cannot doe without my lordes protection.[4]

The loss of the villagers' horses, and the collections to buy more, became the single most recurrent item in householders' expenditure for 1644, virtually every Stratford resident contributing to the fund, specified hopefully as being 'for the safety of the County'. The more wealthy contributed generously, Nicholas Ryland 10s., William Walker 12s., Edward Wells 14s., Baldwin Brooks as much as 18s., down to the modest 1s. 6d. of many others, the money going via the now usual channels of village constable and delegated officer: 'Our Constables collected the money & paid it to Capt. Acocks', reported Peter Holland. Easily the most outstanding contribution, however, was that of Thomas Nash, who, in addition to all his other gifts, now gave an astonishing further £110 to the Earl of Denbigh 'when he came downe Generall of this County'. One can but speculate on the reasons for the diversity of these sums, but it seems likely that, whereas Nash's contribution signals clear political commitment, the more modest sums from almost equally wealthy neighbours represent the minimum expected, and were given in the hope that they might safeguard the district (and the donor) from violence. There was to be no organized neutralist movement in Warwickshire to match that later in neighbouring Worcestershire, but increasingly, as the war dragged on and the toll mounted, civilians turned to whatever or whoever might be thought likely to protect them, or at least spare the countryside further disruption. At the same time, several of Denbigh's officers are reported quartering their men throughout the Stratford district during the spring and summer of 1644 – whether on convoy duties, minor local initiatives, or in readiness for the king's expected arrival or the forthcoming assault on Banbury is not always clear – and some villages were involved in further obligations towards the Earl of Denbigh, like sending supplies for his campaign in the north Midlands.

To such burdens another, unforeseen one was now added, in the form of a further, one-off tax on Stratford, levied seemingly overnight by the unbending William Purefoy in early June. After service throughout the spring with the convoys and then aiding Massey in Gloucestershire in countering royalist offensives there, Purefoy's cavalry were hastily recalled to Warwickshire as the king set out on his northward march already referred to. His return coincided with a new spate of provocative royalist raids in the district. From the Earl of Northampton's seat at Compton Wynyates, an outpost of the Banbury garrison, a group of Cavaliers attacked a parliamentary regiment marching towards Burford, while another royalist force, this time from Banbury itself, fell upon Essex's rearguard loitering at Chipping Norton, taking many prisoners and a consignment of their letters to 'friends in London', causing much hilarity among royalist journalists. Hurrying north through Chipping Campden and Bidford, Purefoy billeted his cavalry throughout the Stratford area and promptly imposed a £10 levy on the town for their maintenance, to be raised by a uniform 5s. from the wealthier inhabitants. Some of Purefoy's men had only recently been in Stratford escorting the convoys, and judging by the wording of the citizens' claims the new exactions ('towards the £10 Colonell Purefoy had in ye towne', 'paid by Colonell Purefoyes commaund towards a sum of Tenn pounds charged upon the Towne', or Stephen Edkins's blunt 'demanded by Collonell Purefoy') were highly unpopular, coupled as they inevitably were with the usual inconvenience for some individuals. Two of Richard Smart's horses were taken away for three days' carting, John Careless's meadow was stripped bare by browsing horses, and as always more free quarter was expected, one night here, three days there, with ten soldiers or more billeted on some households, like Robert Molineau's. An undated item in the chamberlain's accounts noting payments to four townsmen for travelling to an unexplained appointment with Purefoy may date from this time, and, in the light of Robert Fawdon's own similar missions, hints at the anxieties of the local community. The situation was repeated with variants in the villages. Bishopton, Drayton and Shottery provided more quarter, and there was the usual random damage, as at Alveston, where Thomas Walton's fencing was smashed up for firewood by Purefoy's men. The practical result of all this was painful for the civilians, but highly satisfying for Parliament. For using Stratford as his base and joining with Bridges' forces from Warwick, Purefoy mounted a blistering attack on Compton Wynyates, eliminating the small royalist garrison there, achieving a highly satisfying psychological victory in capturing the Comptons' ancestral home, and promptly establishing a new parliamentary garrison there under his zealous puritan kinsman Major George Purefoy. From now on, the Stratford neighbourhood played host periodically to the soldiers from the new garrison in addition to those from the long-standing ones, besides being forced to contribute regular sums to their maintenance alongside existing commitments.[5]

Even without these new ordeals the tax burden on Warwickshire as a whole was by now universally recognized as intolerable. Petitions from its suffering citizens lobbied Parliament, the Earl of Denbigh himself recognized the state of affairs by deliberately quartering his men outside the county border, at Bromsgrove, specifically 'to ease the county of Warwick', while it was left to one of the more humane of his officers, Captain William Acock, to plead on behalf of one ravaged town, Alcester, for special concessions. Acock had been busy since the spring collecting money for Denbigh's dragoons in and around Stratford, and had seen for himself the effects of the war on the community. In May he begged Denbigh 'to consider the estate of the towne of Alcester, not only oppressed with various taxes but also much awed by the Tirrany of the adverse partye [the Royalists], by whom they have bin often plundred'. The plight of Alcester was far from unique, however: throughout the neighbourhood the increasing dislocation of ordinary life was only too evident. A letter dated 13 May 1644 from a Parliamentarian, although clearly biased, described the continuing recruitment of yet more soldiers as disaffected civilians felt they had little to lose by enlisting, the scarcity of horses, interference with farming, and extortion:

> Most of the inhabitants in those parts [Warwickshire] doe now grow sensible of the miseries which they have a longtime indured by reason of the violent and outragious courses of the Cavaliers, and as a manifestation of their affection to the cause of Religion and Liberty undertaken by the Parliament, many of them doe daily repaire to the Castle at Warwicke and to divers other places, so that within lesse then this moneth past there have beene foure or five compleat Troops raised as an addition to the Garrison at Warwicke Castle; and they might have many more men . . . if they could but get horses for them. One Captaine Chamberlaine, with divers others . . . have lately raised a Troop of Horse . . . and about a week since . . . came to Admington to gather contribution Money . . . whence they tooke many Cattell which they drave away with them. But upon the Composition of the owners, who paid them the Money they required, they restored the Cattel unto them. Many Souldiers come daily from the Kings Army to Warwicke Castle, and divers unto Colonel Massie at Gloucester.[6]

By now, commerce was being adversely affected, not only as a direct consequence of the fighting but also by measures taken by both sides to restrict or even halt cross-country trade lest it should benefit the enemy. Clothiers were particularly hard hit and repeatedly protested that their livelihoods were at risk. Traders and even substantial gentry hoping to travel required permits from wayward local military chiefs before doing so. Margery Davies, a Dudley haberdasher, received permission from Parliament to journey to Coventry to sell her hats in June only on condition 'she carrys nothinge with her prejudiciall to the state, or doth not convey any of her hatts to the enemyes garrisons'; while even the Parliamentarian Richard Lucy needed authorization from Sir William Waller before venturing from Charlecote with his servants and horses 'aboute his necessary occasions to Warwicke, & to repasse thence to London', lest he should be molested by supposedly friendly guard posts in the district. Surprisingly, perhaps (although hard evidence is sparse), local markets at Rugby, Banbury, Alcester and Stratford survived, albeit with reduced turnovers; though Stow fair, as already noted, had become a shadow of its former self and Evesham's was cancelled in September 1643 because of the dangers from royalist soldiers in the area after the siege of Gloucester.[7] Even the controversial local olympics, held annually on Dover's Hill outside Chipping Campden, had apparently by now fallen victim to the conflict.[8] Finally, at this midpoint of the war, illustrious society leaders were themselves succumbing to the intolerable pressures. Although each case is different, Viscount Conway of Ragley, Lord Chandos of Sudeley, and Robert Sidney, Earl of Leicester, of Wormleighton, all abandoned the king's cause in the summer of 1644 and took no further part in the war. Leicester, one of those genuinely torn between personal loyalty to the king and rejection of the king's policies, had, like the elderly Earl of Middlesex at Milcote, watched the rents on his Warwickshire estates, at Temple Balsall and Long Itchington, for example, plummet to half their pre-war value; and although details have not survived, each of Stratford's own landholders and their tenants must have experienced similar hardships to those already catalogued barely a mile away, at Milcote, Welcombe and elsewhere. For, above all, by midsummer 1644 the list of local gentry suffering from increasingly harsh sequestration measures was lengthening by the month. Prominent among them was Old Stratford's own ex-lord, Sir Charles Smith, already a suspect in the Popish Plot of 1641 and now sequestered for recusancy and delinquency; his goods and cattle were sold and his estate was secured when he offered no defence.[9]

On the face of it, however, Stratford's life continued much as usual during this period. Whereas there is evidence from Worcester and other towns of internal dissension amid periodic interference from military authorities on both sides in municipal government during the war, the lack of this from Stratford suggests a reasonable degree of stability in the governing establishment.[10] In spite of all, Stratford was never a garrison town, nor was it occupied in any strict sense, and, whatever the tensions, members of the corporation continued to coexist, meet together and elect their officers in the time-honoured way throughout the war years. There were no obvious political purges, only two aldermen being disciplined much later, in the 1650s, for unspecified offences unlikely to have been directly political, and who were soon reinstated anyway.[11] Moreover, disruption to church life caused by the disappearance of the vicar (belatedly expelled by the county committee in 1647 in his continued absence; see chapter 12, pages 150–2) seems to have been minimal, although Puritans in the town were admittedly unhappy that the weekly lecture was replaced by a monthly sermon and accordingly stopped paying contributions towards it. Trouble was still brewing over this in 1646.[12] Burial registers were interrupted for several years too. Yet the curate William Hawling, described by a possibly significant slip of the pen in the vestry minutes for April 1644 as 'minister' rather than 'assistant', evidently deputized competently and enjoyed the full confidence of the elders. In September 1643 they had ordered his rent of £6 to be continued to be paid by the chamberlain 'for the house he liveth in of Widow Bellamy' before at some later date the corporation allowed him and his young family to move in to the vacant vicarage. Taxes he paid to Warwick garrison were later refunded, and (a particularly delightful gesture amid the tensions of the war-torn district) a generous gift of £4 was voted to his wife in September 1644 'to buy her a Fairring at Stratford Faire'.[13]

Outside Stratford, however, some parishes fared less well as divisions deepened in the strains of war and as the efforts of the parliamentary county committee at Coventry to purge alien clergy began to take effect. Although it is impossible to estimate the precise degree of disruption these caused in the parishes of the neighbourhood, many south Warwickshire parishes were undoubtedly affected as the war dragged on and their parsons were subjected to harassment, abuse, imprisonment or actual ejection – as happened at Snitterfield, Temple Grafton, Welford, Wellesbourne and Whitchurch, as well as Stratford's own case (*see Map 5, page 97*). Many incumbents managed somehow to steer a neutralist course, though that did not in itself necessarily guarantee a quiet life. But others, activists or those known for their outspoken views, had made enemies from the start. The perfect illustration from the district of the bitter antagonisms in the underlying spiritual conflict is provided by the neighbouring parishes of Welford and Weston-on-Avon, where for once surviving fragments of documentation allow a fairly clear reconstruction of events spreading over many years. The rival parsons, both equally determined and contentious, had long been at daggers drawn. Welford's rector, Dr Jenkin Bowen, was a conspicuous royalist sympathizer, formerly chaplain to the Earl of Middlesex at Milcote and one of several local Gloucestershire clergy opting, in a clear political gesture, to send their clerical taxes directly to the king at Oxford rather than war-torn Worcester, where diocesan administration had broken down. He had gained his doctorate from Oxford the previous year in recognition of his support for the king's cause. Across the fields at Weston was the stern puritan Stratford schoolmaster John Trapp, known to his enemies as 'the preaching rebel'. As reported earlier, he had already spent a night in captivity on the queen's arrival in Stratford the previous year, and had had his house pillaged and his horse taken away. In early May 1644, probably through the efforts of Trapp via a deliberately organized and vindictive raid when the district was swarming with parliamentary troops, Bowen was seized and imprisoned in Warwick Castle, where he was placed in the custody of one of the

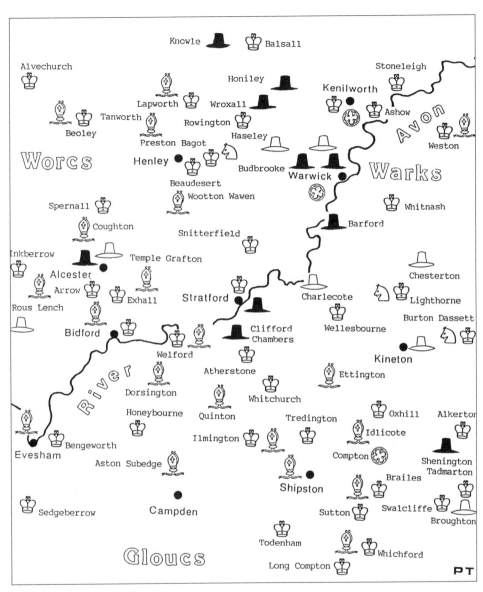

Puritan clergy threatened by Archbishop Laud in 1630s

Major puritan gentry, patron or estate

Major catholic gentry, estate or community

Royalist clergy victimised by parliamentary authorities 1640–50

Clergy abandoning parish to enlist

Parliamentarian church vandalism

Map 5. The Religious War, 1630–50.

John Trapp (1601–69). A highly-respected intellectual and biblical scholar, Stratford's schoolmaster, John Trapp, shown here aged fifty-three in a post-war engraving, was prominent in local puritan circles and minister of both Weston-on-Avon and, later, Welford. Fearing for his life, he fled from Stratford in May 1644 to take refuge in Warwick Castle for eighteen months, becoming chaplain to the garrison there, writing theological works and corresponding with puritan friends and relatives who had migrated to the New England colonies. Shakespeare's son-in-law, the physician John Hall, who had treated him in 1633, described Trapp as 'second to none' in 'his remarkable piety and learning'. See biographical note, Appendix 3, page 161.

(The Shakespeare Birthplace Trust)

governor's trusted officers, Captain Thomas Wells. His horses disappeared, some stolen by Samuel Cox, a trooper in Wells's company (significantly, at harvest time, to cause him maximum hardship), his rectory was seized and a prohibitively high £200 ransom set. Bowen was quite unable to raise even one-tenth of the sum demanded, it was stated, while at least one request for leniency, made by an elderly parishioner, William Chandler, who travelled to Warwick on 12 June to plead with Wells for his parson, fell on deaf ears.[14] Trapp, meanwhile, anticipating an official decision by the parliamentary authorities by two years, took over Bowen's parish though he was evidently ill at ease, since he was afraid of reprisals and admitted 'sometimes I have been put to my shifts'. On 16 May he drew a gloomy picture in a letter to an old friend. Not only was his beloved church torn by conflicting sects, but politically things were as bad as ever: recent peace proposals were doomed and both sides were renewing hostilities afresh. His hated rival, the 'rotten Doctor my neighbour . . . being prisoner, thinkes to free himselfe by me, if I could be laid hold on, so that [of] late I am forced to keep out of the way till he have bought, or otherwise got, his freedome'. His wife Mary, he concluded, could not put pen to paper 'for weeping the sadnesse of our times & state at this present'; her sister, Sarah Hunt, had been plundered and a Shottery friend, Widow Burman, 'hath lost all she hath, almost'. Trapp's fears for his personal safety were well-grounded. On Sunday 8 September a party of Royalists from Worcester burst into Welford church as Trapp (in a royalist report) 'was advancing towards the Pulpit with a case of Pistols for his guard because (as he told the Parishioners) he had that day some Orders to read against the King'. He was seized, taken to Worcester, somehow released but shortly after, 'being by them driven from house and home', he fled with his family to sanctuary at

Warwick, where he 'found comfortable employment and encouragement' as garrison chaplain for the next eighteen months. As he wrote in May 1646: 'We have lived at Warwick-Castle this yeare & halfe, and . . . are yet, till the Lord shall give us liberty to returne home againe, which we hope wilbe ere long.' At Warwick he used his leisure serenely by composing a renowned commentary on the New Testament 'in the midst of the noises and drums', dedicated to the Worcestershire Puritan Sir Thomas Rous, patron of the celebrated divine Richard Baxter, and his Stratford ally William Combe. Some time after, when the royalist cause was disintegrating, Trapp was officially nominated to Welford by the Westminster church authorities, but only to be challenged again by Bowen, still evidently lurking in the district nursing his grievances and who 'doth in contempt of the sequestration order interrupt and disturb the said Mr Trapp in his receiving of the tythes'. For this offence Bowen was ordered to appear before the church disciplinary body on 17 August 1647, who duly referred the case back to the Warwickshire authority where it dragged on for several more years, with witnesses for both sides being called for cross-examination and new evidence periodically presented. During this time, Trapp evidently retained his comfortable position at Welford, including the benefits of rectory and tithes, widely respected but maintaining an uneasy relationship with the corporation of Stratford (he complained later that his 'small pittance' due from the town had been 'detayned'), until the political pendulum swung again and his enemy Jenkin Bowen was finally reinstated at the Restoration. The entire saga is probably far from unique in the district, but is simply better documented than most; other parishes almost certainly presented similar, if perhaps less clear-cut, cases.[15] Stratford, however, in the light of this tale, seems to have been fortunate in having the obscure, conscientious, but no doubt less controversial William Hawling as effective minister at this time, who, when occasionally absent, seems likely to have made provision for a substitute preacher: an undated item in the chamberlain's accounts notes a payment to 'one Mr Wills, & one to feche him with a horse, to preach in Mr Hawlins absence'. Stratford thus seems to have enjoyed a degree of much-needed continuity lacking in many other parishes during these troublesome years. Three years later, when in 1647 a new minister was finally appointed, Hawling left the parish 'in love' having, all agreed, 'taken great paynes in preaching'. The contrast with the prickly relationship between the corporation and the pre-war Thomas Wilson could not be more marked.[16]

The defining character of the early summer of 1644 throughout the neighbourhood is therefore one of uncoordinated isolated skirmishing in sporadic actions. These were often initiated by local commanders eager to make their mark irrespective of wider national concerns, but left Stratford relatively untouched – though not, of course, by the continuing heavy burdens of taxation, collections and demands for free quarter for passing soldiers. As autumn approached, however, more unsettled times returned.

CHAPTER 9

Cotswold Excursions

None of the events of the summer of 1644 – the parliamentary capture of Compton Wynyates, the nearby passing of great armies, apparently trivial incidents here and there like those at Lord Leycester's Hospital or Welford, the new financial pressures weighing on the district – can be separated from the wider struggle. These are an integral part of the renewed militarization and the intensification of the underlying ideological struggle which continued into the autumn and winter. Once the king had finally moved away from the area, in July, local Parliamentarians made strenuous efforts to regain some kind of credibility after what the press called the king's 'dance beyond Worcester' which had led to Cropredy. The new-found determination was channelled into two main directions: an assault on Banbury Castle, long a major irritant, and a simultaneous offensive against Royalist-held Worcestershire. The Earl of Denbigh had been kept fully stretched in Staffordshire over many months, and nothing had come of his earlier plan to launch an attack on Banbury. Meanwhile the battle of Cropredy had dramatically dashed Sir William Waller's own rumoured hopes of capturing the town and thereby, it was imagined, boosting parliamentary recruitment after recent large-scale desertions. But although Waller's army had effectively disintegrated, sufficient local forces under able commanders like John Bridges at Warwick, William Purefoy at Coventry, and Denbigh's own chiefs of staff like Colonel Thomas Archer and the local Edward Peyto remained in the district to warrant a new initiative. The ensuing long, drawn-out siege of Banbury turned into another costly fiasco for Parliament, however, dragging on for fourteen futile weeks before finally being abandoned in late October in a welter of personal recriminations between the commanders. The immediate neighbourhood of Stratford was left largely untouched by these events, though an inhabitant of Broad Marston, Henry Cooper, spoke for many when he wrote despondently in August of 'the Common Calamities and Hardnesse of these sad times, wherein Every Honest man is a sufferer' amid 'the Great Danger these parts are in by the passage of Armies and Souldiers'.[1]

The second initiative, that in the Worcestershire sector, presents a very different and even more confused picture. Here, the Earl of Denbigh had long hoped to liaise closely with Bridges at Warwick and Massey at Gloucester in order to squeeze the Worcester Royalists between them, a threat which had caused sufficient alarm in May for the Worcester governor, Sir Gilbert Gerard, to appeal to Prince Rupert for help. Once the king's army had vacated the area, Parliament renewed the pressure by ordering the capture of Evesham, already assaulted successfully by Massey in

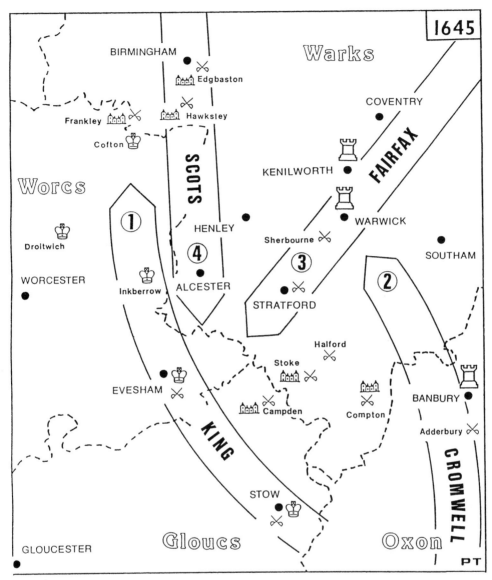

Map 6. Major Events in 1645.

✂ Siege or skirmish

🏰 Mansion plundered or attacked

♛ King's lodging

April and now, after being vacated by the Royalists in June on the king's march north, vulnerable to a determined attack. The plan was for Colonel Thomas Archer to garrison it temporarily until Massey could send a permanent occupying force from Gloucester and thus secure it as a base which would at once, it was argued, neutralize royalist Worcestershire, cut off the Cavaliers' main supply route between Oxford and the west and keep open their own Warwick–Gloucester corridor. But as so often, plans were one thing, implementing them another. Massey was so hard-pressed in Gloucestershire as to be unable to help, despite repeated requests, while the Earl of Denbigh was unexpectedly recalled to London to face serious political charges. In Denbigh's absence any semblance of unity among the local parliamentary commanders quickly evaporated, and it seems to have been left to Archer, one of his ablest officers, to attempt to coordinate efforts towards Worcestershire, using unpaid, starving and therefore mutinous troops. The result was a confused campaign which soon degenerated into a series of largely unproductive skirmishes, raids, advances and retreats. Although some units, like those of Colonel Thomas Stevens and Archer's own, had already been in Stratford on and off since at least May (coinciding with the abduction of Bowen from Welford), the peak of the activity for the town and countryside came in late July and August, when large numbers of Denbigh's troops under Archer on the way to Evesham 'lay in towne' and in the surrounding villages on at least three separate occasions – or even four, according to John Smith and Thomas Nash. It was probably at this time, on the way to Stratford, that Archer and about sixty of his men with their horses, 'the greatest partt of his regimentt', quartered at Henry Parry's at Edstone, 'partt of one night, hay and provinder for theire horses', with 'horse meate & some provisions partt of another night'. From Stratford they moved on to Alcester, on about 24 July, receiving provisions sent on from Snitterfield and other villages, to initiate the hoped-for capture of Evesham. At one point Archer routed attacking Royalists, who fled back into Worcestershire, many, reportedly, 'escapinge with much difficultie through dangerous waters'. After occupying Evesham for a night, however, hearing of the approach of royalist reinforcements, Archer thought it best to return to Alcester, where in evident alarm he reported to Denbigh on 27 July that he was expecting an attack, was barricading the approaches to the town and – as though that were not enough – that his men were mutinous. The next few weeks were evidently chaotic, spent advancing as far as Chipping Campden on 11 August and sending more fruitless appeals to Massey for help, before finally retreating to Alcester once again, on about 16 August. During this time there were nevertheless some limited parliamentary successes, Gerard at Worcester reporting that Denbigh's forces had 'made a strong Inroad upon us', that he needed reinforcements desperately and that even Worcester was in some danger.[2]

At Stratford, Colonel Stevens's men had apparently moved on fairly briskly, requiring only 'a night & dinner on the morrowe' from some of the townspeople, but Archer's own were evidently in larger numbers and in less of a hurry. They established a sentry post at Thomas Horne's, requiring meals for themselves and provender for their horses (described as 'diett and horsemeat' by Alice Halford), receiving additional supplies from outlying villages like Snitterfield, Luddington and Binton 'when they lay att Stratford and Alcester', staying for as much as five days and returning more than once, some groups relaying others. Villages nearby also reported Archer's men quartering several times, and the troops were evidently in sufficient numbers as to commandeer all available accommodation. As usual, a few inhabitants, like William Lindon and Thomas Green, took the trouble to record names and dates: in May, Colonel Stevens's men; in June those of Captains John Gyles and Cotton; 20 July, Colonel Stevens's again; 25 and 28 July, Captain Burbank's. Thomas Horne's entry is one of the most explicit: 'Charges with the Earle of Denbighes soldiers at severall times, horse meate & mans meate & for fire & beere when they kept Court of Guard: £3.' On the whole there was surprisingly little theft this time, though sheep were taken at Bishopton, and in Stratford 'spurres & other wares' from Francis Smith's, horses from Richard Smart, William Hiccox and William Abbott, and a saddle and bridle from Abraham Tibbott. As usual, too, the presence of one company of soldiers did not exclude others: swelling numbers in Stratford at this time were Warwickshire troops from Bridges' and Purefoy's regiments under captains whose names were by now becoming wearisomely familiar to the people: Potter, Hawksworth, Cheshire, Pont, Otway, Wells, Castle, either ready to lend Archer assistance in Worcestershire or as a reserve to reinforce colleagues at the siege of Banbury. Yet despite this sizable parliamentarian presence, royalist raids continued from time to time, provoking an emotional protest by Warwickshire gentry in a petition taken to Westminster in September and the seizure of Trapp in Welford church in the incident reported in Chapter 8.[3]

This unsettled state of affairs continued throughout the autumn, with each side claiming victories but neither gaining any real territorial advantage. Mid-September saw both sides attempting to reinforce their men at the siege of Banbury, with Royalists approaching Stratford from Evesham at one point but deterred from continuing by a threat from the ever-active Massey (not Cromwell, as incorrectly reported) in north Gloucestershire,[4] while there was frequent feuding in the district between the parliamentary governor of Edgbaston, Colonel John Fox, and Colonel Sandys' Royalists from Evesham. Illustration of the persistent violence which dogged the area at this time is provided by the parliamentary plunder of Redditch in September, a dramatic and picturesque episode at Alcester in October and a vicious encounter near Pershore in November, in all of which units recently stationed in Stratford were involved. Following Archer's earlier activities, Alcester had been converted into a virtual garrison town, commanded by two local men much scoffed at by royalist journalists as upstart tradesmen now absurdly promoted beyond their station into 'pilfering shop-Captaines' and 'High-way Commanders who have cast aside their Aprons and made Robbery their trade'. These were John Smith, reputedly a cobbler (and likely to have been the same captain in charge at Coughton and charged with much theft and kidnapping there during its brief occupation by Parliament the previous November); and John Cheshire, an Alcester chandler who had been in the Stratford district for some time, collecting taxes at Alderminster, quartering at Bishopton and stealing Edward Greene's horse at Great Alne 'uppon promise I should be payd for him'. Their activities at Alcester were scathingly reported in the contemporary tabloid style beloved of both sides, clearly biased but probably fairly accurately:

The Chandler keepes his Horses in the Church, and his Troope are maintained by plundering sheepe, which they rost in the Church (where the Captaine hath a double share in the Mutton, besides all that which may advantage his Trade). These two pilfering shop-Captaines have already made thin Sheepfolds in the Country thereabout. The Cobler ranges about and descends so low as stealing geese and henns.

Things came to a head on the night of 8 October when the 'Captaine Chandler' was loitering at his father Anthony Cheshire's, and was caught unawares by a sudden royalist incursion into his home town by Worcestershire soldiers under Colonels Samuel Sandys and John Knotsford, and was forced to take refuge in the church, already apparently being used as a stable and cookhouse. After more jeering at the 'governor of Alcester Church' the royalist account continues:

One of these is Captaine Chandler, Governour (forsooth!) of Alcester Church in Warwick-shire . . . This Chandler had for 10 weekes last past made the Parish Church a Garrison for his horses and (which is worse) for himselfe and foot-Rebells, out of which Church (now if ever a Den of theeves) he still sallied to steale sheepe from the Country. Whereof Sir Gilbert Gerard taking notice, sent out a strong party of horse . . . who advanced to Alcester to the Chandler and his sheep-stealers, and on Tuesday night last encompassed the Towne round, drawing out a certaine number to assault the Garrison in the Church. The Chandler at that time was in bed with a woman in the Towne, and upon the Alarme fled in his shirt to the Church; but that place which they had so much abused before protected them not an houre. For the valiant assailants . . . forced their entrance into the Church; whereupon the Rebells fled all into the Steeple. But the Colonell fired some wet Straw and so smoaked them downe, which forced them all to submit themselves to mercy, Captaine Chandler himselfe leading the way; who with his Officers, 38 Souldiers, 50 Muskets, 30 horse, good store of Pistols and Carbines, all their Powder and Baggage (except the Chandlers Bedfellow) were brought safe to Worcester.

A parliamentary report of the same incident adds that the Royalists 'burned some part of the Church, and having plundered many Houses did carry [their] Prisoners unto Worcester'.[5] Such skirmishes could at times take on the character of a local derby, given an additional edge by the involvement of local rivals eager, no doubt, to settle obscure old personal scores as well as ideological differences. Just as the intense personal rivalry between Lord Brooke and the Earl of Northampton was a feature of the early stages of the Warwickshire conflict, so here the parliamentary commander at Warwick, John Bridges and his subordinate, Cheshire, were both from Alcester (with Bridges, moreover, formerly Lord Brooke's solicitor), while Sandys was from Fladbury and Knotsford from Studley, both probably connected with the Earl of Northampton and the Sheldon family. It was this sort of feuding, not unlike the baronial wars of the Middle Ages, which ultimately fuelled the popular revulsion that created the neutralist, so-called Clubmen, movement in Worcestershire, and there is a hint of the general hostility to the soldiers' presence in an interesting contemporary parliamentarian comment that one Monday, the Royalists 'marched towards Aulcester in Warwickshire, but it being the Fayre-day, they durst not enter the town'. Nevertheless, royalist aggression at this time was so widespread that another petition of Warwickshire gentry, signed, it was claimed, by more than 3,000 residents of the county, was submitted to Parliament on 10 October asking for the urgent return of the Earl of Denbigh to prevent untold tragedy.[6]

Even more dispiriting for Parliament at this time was a costly attempt by the Warwickshire forces to 'regain their honour woefully lost' at the siege of Banbury, as Colonel Bridges put it candidly, which went badly wrong. By his own admission, his regiment was shattered and one of Parliament's ablest local commanders, Major Abraham Pont, 'a Scottishman of brave resolution and courage' who had recently been in action at Banbury, killed in a violent encounter near Pershore. On 11 November the Warwickshire forces under Hawksworth, Wells and Pont had blocked Royalists from Shrewsbury and Worcestershire attempting to cross the Avon near Evesham in order to join the king at Oxford and had chased them back towards Worcester, until at Pinvin a further force of Royalists intervened, crushed the outnumbered Parliamentarians and 'villainously killed' Major Pont, who was refused the gentlemanly quarter accorded the ordinary soldiers. Many Warwickshire villages, and a number of Stratford's inhabitants, had regularly quartered Pont's men in the past, either when escorting the Gloucester convoys or on regular tax collection operations over the wide area assigned to him, from Salford Priors in the west to Mollington in the east, Binton's constable speaking for many when he recorded Pont's regiment 'quarteringe very often uppon us when they gathered their Contribution in our parte of the Country'. Now, town and countryside witnessed parliamentary soldiers fleeing back to Warwick from the two encounters at Alcester and Pershore, followed shortly after by the melancholy spectacle of the major's funeral cortege passing on its way back to Coventry. The procession, as usual, inevitably involved more charges, for 'Major Ponts Company when hee was brought to be buried', as Stratford's John Spires recorded, or 'Coventre soldiers at fetching of Major Pont', as Robert Fitzhughes put it even more starkly.[7]

Thus the tit-for-tat raiding and counter-raiding continued throughout the autumn, with the Earl of Northampton threatening to wrest back his seat at Compton Wynyates from the infamous Major George Purefoy and being contemptuously rebuffed in late October; a party of Archer's men seizing a group of 'the King's stragling souldiers making merry' in a house at Henley-in-Arden in early November; and more Royalists pouncing upon Gloucester carters refreshing themselves one night at the Spread Eagle tavern 'at the end of the Bridge that goeth into [Warwick]', seizing their consignment of 120 yards of red cloth to clothe themselves before taunting the Warwick defenders by blowing trumpets under the castle walls and then careering off through Tachbrook Mallory, Southam and Priors Marston, kidnapping and pillaging along the way.[8] Late November saw Stratford still billeting parliamentary troops, payments of 15s. being recorded 'for souldiers which quarters [sic] in Stratford aboute ye 27 of November 1644', along with Pont's regimental chaplain, Simon Moore. Yet shortly after – illustrating again the town's vulnerability to invasions from both sides – Royalists stormed into town in what was evidently a reprisal against local Parliamentarians. These included Thomas Nash, well-known by now as a regular member of the parliamentary committee sitting at Warwick:

> From Warwick I have intelligence that the Enemy still makes incursions, not onely into the out parts of the County, but into the heart of the County; for the last week Master Nashes house at Stratford, with divers others, were plundered, and Mr Nash himself hardly escaped, at whom they chiefly aimed; and that one Tibitts and his son and divers more, as they were coming from Coventry Market to Warwick, were taken prisoners neer Killingworth [Kenilworth] and were carried away to Liechfield.

Colonel Archer remained active in the district right into December, and was extravagantly praised in the parliamentarian press for 'his remarkable service'. But it is clear, from incidents like those just reported and other references to 'honour woefully lost for want of conduct and order', 'the miseries of our friends at Warwicke' and 'the roots of Contentions' still bedevilling the parliamentary efforts, that, if anything, the Royalists had the better of these inglorious and largely unproductive encounters. But certainly there was no change in the civilian perspective on the war. On 1 December one Stratford inhabitant wrote unambiguously: 'We live in more & more feares daly, the Armies coming verie neare us, and many not farr off us doe suffer daly'.[9]

By December, royalist activity seemed to be intensifying to the extent that Parliament began to suspect a concerted campaign across the Midlands in an offensive from the Banbury and Evesham sectors simultaneously, likely therefore to threaten Warwick and, perhaps, even Coventry. In the east, the Earl of Northampton was as active as ever and continued to dominate the entire Banbury and south Warwickshire district; it was clear that he would sooner or later mount an attempt to recover Compton Wynyates. In the west the Royalists patently had the upper hand, the dependable Sir Samuel Luke warning his parliamentary colleagues that they were fortifying everywhere and lay 'all there and about the Vale of Evesham'. Although it is far from clear whether such a royalist plan existed (and, in fact, though unbeknown to Parliament, local royalist units were in a state of confusion equal to their own, exacerbated by imminent changes in the command structure between Prince Rupert and his brother Maurice), further news in December seemed to confirm the worst. To add to the strong royalist presence at Worcester and Evesham under Sir Gilbert Gerard, his able nephew Charles Gerard was now quartered at Moreton-in-Marsh and Prince Maurice at Bourton-on-the-Hill, while Chipping Campden, Lark Stoke, near Ilmington, Broad Marston house and even Pebworth church were all now occupied by the Cavaliers. Such frenzied activity, reported and gossiped about throughout the district, clearly added to the widespread apprehension besides involving local residents in unforeseen obligations: for some unexplained reason the vicar of Alveston, John Dowley, found himself reimbursing Joan Cooper of Pebworth the sum of £20 which she had lent to maintain the new royalist garrison occupying Pebworth church at Christmas. But it was the newly established garrison at Chipping Campden which caused Parliament particular alarm, staffed as it was by a succession of Rupert's devoted protégés on his instructions, with its outpost at Lark Stoke having long been a minor irritant and notorious as a supposedly strongly fortified papist cell.[10] The addition of these further enemy garrisons in the strategic north Cotswolds, threatening to cut the Warwick–Gloucester route, caused near-panic among the Parliamentarians, but instead of attacking them before they could be consolidated, the Warwickshire authorities decided to pre-empt matters in early December by seizing other potential garrisons, and for reasons which are not otherwise entirely clear the Earl of Middlesex's great Tudor mansion at Milcote, south of Stratford, was selected for immediate action, even though neither it nor its elderly owner who had long abandoned it had played any aggressive role whatsoever in the war. An order dated 4 December and signed by six members of the Coventry committee headed by William Purefoy instructed Major Joseph Hawksworth: 'with three barrels of Powder to blow up the roofe of Milcote House, thereby to unfitt the said house for the use of the Enemy, and so to disappoint their design of garrisoning it.'

Hawksworth lost no time in acting, nor in interpreting his orders as he thought fit. A unique account of the next day's events at Milcote has survived, due to the conscientiousness of the loyal steward, Robert Fawdon, and is worth quoting at length for the clear, stark light it throws on the nature of this war and its sheer human interest:

On Thursday the 5th of this Month about 12 of the clocke their came to Melcott house as neare as I can guesse about 200 of horsse of Collonell Purefoy Regiment, comannded in cheife by Major Hauckesworth, with dyvers captaines & other officers, as Captaine Welles, Capt. Potter & others. After they had sumoned the house [wth 5 or 6 Trumpetts] (when God knowes their was no men in it but my person, [beinge much amazed with their suddaine approach]), Captaine Welles told me then they weer comed [sic] to putt a Garrison in the house, by order from the Committee, & called the Major, who Comaunded mee to show them the house; which I did, everie part, within doore & without. [And after they had seene what they desired, the Major wth the Rest of the Commanders went to Consultacon in private, but in the Intrim the House was full of their unruly souldiers, notwithstanding the Majors comand to the contrary, who many of them tooke what they liked] . . . The Major then told me they must either pull down the house or fyre it, for they had certaine Intelligence that the enemie was verie neere & coming to Garrison the house, wch would undoe the Cuntry and Indanger their safetie. To which I answered And desired That they would consider me as a servant, [as alsoe, what such a greate Fabricke as that would cost in buildinge, wch would all be consumed and many Good Moveables therin & benefitt to noe body], and to give me some short time to send to yor honr; for I was confident the Kings Armie had noe such intention, for their had been such false reports above this twelve monthes, yet never any, either officer or other soldier, ever came to survey the house or ever any of that side was in the house since the warres began . . . save onely Prince Rupert, sixteene monthes agoe, when the Queen lay two nights att Stratford, who then brought with him a Coachfull of Ladies to looke for Fruit. I further desired, if they would not grant me time to send to yor honr, to give me [some litle tyme to

*Lionel Cranfield, Earl of Middlesex (1575–1645). Of humble origins but industrious and astute,
Cranfield rose to power rapidly under James I whom he served as a commercial and financial
magnate, becoming Privy Counsellor and finally treasurer. Making powerful enemies in the process,
he was disgraced in a complex corruption scandal, stripped of office in 1624 and temporarily
imprisoned in the Tower of London. Released and pardoned, he lived mostly in retirement thereafter
at Copt Hall, Essex, but paying frequent visits to his other seat at Milcote, outside Stratford, where
he was lord of the manor as war broke out. Then nearing seventy, he played no active role in the
conflict but paid the penalty for studied neutrality by having his Warwickshire and Gloucestershire
estates pillaged by both sides and his great mansion at Milcote burnt to the ground on the orders of the
Warwickshire parliamentarian chief, Colonel William Purefoy.*
                    (Private Collection; photograph: Courtauld Institute of Art)

pull it downe]; but that would not be granted neither. Then my request was to have Libertie untill the next morning to take away the goods that were in the house, wch would otherwise be Lost; but all the favor I could obtaine was to goe about presently the takeing out of the Goods. The Major told me he would give what time he could, & was sorry to doe what he must, being Comaunded by the Comittee att Coventry to pull it downe or fyre it, and now time would not give him Leave to pull it downe, and he must obey their Comaunds. [For they would grant noe certaine tyme, but spare it as Long as they could and wished me make Hast, when God knowes I had litle help, it beinge Market Day. Neither Durst the Neighbours help, for feare of giveinge offence unto them, assuringe themselves such a Horrid thinge would not been [sic] committed wthout some great fault committed by Yor Honnr. Thus helpless & merciless I was left, and not above two Houres Libertie to gett what I could of Yor Honnrs Goodes into the open feilds, where the most part Lay that night; and betwixt souldiers & other badd people, a greate deale thereof was lost . . . And many good moveables were burnt in the House for want of a Litle tyme to save it]. And as I understand since, they sent to the Comittee (for indeed I was putt in hope they would not fyre until midnight), yett stayed nott the retourne; but within two houres after [before foure of the clocke] the house was sett on fyre [in 3 or 4 severall places, and ready to fall upon our Heades while wee were gettinge out the Goodes], saying the enemie was att [Chipping] Cambden, [and yet, God knowes, noe Enemy neerer for ought I could ever yet learne then their Garrisons at Banbury & Worcester] . . . Those who made readie the Fyre & sett it on Burning was one Thomas Bovie a Trumpetter to the Major and dyvers other of their soldiers comaunded by the Major & his officers, who himselfe & other of his Captaines stayed within night to see it unquenchable before they went away, haveing taken the benefitt of the wind to helpe the fire, [protestinge their owne sorrow in this their merciless Act, wch is yet the Lamentacon of the whole country]. Ther came Also after their consultation Colonell Archer with his Regiment, whose men began to take what they could; but upon complaint he comaunded them away and did not stay himself [to be an Actor in that fearefull desolacon], and for ought I can understand he had no part in the Fyreing. And thus without mercie [to the greife of all Good men, did they in a short tyme destroy this great & goodly buildinge wth many Good moveables, wch want of tyme would not give me leave to prserve] . . . And this is the Truth of that mischeifeous Act, soe farr as I know, which to my continued Sorrow I was a wittnesse of and sufferer in; which with my bounden dutie I most humbly prsent to yor honr.[11]

As news of the destruction of the great house spread, Parliamentarians made a feeble attempt to claim the act as one of royalist vandalism, but the court newspaper lost no time in pointing the finger at 'the Brethren at Warwick'. The Earl of Middlesex, friend of John Donne and Inigo Jones in happier times, was by all accounts a hard, unpopular landlord, and there is more than a suspicion that his tenants' reluctance to help with the salvage operations was more than diplomatic. But the sick old man had done little to deserve this, other than to have accumulated wealth and power as former treasurer to James I, counted the court poet-gallant Sir John Suckling among his near-relatives, been a close friend of the royalist Bishop Goodman of Gloucester and held strong views on silencing Puritans 'that will not conform themselves'. He had tried to steer a neutral course, and had paid the penalty by being financially harassed by both sides before and after this final catastrophe. Besides the religious zealots, William Purefoy and Joseph Hawksworth, the other figure in the puritan trio directly implicated in the destruction of Milcote was, probably, none other than the Stratford schoolmaster John Trapp, described by Robert Fawdon as an intimate of Hawksworth. As we have seen, Trapp had very recently been victimized by local Royalists at Welford, and his failure to warn Fawdon of the impending assault on Milcote, of which the bailiff was sure he must have known, looks deliberate. Trapp later claimed (not necessarily insincerely) that the tragedy was divine retribution for the mansion's past iniquities – perhaps a reference to the fact that before the war the Bishop of Gloucester had sent his friend Middlesex a chorister, virginals and wax candles, and that the house had often seen unbecoming merriment involving courtly entertainments at successive Christmases. Already terminally ill, the seventy-year-old earl soon succumbed to this final blow to his declining fortunes and died in London in August 1645. As for his great old mansion in the meadows sloping down to the Avon, which had echoed to the sound of dancing and music, where Suckling had delighted in the pipe and tabor in the great hall and where Prince Rupert had ambled with his ladies through parlours and gardens only the year before, it vanished like a ghost at cock-crow.[12]

Later, an inventory was drawn up of those contents of the great house which Robert Fawdon somehow managed to salvage and dump hastily in the meadow on this December afternoon before the flames took control and the great pall of smoke rose over Stratford. As he explained, many items were promptly stolen by the soldiers or idle onlookers, but the residue, still substantial, was eventually packed up in trunks and blankets and sent in consignments to the family estate at Copt Hall in Essex. Some goods were despatched shortly after the tragedy, but the bulk did not follow until October, without any explanation for the long delay (though the old earl had just died):

> Imprimis, one greate trunke of Lynnen for tables & beds
> Item 10 peeces of hangings of Antiq worke
> Three greate peeces of hangings, of the Passion storie
> One great Standerd of fine Linnen & silke quilts
> One little Box with all the plate loste at Milcott
> One Trunke with small Carpetts & 2 riche cushions
> fowre Cabbinetts of my Ladyes packed up in one Rugge three blancketts and a packclothe
> More sent from Milcote 1 Octo 1645
>
> Five trunkes
>
> In the first trunke 4 fine ruggs
> foure small peeces of [ ] with hangings
> one bigger peece of fine hanging
> one silke Curtaine

In the 2d trunke.
The furniture of the purple bed
The furniture of the great red bed
The furniture of the yellow quilt bed
The red taffatie Canopie Curtaines & Vallance
3 Damaske Curtaines
Three Curtaines of India stuffe

In the third trunke. 19 paire of sheetes
one dozen of napkins
one sweete bag imbroydered
three wrought pillowbeeres with blacke, and a
Cover for a bed of the same worke
one greate Cushian

In the fourth Trunke. 13 pewter dishes with my Lords Armes ingraven two
dozen & eleaven plates
9 sawcers
two greate chargers of old pewter
one greate bason
two old dishes
2 pie plates
one pastie plate
one Salte
8 Chamberpotts
8 stoole panes
2 bed pannes
5 greate Cushions
5 small carpetts

In the 5th Trunke, the furniture of the Red clothe bed
three greate Cushions

Alsoe sent my Lords deske

Throughout November further consignments were sent, this time by Stratford's John Bellamy, 'after the Inventorie was made'. These included twenty-two tapestries, six Turkish carpets, fourteen 'little picktures', many more blankets and rugs, 'one painted boxe & Cover', and 'one Blankett to packe them in'. The house had long disappeared, but at least some of the furnishings, and the priceless tapestries of mythological and Biblical scenes, were rescued from the damp wintry fields.

Almost as though stung into some kind of spectacular retaliation for the destruction of Milcote, the Banbury Royalists under the Earl of Northampton's brothers the Comptons finally decided to implement the long-expected recapture of the ancestral home at Compton Wynyates from the detested puritan zealot George Purefoy, dubbed the local Wat Tyler by hostile journalists. Following the earl's failure to intimidate the governor in December, the Royalists had been thought to be planning an attack, and the garrison was warned to be on guard. It was not until well into the New Year that an attempt was finally mounted. The Royalists left Banbury by moonlight at midnight on 29/30 January 1645, and they took the sleeping sentinels completely by surprise. The graphic account of the fierce engagement, and the ultimate royalist failure, written by Purefoy himself at 9.00 p.m. the same evening, is among the most detailed and dramatic of local actions in the war, and is worth quoting in full:

> This night, about two of the clock, about a 1,000 or 1,200 Horse and Foot fell upon me at Compton, storm'd my outworks, gain'd the stable and cut down my great Draw-bridge and possest themselves of all my Troop horses, and took about 30 of my foot Souldiers in their beds who lay over the stables, almost before a man could think what to do. We received that alarm as we had good cause, and presently made good the new Sconce before the stone Bridge & beat them out of the great Court, there being about 200 entred and ready to storm the Sconce. But we gave them so hot a sallie that we forced them to retreat backe to the stables, Barns and Brew-house, where from the windowes they played very hot upon us. I then commanded Lieutenant Purefoy & my quarter-master (having no other Officers of quality at home, the rest being abroad with about 30 of my best Troopers) to sally out upon the enemy with a partie of some 40, & to attempt the regaining of the Brew-house and the roomes above, which they did with gallant resolution and courage. Sergeant Bird was one who came not short in bravery of any. This party fought with the enemy and came to push of Pike, nay, to swords point, and did lay about so bravely that they forced the enemy to retreat from chamber to chamber. I then sent out my youngest brother the Ensign with my three corporalls of horse and about 40 more men to relieve the first partie; and I will assure you, the young boy will fight: he led on his men bravely, and relieved his brother, by which meanes all the upper roomes were gained. And the enemy kept onely the stables and barns, stoutly, [but] my resolute soldiers did then thunder their horses and reserves of foot that stood within pistol shot, that Sir William and Sir Charles Compton began to give ground, which my souldiers easily perceiving, some leapt out at the windowe and so into the out-works, by which means I recovered my out-works againe, and made good a sally port, by which the enemy endeavoured to retreat at; but finding they were frustrated of their hopes, and that my Musketeers did play so hot upon the great Draw-bridge that they could not be relieved; & withall having beaten the enemy out of that worke, which we stormd when you took the house, I had time to recover the great Draw-bridge and presently got new ropes and new lockes, and drew it up againe in spight of them all. Now these whose names you have here inclosed were all in Cobbs pound, having no meanes in the world to retreat. Whereupon they fought desperately for the space of 3 houres, & the valiant Comptons perceiving their extreame losse

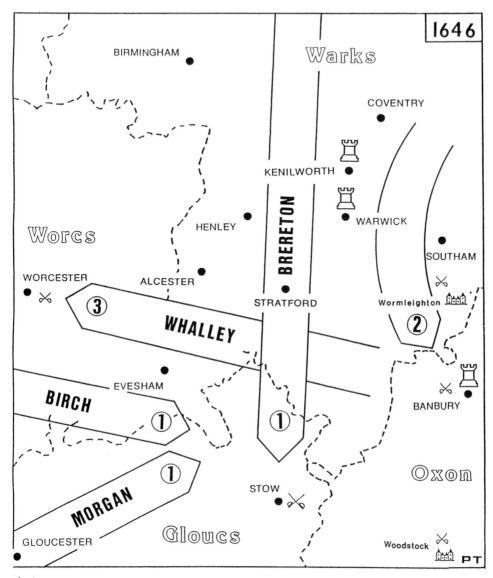

⚔ Major battle

⚔ Siege or skirmish

🏰 Mansion plundered or attacked

Map 7. Major Events in 1646.

attempted three severall times to storm and to regain my outworkes, but all three times were beaten off with as much resolution and gallantry as could be. The enemy within set fire on the hay, straw and all combustible stuffe, to smother my men out of the upper rooms, which did indeed much annoy them; and the Enemy without threw at least 100 hand Granadoes upon the houses that they set them on fire in divers place. Sir Charles and Sir William Compton then thinking all was their own sent a Trumpeter to parlie, but I commanded that none should parlie, nor would I permit the Trumpeter to speak at all, though faine he would have said something to my souldiers, but commanded him upon his life to be gone and return no more at his perill. We continued in fight still, and the fire did so encrease that I thought it fit to offer quarter to all those in the stable, for their lives onely; but they would not hear me. Upon which I drew all my men together and fell violently in upon them, wherein were slain and taken prisoners all whose names are in the insuing list. This did so dishearten the Comptons and all their forces that they did draw presently off all their foot, and onely faced me with their horse, and sent another Trumpeter to parley. But I commanded to give fire upon him, so that he returned with no other answer but what a Musket could speake. Sir, this is as true and as short a Narration as I can give you. I am, as we all are,

Your obliged servants & kinsmen

George Purefoy
William Purefoy

After listing the prisoners taken, Purefoy added a summary: 'The fight began about two of the clock in the morning and continued till about nine, in which they stormed us foure severall times, and were beaten off.' In the process, stables, barns and brew-houses were all burnt. Further accounts of the siege, including one by John Bridges, give similar details, with interesting minor variations. One speaks of the governor 'making good the Draw-bridge, for the House is moated about', and specifies that the royalist assault party was finally 'inclosed in betweene the Hils and the House'. Several report that the prisoners taken outnumbered the garrison to the extent that Major Joseph Hawksworth was called out from Warwick to help escort them away, while one concludes with a self-congratulatory flourish: 'The enemy carried away with them eight Cart-loads of dead and wounded into Banbury, and it is believed will hereafter have but little stomacke to make an onset upon Compton house.' Shortly after, an official communiqué from the Coventry authorities congratulated Purefoy on his success in repulsing the royalist onslaught. The remaining Cavaliers, for their part, had barely regained their quarters at Banbury and Kings Sutton when they were set upon by a strong cavalry force from Northampton, losing more prisoners and horses, sold the following day at Northampton.

After successive restorations over many years, the precise extent of the damage to the house is impossible to estimate, but it was probably no more severe than that already caused by the parliamentary garrison in residence. However, at some point the Comptons' alabaster effigies in the church nearby were vandalized and the church itself wrecked, to await rebuilding at the Restoration. The moat was later filled in following a government decree, to prevent the house ever again being used as a fortified garrison. Centuries later, Henry James described the opulent setting of the great house, its air of solitude and delicate decay – of having been dropped into its grassy hollow 'as an ancient jewel is deposited upon a cushion, and being shut in from the world and back into the past by its circling woods.' It is indeed difficult to imagine today the murderous activity on those green slopes of that moonlit winter's night of 1645.[13]

A week after the siege of Compton, John Bridges, eager to capitalize on new-found parliamentary confidence, successfully stormed Lark Stoke house, occupied by the Royalists as an outpost of their new garrison at Chipping Campden under the colourful (and notorious) war-scarred veteran Colonel Henry Bard. Situated on an eminence near Ilmington commanding extensive views across the countryside, it was clearly a threat to the Warwick-Gloucester route, and was equally pernicious to the pious Bridges as the home of the noted local Catholic Richard Brent. Among the royalist prisoners taken back in triumph to be ransomed at Warwick Castle were, it was claimed, captains from the major catholic land-owning families of the district, not only Brent himself but the Keytes of Wolford and the Cannings of nearby Foxcote. As was increasingly usual at this stage of the war, Bridges promptly destroyed the mansion by fire, 'to prevent the building of any more such Rookes nests', as he explained. Bridges' men had passed near Stratford on their way to Stoke, and now, their mission succesfully completed, refreshed themselves at Loxley on the way back. In one more fascinating contemporary insight into the nature of the war, into the conduct of garrison commanders of both sides and the way local people were kept informed of events, a Parliamentarian in Stratford reported shortly after that Richard Brent, 'the great Papist of Stoak-house',

> . . . gave intelligence of a Constable at Qurniton [Quinton?] and enforced him to bring his collection money to Colonell Bard, Governour of Campden. The poore Constable brought as much as he could get, and certified the Governour (then in bed) thereof. The Governour demanded if it were all. The Constable answered, 'He could not bring all, for the plague was in some houses.' The Governour replied, 'That if the Plague were in one, and the Pox in the other, he would have all the money, and would talke with him further when he was up.' After he rose, he commanded the Constable to be throwne into a pond to swim for his life, where he had been drowned had he not beene helpt out by one of the souldiers . . . They are now fortifying of Cambden stronger than ever.[14]

Such incidents as these, however, insignificant in any wider perspective yet traumatic enough for the local communities who lived through them, were soon to be overtaken by more important events on a truly national scale. It is to these that we now turn.

CHAPTER 10

Before and After Naseby

Although great things were in the wind, the first months of 1645 gave little hint
that anything had changed; the general picture remained one of sporadic
skirmishing, of a futile expenditure of energy, resources and men with no obvious
overall strategy, of militarily unproductive alarms and excursions. The planned
parliamentary army on a 'new model' was not yet ready, the Self-Denying
Ordinance to replace tired aristocratic officers with trained professionals from all
walks of life had not yet had an effect, and the king, although reported to be
preparing to take to the field, was as yet stationary in Oxford. Although it did not
necessarily appear so to the combatants, early 1645 seems in retrospect to have
been a period of waiting for both sides. For the moment, then, all continued much
as before in the Stratford district, with the occasional raiding and violence, as at
Compton Wynyates and Lark Stoke, vicious though they were, of less overall
consequence to the local civilian population than the unprecedented tax burdens
and the general economic depression caused by the unstable times. New royalist
garrisons, as at Chipping Campden, added significantly to the hardship facing
landowners and tenants alike, who were being taxed simultaneously by both sides,
'both from the Kings forces in Worcestershere and the [parliamentary] Comittee
of Worcestershire now sitting in Warwick', as one local resident grumbled to a
Stratford friend away on business in London. This was not, in fact, the whole
story: as the Milcote bailiff made clear in February, things were even worse:

> The demaunds on both sides were never soe vyolent as now, both from Cambden,
> Glocester & Worcester, and to add to those great Taxes everie high Constable (by
> Authoritie from the Comaunders) will rate those great somes as they please, and
> no remeddie, for the soldier cares not who paies soe they may have it.

A hint of the ruthlessness underlying the local conflict is given by the fact that no
allowance was made to the Milcote bailiff for the destruction of the great house, as
peremptory demands for money continued to pour in from both Coventry and
Chipping Campden after the mansion had been reduced to embers. He pleaded
with the parliamentary authorities for arrears to be waived since, he thought 'they
could not for shame, I was confident, have demaunded these'. But he misjudged
William Purefoy, for the puritan colonel was unyielding, and Fawdon had no doubt
that 'this sudden calling for all those monies certainly come from the Colonells
orders'. His plight deepened during the spring, when royalist cavalry from Banbury

were once again in Stratford collecting contributions; not for the first time, April found him forced to travel far to plead with local royalist commanders and, receiving no satisfaction, planning to take his suit to the court itself, at Oxford.[1]

Perhaps more than anywhere, Banbury continued to be the focus of violence throughout a wide radius. Although this did not directly affect the Stratford neighbourhood, the whole area was militarized to the extent that the movement of any group of soldiers or even civilians in a given direction was likely to attract interference from enemy patrols collecting money or simply looking for trouble. To remedy the chronic lack of gunpowder, saltpetre was being dug by Royalists near both Banbury and Chipping Norton, and the latter town was reported by parliamentarian journals to have been systematically plundered by the Cavaliers in January.[2] There was such a congregation of Royalists throughout the area that a nervous Coventry committee was alarmed at the prospect of a renewed attack on Compton in late February and appealed to Sir Samuel Luke at Newport Pagnell for help for 'our friends [in Warwickshire] now in danger'; while the expected arrival of Prince Rupert in Stratford announced by Luke on 6 March did little to calm fears. Surprisingly, neither threat materialized, though royalist troops were much in evidence around Stratford, particularly those from Banbury collecting money. An anonymous parliamentary soldier whose company was travelling west to join Massey at Gloucester had no fears for the relatively safe Northampton–Warwick stage of the march, but admitted 'I feare the way is something dangerous from Warwick to Glocester'; and confirming this picture from Stratford, Richard Chandler succeeded in prevailing upon his elderly father William, at Milcote, 'to Remove him selfe and Famaly out of that eminent danger he was in at Milcoate in Regard of the Kings forces'. And to these dangers a new, even more chilling one was added in the spring of 1645 as a new outbreak of plague settled on Stratford and began to make inroads among the population.[3]

The kind of danger feared by Richard Chandler, however, that could erupt literally anywhere, may be well illustrated by a succession of incidents that took place within a few miles of Stratford, at Loxley, Halford and Sherbourne, all inside the space of a few weeks in the spring of 1645, and provoked by Royalists ever on the watch throughout a district supposedly under parliamentarian control. At nearby Loxley one February night, when Warwick garrison's cavalry had left to assist Sir William Brereton in Staffordshire, the Parliamentarians had not got far when Worcestershire Royalists promptly looted the village, while colleagues from Banbury were also busy outside Warwick stealing horses. Ten days later, Banbury Royalists under Sir Charles Compton were again in action, this time collecting taxes near Ilmington, when their scouts routed a small enemy party only to discover that they were the advance party of a much larger contingent escorting a huge convoy of cloth from Massey's Gloucester garrison towards Warwick via Chipping Campden. Hastily calling up their main regiment, the Royalists successfully ambushed the convoy of heavily laden pack-horses as it negotiated the narrow Halford bridge, evidently either patched up or less than effectively damaged the previous year:

Six or seaven of their packs got over the narrow Bridge at Hawford Mill; the other 72 Sir Charles and his Souldiers seized, three or foure whereof the

Souldiers presently opened, and found to be broad Cloath of 20 shillings a yeard. In those packs which the Souldiers opened were wrapped in the Cloathes Mony, Plate, fine Linnen and rich Apparell . . . Sir Charles slew 12 Rebels in the place, tooke neare 70 of them Prisoners, and almost six score Horses.

The Royalists claimed the booty to have an estimated value of £10,000. An interesting postscript to the incident came eight years later, when the Earl of Northampton petitioned against penalties imposed on him by the clothiers for his brother's theft. Far from denying that it took place, he defended the action as a legitimate military one, the traders' consignment being not an innocent one 'but defended by a convoy under whose protection they had placed themselves'. The king himself had, moreover, approved the seizure in order to clothe his troops. Finally, in April, another dramatic encounter took place at Sherbourne and Longbridge, along the Stratford road just outside Warwick, when Prince Maurice moved to intercept another large parliamentary consignment, this time of gunpowder and match, going in the opposite direction, from Warwick to Gloucester. Frustrated at arriving too late at Quinton, the convoy having already passed by 'some houres before', and aware that most of the Warwick cavalry were well out of range escorting the now distant carts, the Royalists decided to vent their anger by pillaging the defenceless countryside. Threatening to plunder Stratford unless £800 was delivered up (though apparently content to accept a mere fraction of that unrealistic sum) and emptying the fields of any available cattle, they reached Longbridge, within sight of the enemy battlements, and 'drew up and faced Warwick upon an hill about a mile distant from the Towne'. They were unaware that the castle was in fact the temporary home of passing Worcestershire and Newport Pagnell Parliamentarians destined to reinforce Massey at Gloucester. The combined allies under Bridges and his able colleague Hawksworth were able to rout the Royalists in a vicious running battle lasting four hours through the springtime lanes about Sherbourne, with much close combat graphically described, as when 'Captain Halford . . . expressed much courage, and . . . strucke off [Major Pilkington's] head-peece and perriwigge with the first blow, and with the next gave him a wound [to] his head'. Many Cavaliers were killed, others fled towards Campden and Evesham, 'many without Hats, others without Horses, and few with swords.' The spoils included fifty prisoners, over a hundred horses, a herd of frightened cattle and 'one cart load of broad cloath', presumably part of the hijacked Halford cargo.[4]

No wonder that, with such incidents, even affluent tenant-farmers like Richard Brent at Long Compton, Thomas Combe at Welcombe and William Croft at Todenham should continue throughout the spring to bewail their 'great losses' in 'these dangerous times', complaining that they were unable to restock or pay rent, of being obliged to demand 'some considerable abatement' of rents in view of 'the loss I have sustained by the quarteringe of Trupers, the plunderinge of six Tunn of my Oad [note: woad] and six horses'. Little wonder, too, that it was at precisely this time that the neutralist movement of civilians banding together to resist the soldiers' outrages in Worcestershire should begin to emerge; or that after the war, when a local inhabitant, William Bisbey, reported many 'friends about Stratford . . . have beene wofully plundered, & soe have most parts of the land', others, like the Stratford clothier and later, bailiff, John Brooks, should be pointedly accused of having 'thriven these bad times', profiteering, it was implied, from lucrative military contracts, as well as from civilian ones like those many cargoes going via Bristol for export to the puritan colonies in New England.[5]

What finally provided a clear focus for all this uncoordinated activity was the king's long-expected departure from Oxford on 7 May. This galvanized both sides into action. It had been common knowledge for some time that 'great preparation' was being made for this move, though the king's ultimate objective remained unknown, and this uncertainty, while filling Parliament's supporters with alarm, also opened up the possibility of trapping Charles between the various regional forces. These were accordingly alerted for what was hoped might be a decisive confrontation somewhere in the Midlands. The basic plan was to mobilize sufficiently to prevent the king from returning south and pin him down whenever a clear opportunity arose, while besieging the now supposedly weakened Oxford. Able regional commanders like Brereton in the north, Massey at Gloucester, Luke at Newport Pagnell and Whetham at Northampton could be counted on to lend wholehearted support, while high-ranking officers like Browne, Whalley, Fiennes, Lidcot, Pye, Vermuyden and Crawford were permanently in the field, eager for action now that the decisive moment seemed to be approaching. Anticipating the royalist move north, large parliamentary reinforcements were ordered on 10 April from Aylesbury, Newport Pagnell and Northampton to converge on Warwick to supplement John Bridges' limited resources and be at Massey's disposal, while some of Massey's own forces began moving north too. A further dramatic stage in the parliamentary preparations came when Cromwell, who had been cooperating with Sir Thomas Fairfax in the far south and was now recognized as being unbeatable in the field, was ordered on 20 April to move north to prevent communications and supplies going between the king at Oxford and the Royalists under Rupert on the Herefordshire–Worcestershire border. His subsequent harrying campaign about Oxford was so successful as to open up the real possibility of bottling the king up at Oxford, an elated Massey boasting that Cromwell had 'frightened them out of their wits at Oxford'. But, just as he had the previous year, the elusive king, having recalled Rupert and Maurice and made elaborate preparations for the maintenance of his army during its early stages through Worcestershire for the north, slipped out of the city on 7 May on what no one could have guessed was the fateful journey which was eventually to lead to Naseby. After holding a council of war at Stow-on-the-Wold, the king was soon marching through Worcestershire directly northwards. As it passed, the royal army grew in numbers by withdrawing units from nearby garrisons, thereby foolishly abandoning useful Evesham and Chipping Campden, while some units strayed well inside Warwickshire, quartering in numbers around Bidford and Alcester and occupying the great abandoned mansions of Beauchamps Court, Ragley and Coughton. Others, considered superfluous, like Campden, Frankley, and Hawkesley, at Kings Norton, were simply burned down to prevent their use by the enemy. Prince Rupert as usual diverged from the main army, passing through Chipping Norton and Alcester to lodge with Old Stratford's former lord, Sir Charles Smith, at Wootton Wawen, while his brother Maurice's regiment similarly moved north, crossing the Avon at Bidford. Each of these towns and countless villages to the west of Stratford must have suffered heavy royalist quartering on this occasion, but, as before, the details were either not recorded by the local communities who saw no point in doing so, or have simply not survived.[6]

Cromwell, meanwhile, was in Warwickshire for the first time since Edgehill. Initially intending to capitalize on his successful Oxford campaign by pursuing the king into Worcestershire, he was instructed by Parliament to march into Warwickshire instead, shadowing the king to the east pending the deployment of other parliamentary units, including the fledgling New Model Army. Leaving Woodstock on 11 May accompanied by General Richard Browne, he crossed north Oxfordshire into Warwickshire west of Banbury at Tadmarton, and halted at Radway, under the brow of Edgehill. Already arrived near Stratford from the opposite direction was Sir Robert Pye's regiment, receiving supplies from Bishopton and elsewhere while enjoying free quarter at the expense of Snitterfield's vicar Edward Nicholls, putting no less than 2,000 horses to graze the clergyman's 'mowing groundes', drinking six barrels of his beer and taking whatever food they needed. 'All this', the indignant vicar later stressed, 'I will affirme upon Oath.' Other commanders, like Colonel Vermuyden, camped about Charlecote, and Massey, who had by now advanced via Sudeley as far as Chipping Campden, were also in the neighbourhood, keenly awaiting orders, while other troops, from Northampton, were 'lyinge at Welford'. By early May, therefore, the entire region to the south and east of Stratford was swarming with parliamentary regiments, demanding the usual supplies and setting up guard posts in the villages, while the Royalists were equally numerous to the west and north. The two armies were now very near each other: at the very time that Royalists were streaming through Bidford and Alcester, an excited parliamentary report from Warwick announced proudly that 'there came a gallant army of horse and foot the 13th of this instant May into our quarters neare this towne, much encreased by additionall forces from Northampton, Newport Pagnell and Aylesbury, to follow the King'. A showdown seemed inevitable.[7] From now on, Cromwell was engaged in a hectic programme of marching, consultation and tactical planning of which, tantalizingly, virtually no more than a few details emerge. While at Edgehill with the main part of his cavalry he is reported as having replied contemptuously to a message from the king warning him of the danger he was courting in approaching too near the royal quarters, and making a lightning dash across Warwickshire to confer with Massey near Chipping Campden. He also sent a detachment of troops under Major Anthony Buller to cover the Stratford district against a surprise royalist attack from the west. Some of these quartered in Stratford, but Buller and the bulk of his unit were scattered in nearby villages, including Sherbourne and Alveston. Despite one report to that effect, Massey, anxious not to distance himself from a weakened Gloucester, probably never joined Buller, as may have been the original intention, but their combined units were dispersed over a wide area around Stratford. Cromwell meanwhile advanced with his colleague Browne via Southam, swamped by large numbers of their soldiers, to arrive on 14 May in a Warwick that was once

Oliver Cromwell (1599–1658). Although his troops were stationed in and around Stratford more than once, and he himself lodged nearby at Warwick and Kenilworth in the weeks immediately preceding the decisive parliamentary victory at Naseby, Cromwell's only known visit to Stratford during the war was on the lightning march to the south-west with Sir Thomas Fairfax after that battle, in June 1645. On that occasion Fairfax, and probably Cromwell too, stayed not at Stratford itself but at Lillington and Clifford Chambers, possibly deliberately avoiding Stratford because of the plague in the town. Cromwell was again at Stratford in August 1651, on his way to defeat Charles II at Worcester.
(The Trustees of the Grimsthorpe and Drummond Castle Trust Ltd; photograph: Courtauld Institute of Art)

more the hub of frenzied activity. The town and nearby villages were being swollen by the arrival of troops, seemingly from everywhere, in excited anticipation of a decisive encounter with the king, who was himself now at Droitwich, within about a day's march, but with reports that some of his troops were much nearer. John Bridges was honoured to entertain his two celebrated superiors, Cromwell and Browne, presumably in the great hall of the castle, on what must have been a sumptuous occasion heightened by a throng of commanders tensed for the expected battle: 'they were pleased with divers other of their officers to honor mee soe farr as to dine with mee yesterday' (14 May), he wrote with a touch of pride. Whereas not so long ago he had complained to his regular correspondent Sir Samuel Luke that Warwick was unusually calm, it was now Luke's turn to envy his colleague his centre-stage role in the coming drama: 'I hope you will not expect newes from hence', he joked from Newport Pagnell, 'when you are at the Fountaine, neere 2 armies the conjuncture whereof is expected hourely.'[8]

Surprisingly, however, after this impressive build-up, the expected showdown never came, and Stratford escaped the major disruption this would certainly have caused. The king's forces loitered aimlessly nearby, and when Sir Robert Pye rode from Warwick past Stratford on a foraging expedition to provoke an encounter with the Royalists he returned despondently without meeting them. Once again, nevertheless, a reminder of the economic cost to the district from the unpredictable military activity comes from reports in May: any land not already ruined by overgrazing cattle deliberately herded together 'to shelter from those last armies', it was claimed, was lying idle for lack of tenants foolhardy enough to take the risks involved in taking out leases. Militarily, however, the tide had ebbed: for Parliament suddenly ordered a major change of plan which averted the immediate prospect of a decisive confrontation in Warwickshire. Believing that the king's ultimate objective was to relieve Chester and reconquer the north, Colonels Fiennes, Vermuyden, Sidney, Pye and Okey were instructed to march north towards the Scots, while Cromwell, still untested but continually in the saddle commuting between Warwick, Coventry, Kenilworth and the bulk of his troops at Southam, was ordered to proceed no further but to return south to join Fairfax in besieging Oxford. Reluctantly abandoning hopes of trapping the king between himself and his colleague Brereton in Cheshire, he obeyed and immediately marched south again. A great opportunity seemed to have been lost. The one positive achievement resulting from all of this otherwise fruitless activity was the parliamentary seizure of Evesham, left vulnerable since the departure of the Royalists a fortnight previously, by the ever-watchful Massey on 26 May. Its capture 'in a storm of fire and leaden hail' was a disastrous blow to the Royalists, the result of a concerted campaign by Massey's own forces reinforced by Warwickshire, Northampton and even Newport Pagnell troops already positioned in Warwickshire. These crossed the Stratford district through Alderminster and Bidford 'when they went to take Evisham', commissioning carts and teams of horses locally for transporting armour from Warwick and eventually helping to construct earthworks for the final assault on Evesham. The capture of the town added almost immediately to Stratford's burden, since money and provision were needed for the returning soldiers as well as items like bedding soon demanded by the new governor at Evesham, Colonel Thomas Rous. Furthermore, the newly-secured Warwick–Evesham route inevitably brought increased parliamentary traffic and quartering in both directions – as suggested by the repeated references to groups of 'Evesham men' in the town under various captains from this time on. And with the whole area now full of their soldiers in the immediate countdown to the battle of Naseby, the parliamentary command wielded its authority to exact taxes more stringently than ever, as illustrated once again by the plight of the Milcote steward. On 1 June he wrote despairingly to his master:

> Now, not only the Comittee att Coventry but att Glocester, and the Comittee for Warr: Sheere likewise hath ordered that all Arreares and weekeley Taxes shall be paid upon demand, and in dyvers places Assigned them to the Soldiers . . . soe that Trulie I know not what to doe nor where to gett monies to pay them.

A few days later he returned to the theme in a letter to a friend, Thomas Bellamy (of Stratford?):

> I have been forced to pay both att Warwicke & Glos. And much more is required. And I feare everie day to have my Lords cattell & my selfe feched away . . . Truly I am att this time in such perplexities about these great Taxes, I know not which way to tourne my selfe.

John Trapp owed him money for sheep, was putting obstacles in the way of paying, and also refused to pay his share of the taxes at Weston-on-Avon. When, shortly after, Fawdon had the temerity to pursue these matters, the schoolmaster responded with thinly disguised threats: 'Consider of this, I pray you, and put me to no further trouble'.[9]

The decisive battle of Naseby, on 14 June, lies well outside the scope of this book. It took place in a remote corner of the east Midlands more than 30 miles from Stratford, and in spite of the intense activity in Warwickshire in the weeks immediately preceding it, as already described, in the event neither of the opposing armies approached the battle area through Warwickshire. Nor, unlike Edgehill, is there any record of the dramatic news immediately reaching Stratford, since after the battle both armies – fleeing Royalists and triumphant Parliamentarians alike – careered away northwards towards Leicester. Once Leicester was recaptured from the dispirited Cavaliers, however, a new situation arose as the king moved rapidly away west through Staffordshire into Worcestershire and Herefordshire, and Parliament decided to follow up its advantage by pursuing him. Fairfax's long and purposeful march south-west from Leicester after Naseby, averaging an impressive twenty to thirty miles a day, is usually dismissed in an admiring sentence or two as though its rapidity somehow saved the country through which he passed from further disruption. Far from that being so, however, one parish after another along his route felt the full impact of yet more soldiers, this time battle-hardened, marching from Lutterworth to Chipping Campden and beyond. The route passed through the heart of the Stratford district, so that barely a week after the battle of Naseby the area was once more host to substantial numbers of troops moving south-west, rejoining many others who, it is probable, had been loitering in the neighbourhood over many weeks awaiting instructions. Following a broad corridor along the ancient Fosse Way, the New Model Army under Fairfax and Cromwell moved directly south-west towards Warwick, Fairfax himself establishing his headquarters at Lillington, with his men crowding into villages everywhere, for days on end, continuing to arrive or remaining long after Fairfax himself was already in the West Country. At the beginning of July, Milverton received Colonel Pickering's regiment of foot, comprising 700–800 men, as well as Henry Ireton's troop of a further 120 and their horses. Leamington billeted Colonel Montague's regiment for two days and nights, with the church serving as temporary dormitory, Whitnash saw the return of Sir Robert Pye's soldiers, no strangers to the district, while Wasperton was chosen for the unenviable distinction of holding one of the frequent rendezvous. This, near John Green's house, cost him and his neighbours much food and drink, and there was much accompanying theft. Robert Bradshaw lost a pint flagon, cheese, butter, bread and his new pair of shoes; Thomas Handy complained that the soldiers 'cut my Geares and tooke away Leathern haulters'. Continuing steadily south, Fairfax's army approached Stratford, Fairfax staying at Clifford Chambers on 23 June with 'his whole army', some units reportedly camping at Cross o' th' Hill, just outside Stratford. It is clear from the individual parish details, though, that many contingents were widely scattered, through Binton, Bishopton, Lighthorne, Tiddington, Luddington, Drayton and Moreton

Sir Thomas Fairfax (1612–71). Courteous, modest and reserved, Fairfax was from the outset active in the north with his father, Lord Fairfax, in organizing opposition to the king. Distinguishing himself as a cavalry commander at Marston Moor in 1644, he was appointed to succeed the Earl of Essex as supreme parliamentary commander in 1645. With Cromwell as his second-in-command, his New Model Army became virtually unbeatable, defeating Charles decisively at Naseby before passing through Stratford to mop up at the last royalist outposts in the south-west and at Oxford. Without personal ambition, he resigned his command in 1650 and withdrew from politics. The medal, one of several of Fairfax struck by order of Parliament and the City of London around 1645 as a military reward, depicts him armoured with, on the reverse, his arms in a garnished shield between branches of palm and laurel, symbolizing peace and victory. (Medal: The British Museum)

Morrell. At Charlecote, Henry Bacon was one who complained bitterly at being obliged to receive more than 300 of Fairfax's cavalry, 'of the arreare guard', 'when the Army passed from Naseby fight', besides having money 'exacted from him'. Each village sent provisions somewhere, to nearby quarters and sentry posts like the court of guard set up at Shottery, while others, like Luddington, had to supply carts 'for carriage of necessaryes for his army'. The men were in no hurry to follow their leaders: Binton received Colonel Okey's men for a whole fortnight.

It is tempting to speculate on why Fairfax should choose to quarter at Clifford Chambers rather than take advantage of the resources of prosperous Stratford, like some of his officers, unless the comfortable late mediaeval manor house of the absent Rainsfords or the company of puritan ministers in the district were the attraction. Such decisions are never explained in the surviving records, and were likely often to be made *ad hoc*, in the light of volatile local circumstances that are now difficult to guess. But local mansions like that at Clifford Chambers belonging to royalist sympathizers were constantly being requisitioned by passing regimental quartermasters. One such, Radbrook, at nearby Quinton, was taken over at this time, when a parliamentary captain was instructed 'to enter and garrison' the vacant home of the Royalist Captain Roger Lingen and to 'keepe and maintain in and about the same for the Defence of the country forty foote Souldiers and a Troope of three score Horse at the least'. This was, after all, a district rich in detested catholic 'delinquents' whose estates were lying either abandoned or effectively confiscated, and whose wealth could conveniently be appropriated to support the local garrison. In Radbrook's case this involved redirecting the tithes of Ilmington and Quinton belonging to Francis Hodgkins and Edward Savage respectively, and taking the income of the Brents, the Rainsfords and (particularly satisfying) the king's court favourite Sir Endymion Porter, at Aston-sub-Edge and Mickleton. At Clifford Chambers, Henry Rainsford's mansion stood temptingly vacant, its master having fled to join the king, and the parson, William Albright, was an uncompromising Puritan.[10]

However, a more dramatic explanation for Fairfax's decision to lodge at Clifford Chambers rather than Stratford has been suggested: that the town was plague-infested. The theory is attractively simple and, although unsupported by any evidence that this influenced Fairfax's thinking, remains plausible. The spring epidemic of 1645, one of many outbreaks in the Midlands during the war, continued throughout the summer and well into the autumn. Collections were made for the victims – the bailiff, Richard Castle, listed sums totalling almost £20 'for the poore infected people' – pesthouses were built outside the town, and the infection was serious enough in August for all the inhabitants living within a five-mile radius to contribute proportionately to a total of more than £6 per week 'towards the relief of the said town, being infected with the plague'. Warwick closed its gates to Stratford visitors, William Combe for one commenting that 'the Towne [Stratford] is soe much visited with the Plague that I would not willinglie goe thither'. On the other hand, there is no suggestion of prosperous residents leaving town, nor of any panic, and officers like Colonel Okey had no apparent qualms about staying in the town.[11] Whatever the reasons, Fairfax lodged at Clifford Chambers on 23 June, and, in the absence of any evidence for

Cromwell's whereabouts other than the unhelpful report that he was 'at Stratford or neere', we must assume that he was with his commanding officer at Clifford. There is no mention of him in the town residents' submissions at this time.[12] But plague or no, the common soldiers had little choice, and Stratford was accordingly reoccupied 'when Sr Tho. Fearfaxe past by' or 'when Generall Fearfaxe went to the West', as the town's scribe put it. Major Buller's company had already been stationed in town on and off for some time, and there was now a new influx with the arrival for three or four days of the New Model's dragoons under Colonel John Okey, variously said to have been until recently a stoker in an Islington brewhouse, a drayman and a tallow-chandler, and so exemplifying the new, democratic military thinking. The usual chorus of complaints arose as groups of up to twenty or so soldiers at a time, with their horses, installed themselves for board, lodging and grazing in most of the more prosperous households around the town centre. Most, like William Lindon in High Street, 'lost in grasse' in overgrazed closes, but some lost household goods too. A few, like Richard Smart in Wood Street, specified the 'drawing of Beere to Clifford for Generall Fearfaxe army', and everyone listed 'charges' of one sort or another. Elizabeth Wheeler's was one more house to be converted into a temporary guard post, while William Greene in Wood Street even complained that he had 'lost a Mare, shott by Sr Tho. Fearfaxe soldiers' – presumably as punishment for some unspecified offence. The Hathaways, Priscilla in Bridge Street and John at Shottery, once again recorded losses. Once more, however, it was Shakespeare's grandson-in-law Thomas Nash, at the poet's New Place, who was one of the most conspicuous victims, with little option but to be host to the dragoon commander: 'Colonell Oakey, from Saterday to tewday[sic], himselfe with servants & 6 horses at house [and] a meadow of Grasse eaten upp at the same time, . . . which in part of satisfaction he paid me £5, soe yt I was dampnified more then he paid me'. Straw was taken from Nash's barns for litter and makeshift beds for the soldiers, and he even insisted on recording 'a dunckart broken & burnt & a gate, when the generalls Army was there'.

At Clifford Chambers, Fairfax held a council of war, which Cromwell must have attended, and at which, according to Sir Edward Nicholas, it was decided to make for Bristol. Attracted by the king's flight towards Hereford, the focus of military activity therefore swung south-westwards, and parliamentary detachments began to converge on the Cotswolds. Fairfax resisted any temptation to deviate from the major task he had set and continued his brisk march. Spending only one overnight stay each time, he quickly moved from Clifford to Chipping Campden, still receiving beer from Stratford and complaining bitterly to his superiors about the condition of his men.[13] His soldiers gradually moved away from the district, to Northleach, Lechlade and beyond, eventually to further spectacular successes in the west. As so often in the past, however, the departure of one army from a district simply meant that another arrived to fill the vacuum. Before Fairfax's army had vacated the region, barely a fortnight after Naseby, a new parliamentarian force was approaching to provide the last major trial for the long-suffering people across the Stratford countryside.

CHAPTER 11

The Final Months

As the months passed it became clear that the battle at Naseby had dealt a mortal blow to royalist fortunes, although for some time after the king refused to believe it as he began busily recruiting more troops in the south-west to renew the struggle. Certainly by the end of the year it was evident to most observers that Charles was losing the war, as dissension intensified in the royalist ranks, the New Model Army brought off a succession of further victories and, one by one, shortly after, the king's garrisons began collapsing like ninepins. But this is to adopt a retrospective and national viewpoint; none of this was immediately obvious in Warwickshire. Busy elsewhere, Fairfax would not return to the Midlands for almost a year, but in the countryside, Naseby, and the absence of the New Model Army, had changed little. As the summer of 1645 wore on, other parliamentary forces were approaching to capitalize on the recent triumphs.

The first of these that the local population had to contend with came in an outwardly new form – for the first time in the region, a large Scottish army. Following a treaty with the English Parliament, a Scots army under the veteran Alexander Leslie, Earl of Leven, had been campaigning in the north for more than a year, and had played a major role in the great victory at Marston Moor. After long months spent trudging through the north of England, the Scots had now reached Nottingham and were preparing to march south with the intention of besieging Hereford, the king's temporary headquarters. As already noted, Parliament had sent various English contingents north from Warwickshire under Vermuyden and others to join them in the weeks preceding Naseby, and other Midland commanders, like Sir John Gell in Derbyshire, had also contributed to what was by now, on paper at least, a formidable army. A bare fortnight after Naseby, Leven was ordered to march with all speed for Worcester,[1] and immediately, the royalist commander-in-chief there, Prince Maurice, took precautionary measures, ordering all able-bodied men aged between sixteen and sixty to report for large-scale work on the city's fortifications, on pain of death. With Evesham now in parliamentary hands but much of the surrounding countryside still under royalist command, an increasingly outraged local community was abused equally by both sides, to the point where apportioning blame to one or the other was no longer possible or relevant to the exasperated people. One lengthy document, undated but reflecting conditions throughout Worcestershire during this summer, provides a veritable catalogue of complaints, ending with a thinly veiled threat of insurrection:

That the Country is fallen into such want and extremity through the number and oppression of the Horse lying upon free quarter that the people are necessitated (their Hay being spent) to feed their Horses with corn, whilst their Children are ready to starve for want of Bread. Their exacting of free quarter and extorting sums of money for the time of their absence from their quarters, mingled with threats of firing their Houses, their persons with death, and their goods with pillaging. Their barbarous seizing men's persons and compelling them to ransom themselves with very great sums of money to their undoing . . . and that, without any order or warrant . . . Their daily robberies of all Market people, killing and wounding men who resist and stand on their own defence, their contempt of all discipline to all orders, quartering where they please and how . . . Their opprobrious and base language [against] the Commissioners, intermingled with scorns and threats . . . That all the country lying between Severn and Teme . . . and also all the parishes adjacent within 4 miles of the City [of Worcester] are by free quarter of the Horse eaten up, undone and destroyed, together with the country lying about Kidderminster and Bewdley, with their several Armies passing to and fro . . . That the Insolencies, oppressions and Cruelties have already so disaffected and disheartened the people, that they are grown so desperate and are already upon the point of rising everywhere.

If these charges, all too familiar, were levelled at the Royalists, threats to at least one Worcestershire parish, dated 14 October 1645, certainly came from the opposite side, from the new Evesham parliamentary authority, urging the constable and tithingmen of Elmley Lovett to produce arrears of taxes immediately, 'at your perils of pillaging and plundering, and your houses fired and your persons imprisoned'. It is, therefore, against such a picture, of a civilian community pushed almost beyond endurance, that the further havoc wreaked by the Scots must be set. With an unenviable reputation preceding them even before they arrived, and heightened, no doubt, by ancient fears, the passage of the Scots was to confirm the worst fears of the local communities. As a modern historian has written, 'The Scots' image was more that of a hostile army of occupation than of an allied force'.[2]

The Scots left Nottingham for Worcester on 2 July, entered Warwickshire at Tamworth and crossed diagonally through Birmingham before being forced to halt at Alcester on 7 July by what Leven described as 'the daily increasing hard condition of our Army', which, as we shall see, was now acute. Joining them at some undisclosed point was a regiment under the indomitable William Purefoy, never one to pass up an opportunity to strike against the king, and who responded with alacrity to instructions to 'send what horse you can spare'.[3] As always in the civil war, this army was no compact, disciplined body but a motley force totalling, according to reports reaching the king's secretary, Sir Edward Nicholas, some 5,000 to 6,000 men, plus another 2,000 English from the regiments of Sir John Gell and Sir William Brereton – and not counting the 3,000 or 4,000 women and children emphasized by possibly mischievous royalist reporting. As usual, too, this army was split into widely scattered groups, so that while Nicholas could inform Prince Rupert correctly on 11 July that many of the Scots were camped about

Alcester and Evesham, others were in fact straggling throughout the country many miles from there, far to the north and east of Stratford, with Gell still at Coventry.[4] The southward route from Birmingham had already proved eventful for the countryside. It was on this stage of the march that the vicar of Hampton-in-Arden, Richard Pretty, was forced to offer hospitality to Lord Montgomery in his parsonage, that Tanworth-in-Arden, Henley and Edstone were occupied by Colonel Stockdale's men, that Morton Bagot quartered Lord Montgomery's regiment for a whole week, during which its constable, Richard Milburn, had to arrange to send on provisions to General Middleton's quartermaster and troops stationed at Great Alne, which, in its turn, sent on more to the main camp being set up at Alcester, and that Studley and Sambourne were heavily invaded and their inhabitants terrorized into giving money to prevent the pillaging of their cottages. As the Scots army approached Stratford it was its sheer size that impressed the local people, persuading Robert Fawdon for one to stay indoors at Milcote on 13 July and to postpone his urgent estate business, 'for feare of this great Armie, part whereof is every day amongst us'. Wasperton suffered large numbers with one single unit, when Captain Leslie arrived at Francis Warner's 'with threscore men & horses', while, as before, some of the soldiers extorted money 'to forbeare the plunderinge of my house', or 'to excuse our houses', and a neighbour, John Greene, victim only weeks before of Fairfax's soldiers who took over his house as a sentry post, now had all his stock of available timber, gates and palings burned for firewood. Temple Grafton quartered another group, providing them with more provision besides having to surrender virtually all of their teams of horses, requisitioned at harvest time for four weeks of transporting cargo to Hereford and losing some of them in the process. Snitterfield too, only lately home to Sir Robert Pye's regiment before Naseby, now received some of Gell's Derbyshire contingent (from an entry in the village accounts helpfully dated 14 July), before sending provision to Alcester and Stratford. Binton, while sending food forward to the guard posts at Exhall and Bidford, and suffering many thefts, included a note of understandable weariness in its own record: 'whilst the Scottish Army lay at Alcester, wee quartered att least six or seaven score men and horses by degrees, but under whose Comannd wee knowe not'. At Alveston the Scots burned Thomas Walton's sheep hurdles, took his cheeses and hams, and extorted money from his wife, while at Luddington John Tarver had to supply them with malt 'when they passed by my house'.

Curiously (unless the continuing plague in the town was responsible), Stratford had another narrow escape, if the king's secretary is to be believed: 'Quarters were taken up for 1,000 of their horse ye last night [10 July] at Stratford on Avon,' he reported, 'but whether they came thither or noe I heare not as yet. They plunder notably in ye Countrey.'[5] That they evidently did not invade the town in large numbers is confirmed by the sparseness of references to the Scots in the parish records – unlike those for most of the nearby villages, which are full of them – though it did suffer some of the usual penalties associated with passing troops. Teams of horses were demanded for 'drawing bread' to distant quarters, like the two-days' journeys to colleagues at Droitwich and Birmingham; provision was imperiously required, usually specified as bread and beer; a little incidental damage was caused; and, inevitably, a few random thefts were recorded, including a sorrel mare valued at £5 from Thomas Nash 'as they went by Stratford', leaving him in its place 'a lame nag' worth less than half that sum, and 6s. taken 'as they past by' from his mother-in-law, Shakespeare's daughter, Susanna. Evidently by-passing Stratford to the north, however, the bulk of the army moved on through Great Alne, where the two colonels Carr, 'with divers officers and troopers', exasperated Edward Greene by staying for four days, demanding 'divers carriadges of haye and grasse fetched out of my meadows and caryed to other places, with 20 strykes of beanes, pease and mault which they gave theire horses', costing him £20, not counting the quantities of bread and cheese which he had to send after them when they left for their next stop at Alcester. If its inhabitants' claims are to be believed, Studley's treatment at the hands of the Scots would alone merit a chapter in itself. Alcester then suffered ten days' disruption from the Scots' camp or 'leaguer' before it moved on to Bidford, where Anthony Gillam again confirmed the size of this 'Grate armee of Scotts, whereof I had the Captin'. A neighbour, William Broad, detailed his own experience, 'a great number quartering with us 4 nights & 3 daies, besides 7 score horse in our mowinge grasse'. Food was demanded from him even for those fortunate enough to find lodging at the spacious Falcon inn, while others took fodder from his meadow near the bridge, as well as twenty-five of his sheep. The innkeeper, William Toupley, confirmed the invasion:

> In July 1645 the Scottish Armie cam who quartered att my housse Lieftenant Georg Monnggomberey & divers other commaunders & sooldiyeares with theier horsses, soe for mans meate, horsse meatte besides to clooses of grasse, to the value of £15 10s [and] free quarter, 3 dayes & 4 nightes.

Unfortunately for the local people, this was far from being the end of the story, for within days of moving off into Worcestershire the Scots were back again, daunted by a royalist show of strength approaching the River Severn. As the king's secretary reported triumphantly to Prince Rupert on 21 July,

> ye Worcester Horse sallying out upon them, gave them soe sharpe a chastisement, having kild & taken about 200 Scots (some say many more) as they presently retired to their former Quarters at Aulcester & thereabouts, where they still remaine.[6]

Back at Alcester once more, Leven pondered his options. His army was in no fit state to confront a determined enemy, his men unpaid and starving, morale at breaking-point and himself despondent and bitter. Parliament had acknowledged 'the great arrear due to that army' and informed him, belatedly if unhelpfully, that nine and a half chests of money awaited him at Northampton, and he had only recently been promised 'good and convenient quarter and accommodation for your army'. But this had proved a mockery as they crossed an impoverished Stratford countryside peopled by a hostile and sullen countryfolk, and he had addressed an astonishingly frank and eloquent plea to his superiors from Alcester on 8 July:

We think ourselves ill-used. We are called to march, march, [told] that a plentiful country is still before us, where nothing will be wanting to us. But we find nothing by the way but solitude – pleasant places indeed for grass and trees, but no other refreshment, the country people looking upon us as enemies to take from them without paying for it, as others do, and so eschewing to bring in any provision . . . Certainly neither ye nor we will be long able to feed the pinching belly of this Army with words, and to starve them with fair promises.[7]

Yet, somehow, Leven mustered his army again and eventually, despite everything, the Scots moved west again, towards Hereford this time, though making a wide detour to the north via Droitwich and Bewdley to avoid royalist Worcester. But, once again, this absence was only temporary, for after spending the whole of August in a frustrating abortive siege of Hereford, thwarted by 'want of gunpowder, match and bullet', by the ominous approach of the king with a strong force of cavalry and, above all, by disastrous news from Scotland, the Scots withdrew towards Gloucester and Cheltenham and were soon re-entering Warwickshire, this time on the long trek home, with 'a resolution to relieve their own distressed country, and unwilling to engage their army in this kingdom'. As Leven put it simply: 'neither officer nor soldier was willing to stay, the soldiers professing openly they would all for their country'. So Bidford and Alcester were again recrossed at the beginning of September and the soldiers were soon in the Stratford district once more: Luddington and Bishopton were again called on for food, required to supply more carts to transport cargo towards Northampton; Alveston added 'losses by the Scotts goeing by' to its other claims; and more than 400 sheep were seized from the Milcote estates alone, according to the reliable Fawdon, before headquarters were established, this time at Charlecote, on about 9 September. There, John Tew was one whose patience was sorely tried: three loads of his hay lost, two of barley, wood burned, sheets and blankets taken, '15 couple of Poultry', and even, by some intrepid recruit, '2 Stocke of Bees'. The relief of the local inhabitants must have been palpable when the Scots finally moved away, through Warwick and Stoneleigh for Coventry, Nuneaton and the north. Doubtless as relieved as any, Leven finally reported from Nottingham: 'I have marched with the whole party for Scotland'.[8]

This astonishing and protracted saga – an eight-day occupation recorded at Sambourne, ten days at Alcester, as many as nineteen at Morton Bagot – of which only the barest outline has been given here, has all the makings of a minor folk epic. With massively ironic understatement the king's secretary had joked that the Scots' leader 'finds the country not well satisfied with their coming', and the Royalists gleefully capitalized on the major propaganda coup that had unexpectedly been handed them by what they mischievously called 'the Invaders now among us'. Such was the impact of this army that an unprecedented level of bitterness was reached and some parishes pointedly listed their 'charges by the Scots' separately from the rest, as a kind of crowning outrage suffered after so much else at the hands of these new barbarian hordes. If the royalist press is to be believed, the parliamentary authorities were so worried at the public relations damage to their cause as to convene a regional conference at Alcester to debate their dilemma, and among those participating in an official enquiry in January 1646 into 'the damage done by the Scotts' were Stratford's own committeemen sitting at Warwick, William Combe and Thomas Nash.[9] Of course, the local people were no strangers to thefts committed by their own soldiers, but the new insults, aggravated, no doubt, by contemporary prejudice, appeared to be at the hands of incomprehensible and interfering foreigners from beyond distant borders for whom pillaging and extortion was evidently a way of life. Everything was vulnerable, from trivial objects like John Davies' pair of shoes at Stratford and Thomas Toone's kettle at Wasperton to more picturesque collectors' items, as in the case of William Chambers at Tanworth-in-Arden who 'had [taken] from his howse a great booke intituled The Turkish History', worth more than 12s. Between the two extremes lay the constant distress caused by routine, day-to-day outrages, typical among which were the experiences of Mr Rogers at Sherbourne and Thomas Walker at Studley:

> Lost by ye Scots in hay, oates and Gates which they burnt, with a range of Pales & 2 new Ladders, with Pulling downe our barne walls, taking away a Gun of twenty shillings Price, and 1 sheepe of a noble Price, besides Linnen which they violently tooke away.

> Plundered by them: all yt was worth takinge, both in Cloathes, Shirtes, Brasse, Pewter, meltinge it for bulletts, with 60 Cheeses & 9 fleeces of wooll & all my workinge tooles, being a Gardner; besides they soe Cutt and abused mee, forcing my flyinge from ye house to preserve life.

Yet in extenuation it is also well to remember the appalling plight of the raw Scottish soldiers on their long and ultimately futile march, deprived of the most basic necessities to survive, let alone fight an elusive and tenacious enemy in an alien land, far from home. It is easy to catalogue the justified complaints of the abused civilian population. Those of the soldiers have usually been neglected in studies of the civil war.

After this experience, one might think that communities throughout south Warwickshire had had enough to contend with. But during their brief respite in August, while the demoralized Scots were disintegrating outside Hereford, a new development occurred to add to their burden when the new northern army under Colonels Sydenham Poyntz and Edward Rossiter was called upon to assist in pursuing the king, marching rapidly through Lincolnshire towards Oxford and eventually Hereford. Returning to Nottingham on the way home, Leven conferred with Poyntz at the end of August and had little option, in view of his men's resolve to return to Scotland, but to see Poyntz in effect replace him in the task of tracking the elusive king. Some time was lost when Poyntz in his turn was obliged to raise the delicate matter of 'the mutiny of my whole army, who would not stir without pay', a delay which allowed the king to move rapidly from Huntingdon towards Oxford and then dash across country via Shipston-on-Stour to Hereford.[10] Poyntz and Rossiter eventually set off in pursuit from Leicestershire towards Evesham, crossing Warwickshire diagonally from Coventry with a force of about 2,000, mostly Yorkshire and Lincolnshire cavalry but soon joined by Warwickshire cavalry and a Northampton contingent under Colonel Leonard Lidcot, at the very time that the remnants of the Scots were wearily trudging back across the same country in the opposite direction. The emotions of tiny communities like Bidford, Butlers Marston and Alderminster, where large quantities of barley and corn were 'spentt & spiltt' or simply 'toocke away' when, as Kineton's spokesman put it, 'Colonell generall Poyntz his Army marched through the Towne in August 1645', many of them so recently penalized by the Scots and now reoccupied by large numbers of unruly northerners, can only be imagined. To show that they needed no lessons from the Scots, the north countrymen imported their own methods. The inevitable thefts were soon being repeated, this time residents at Radway, Chadshunt and Pillerton being victims, and even a friendly journalist admitted that 'the Yorkshire horse behaved themselves verie ill in Warwickshire, which I sorrow for'. Rossiter's Lincolnshire men, meanwhile, evidently behaved similarly in Knowle and elsewhere. Milcote, already virtually emptied of sheep by the Scots only days previously, as already noted, now suffered two whole troops of Poyntz's men on 5 September, amounting 'at the least [to] 120 men & their horses', who took yet more precious livestock. Little wonder, with such distractions, that a parliamentary complaint was voiced on 3 September that Poyntz's soldiers were still 'at a great distance' from their destination, Hereford, at the very moment that the king was about to enter the city in triumph. Interestingly, the king's march from Lincolnshire had taken him through Huntingdon, where he had been received 'with much complementall hatting and bowing, reciprocall expressions of Joy and such Acclamations and Whoopings as have not beene heard in [that] place'. It is fascinating to speculate on whether Stratford's vicar, known to be in residence at Haddon, situated directly on this march between Stamford and Stilton, was among the throng greeting Charles on what was effectively his last campaign in the field.[11]

Despite all the parliamentary action, the Royalists, particularly what parliamentary newsletters described as 'the hellish crew of Banbury', were far from dormant, taking advantage of the absence of the Warwickshire forces assisting Poyntz in the west – even if their activities look suspiciously like mounting desperation over a lost cause. In September, one of the Fiennes's houses in north Oxfordshire, at North Newington, seems to have been destroyed by them, as was certainly the great mansion of the Cartwrights, the 'fair goodly building' at Aynho; Colonel Robert Phipps, a Coventry physician turned soldier, was almost killed in an ambush as he left Charlecote one day after ministering at Lady Lucy's sickbed; Rugby was plundered on market day and Sunday worshippers listening to the sermon were kidnapped in a nearby church; and a confused skirmish was reported at Stratford between Major George Purefoy's men and those under the Earl of Northampton. But that outrages could be perpetrated by either side was confirmed during this autumn by the renewed pillaging of the great Sheldon mansion near Long Compton by Lord Grey's Parliamentarians; and a veritable atrocity, the slaughter of an elderly royalist clergyman, the gentle and scholarly vicar of Adderbury, Dr William Oldys, on 12 September, in an ambush near his home after a tip-off by a malevolent

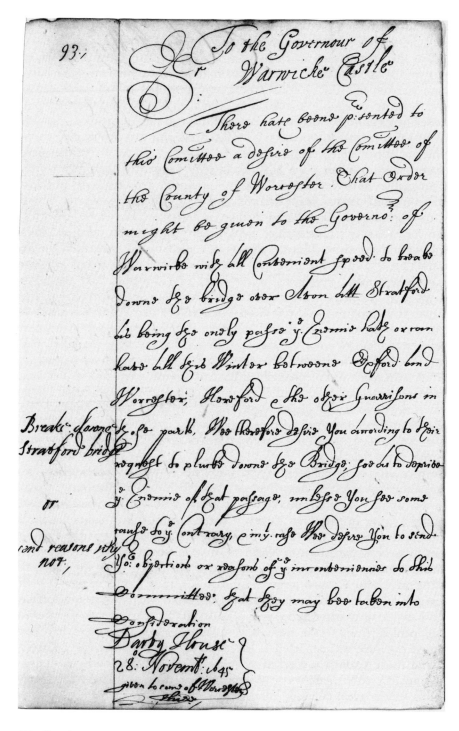

The Breaking of Stratford Bridge. For transcript, see page 136.

(Public Record Office)

Clopton Bridge, Stratford. *River crossings being few and far between in the seventeenth century, bridges were fiercely contested during the war for their military value, and consequently often deliberately sabotaged to pre-empt use by the enemy. Although many Midland bridges were destroyed, that at Stratford escaped until late in the war when Worcestershire Parliamentarians, fearing renewed royalist incursions, petitioned the authorities to render it impassable. Parliament agreed, and ordered the governor of Warwick Castle, Major James Bridges, to 'plucke downe the Bridge'. Only one arch, apparently the second from the south (second from right in this photograph), was demolished, though there is no visible proof of this today. The bridge remained derelict for several years before eventually being repaired in 1651.*
(Public Record Office; photograph: The Shakespeare Birthplace Trust)

parishioner, when riding to take his son to school in Oxford. These closing months of the war were as vicious as any.[12]

The alarms and excursions intensified with the news that the king had finally returned to Oxford on 5 November, after riding well over a thousand miles since Naseby, and Parliament became increasingly alarmed at the prospect of renewed royalist aggression in the Stratford area. As so often recently, Bidford was a hive of military activity that autumn, occupied by a succession of parliamentary regiments from Evesham, including Colonel William Lygon's men, who set up a guard and, according to one inhabitant, William Broad, 'burnd gates, Doors, pales & hedges'. The parliamentary fears focused particularly on the likelihood of renewed royalist thrusts westward across the Avon from Oxford and Banbury into Worcestershire and beyond, threatening their Evesham garrison. A further strong force under Colonel Thomas Morgan was sent to Bidford on 30 November to guard local bridges and fords which could be used by the enemy, the husbandman George Brandon reporting that 'there came a partee of horsse and foote, about

4 hundered, to stope a passage, who quartered att my housse'. The conduct of these Worcestershire men was evidently no better than that of their Scottish or Yorkshire counterparts, as William Paynton made clear with graphic simplicity: 'Colonel Morgones men took Bacon, bred, chise, beare, & when all was spente & gon, then they broke the glass windowes.' Parliamentarians felt particularly vulnerable to royalist attack in Worcestershire, where their hold was precarious, and in late November they were sufficiently alarmed to send an urgent petition to the London authorities to break down Stratford bridge 'for the securing of this county from the incursions of the enemy's forces', as a later directive recollected. The text of the original Worcestershire plea does not survive, but by 28 November the London committee accepted the request and instructed John Bridges at Warwick to see that the bridge was rendered impassable (*see illustration, page 134*):

> To the Governour of Warwicke Castle
> Sir:
> There hath beene presented to this Comittee a desire of the Comittee of the County of Worcester That Order might be given to the Governor of Warwicke with all Convenient speed to breake downe the bridge over Avon att Stratford, as being the onely passe ye Enemie hath or can have all this Winter betweene Oxford and Worcester, Hereford & the other Guarrisons in those parts. Wee therefore desire you according to their request to plucke downe the Bridge, soe as to deprive ye Enemie of that passage, unless You see some cause to ye Contrary, & in yt case Wee desire You to send Your objections or reasons of ye inconveniencies to this Committee, that they may bee taken into Consideration.
>
> Darby House, 28 Novembs 1645 given to some of Worcestershire

A marginal note in a different hand summarizes: 'Breake downe Stratford bridge, or send reasons why not.'

Major James Castle was entrusted with the task, several groups of his men quartering in numbers up to twenty or so in the cottages of John Cooke, Roger Grey, Francis Fletcher, William Rawlings, Thomas Redwell and Robert Simcot in Luddington for two days in December 'when they tooke up Stratford bridge'. There are no surviving records for the Bridgetown district, but the fact that neither the major nor any of his soldiers are reported in Stratford might be further acknowledgement of continuing fears over the plague in town – though this did not prevent Richard Castle in the High Street from having to send 'a labourer, working at ye Bridge', nor Richard Smart's horses and carts from being commandeered 'for drawing ammunicon to Warrwick when the bridge was puld downe'. Major Castle's accounts show that he had seventy-one men under his immediate command in November and December 1645, but the destruction of what turned out simply to be one arch of the ancient Clopton bridge, already broken and patched up many times over the years and repaired as recently as 1637, cannot have been a major operation, nor, coming at this late stage in the war, could it have had any impact on the course of things. It is more likely to have had an effect on the local community in disrupting civilian traffic and market-going, though even this is far from certain since Stratford's other bridge, the footbridge at the mill half a mile downstream, probably remained open and local fords were often passable as alternatives, Thomas Nash himself being required at some point by the authorities to assist in 'drying up the fords about Binton'. Nor does the town seem to have been in a hurry to repair the bridge once the royalist cause had evaporated, for not until 1650, by which time its general condition had seriously deteriorated, as 'the breach hath much weakened the other part of the said bridge', were repairs put in hand, along with those to the still roofless market house and also, incidentally, to Halford bridge, still apparently lying useless. It then fell to the local parliamentarian Justices of the Peace William Combe and Edward Peyto to arrange to have the bridge surveyed, repair estimates submitted and a contract drawn up and eventually awarded to the Coventry mason Thomas Sargenson, who had already been involved in the construction of Stratford's market house before the war and had since prospered through lucrative building and repair projects throughout the conflict. Nominally at least, therefore, Stratford's joins the catalogue of other local bridges, like those at Halford, Bidford and others in Worcestershire, which were deliberately destroyed by both sides during the war. Curiously, however, the records have so far remained silent on the fate of the bridges at Hampton Lucy, Stoneleigh, Shipston-on-Stour and elsewhere. The bridge at Barford, evidently guarded by a fortified sentry post to which provisions were periodically sent, was the scene of an interesting incident at this time, when a quantity of coal awaiting transportation for Lady Lucy at Charlecote was stolen from Barford on about 30 November by parliamentary soldiers, probably those guarding the bridge. The coal merchants, who included the traders William Shakespeare and Richard Shuter of Rowington, successfully petitioned the Coventry committee for compensation for their lost revenues. The case highlights the problems facing traders attempting to conduct business as usual in the face of constant military interference, as well as the praiseworthy efforts of the parliamentary authorities to safeguard the livelihoods of ordinary citizens – even of those who, like William Shakespeare, were known to be political enemies. As for Warwick's bridge, lying in the shadow of the castle walls, it must have been almost permanently guarded by the parliamentary garrison and survived the war apparently intact.[13]

Initially, the parliamentary fears of royalist incursions seem to have been justified, for on 7 December, shortly after an alarm in Coventry, 'the Kinge being neere this Citty' and unpaid parliamentary troops there 'ready to Muteny', a sizable royalist foraging party of 400 to 500 men from Banbury was reported approaching through Broadway and Chipping Campden, supposed, mistakenly, to be the king, intent on clearing a way to the west by 'seeking passage over Avon, which they endeavoured at Bidford, Hampton [Lucy] and Stratford'. It is unclear what occurred and whether this was before or after the breaking of Stratford bridge, but a parliamentary report claimed a decisive victory, 'those bridges, fords and passages being strongly fortified', and that consequently the Cavaliers 'were easily blown off'. As noted, Barford's bridge was one which was evidently being guarded, so the report that others were too is entirely plausible. If some skirmishing did take place at this time at or near Stratford, it marked in effect the last real military action here, for Stratford's involvement in the civil war ended not with a bang, but a whimper.[14]

As it happened, the partial destruction of Stratford's bridge was irrelevant to the remaining course of the war and marked the beginning of the end both for Stratford's involvement and for the war as a whole. The role of the town would be confined over the remaining months to providing occasional overnight accommodation to parliamentarian officers on a few last missions. Since Naseby, the New Model Army had become virtually invincible, with royalist morale collapsing everywhere, and what followed were simple mopping-up operations in which Stratford was only slightly implicated. The first of these was the battle of Stow-on-the-Wold, on 21 March 1646. Once Parliament had secured both the south-west and the north-west, by February, and it was clear that neither the French nor the Irish reinforcements desperately awaited by Charles would materialize, it could turn to crushing the last royalist attempt to assemble a field army, by Prince Rupert's old tutor, the loyal veteran Lord Astley. By heroic efforts in Shropshire and Worcestershire, Astley had succeeded in staving off the total disintegration of the royalist cause in the region and even managed to collect some 3,000 bedraggled royalist soldiers. He marched them from Bridgnorth through Kidderminster to Worcester, his every move watched by Colonels John Birch and Thomas Morgan at Hereford and Gloucester and by Sir William Brereton in the north, who, having captured the great prize of Chester (thereby cutting off the Irish link), was now eager to join his colleagues in the south to trap the king, as he had hoped to do the previous year with Cromwell in Warwickshire. Astley crossed the Avon at Bidford, making to join the king at Oxford. Birch and Morgan had moved to Broadway to prepare to intercept, some of Morgan's troops advancing as far as Alveston, Tiddington and Charlecote lest Astley should attempt a diversion that way. Some of the Gloucestershire men were even recorded at Avon Dassett in early March, in Colonel Fleetwood's regiment, where Captain Zanchy had been for some time, merging with colleagues under Colonel Whalley still engaged in the protracted siege of Banbury. With Astley still skilfully eluding them, Morgan appealed urgently on 19 March to Brereton, already in Warwickshire, to rush his cavalry forward to join them in intercepting Astley. Brereton responded promptly: large numbers of his men quartered at Great Packington 'as they passed by my house', as William Dyall recalled, with others of Sir Thomas Middleton's 'when they kept their Randezvous on the greene before my doore', before moving on to Knowle and Lapworth 'ye daye before Stoe fight'. Oliver Weigham at Knowle was one who had reason to remember this day: 'I quartered Sir William Brearton with divers Captaynes & souldyers & their horses when they went to Stow fight and tooke Sir Jacob Ashlye [Lord Astley].' From Knowle, Brereton continued rapidly south, followed the precedent set by illustrious predecessors by lodging with Thomas Nash at New Place ('Sir William Bruerton quartered at my house', he carefully recorded), and finally joined his colleagues in crushing the Royalists near Stow. 'You have now done your work, boys,' the weary old man told his captors as 1,500 of his men were taken prisoner and locked in Stow church for the night, and he was taken off to imprisonment in Warwick Castle, 'you may go play, unless you fall out among yourselves'. Apart from entertaining Brereton, Stratford's involvement was slight, but the soldiers were near enough for Thomas Smith at Tiddington to complain of food and drink being taken by Morgan's men on 17 and 18 March and for William Hopper at Alveston to specify bacon, cheese and barley being stolen from him to be carried to Stratford 'before the fight'.

Stow was immediately recognized as the decisive last battle of the civil war: 'This year very fatal to his Majesty's Interests concluded with such a Sparring-Blow as destroy'd almost all Hopes of Resource; and this was the Defeat of the Lord Astley, who had the only standing Force abroad for the king.'[15] Clarendon was in no doubt that the end was in sight, 'nor did there remain from that minute any possibility for the King to draw any other troops together. Every day brought the news of the loss of some garrison'. Stow was indeed followed by a rapid royalist debacle. Six weeks later, in a desperate bid to exploit existing dissension between the quarrelling allies, Charles slipped out of Oxford in disguise, riding 'at night, like a broken king', via the temporary sanctuary of Little Gidding's peaceful community,[16] into the Scottish quarters at Southwell in Nottinghamshire to surrender, though, facing the military reality as he had not always done, Charles ordered the governors of his surviving garrisons to capitulate. With the king gone, the final hammer blows to the cause fell in quick succession. After a long and heroic siege, Banbury finally capitulated on 6 May, followed shortly after by the even more shattering blow of the fall of Oxford. Once Banbury had surrendered and Colonel Edward Whalley's victorious forces could be hastily transferred the forty miles west, the siege of loyal Worcester began on 21 May. For this closing campaign, large numbers of parliamentary troops crossed south Warwickshire for the last time, to join in what must have seemed, even to the participants, the final major campaign of the war in the neighbourhood, as Whalley, Brereton and combined forces from Warwick, Coventry and elsewhere converged on Worcester. Most of these moved across the country too far south to affect Stratford, though across the fields, villages like Alderminster, Binton, Drayton and Luddington all quartered passing soldiers, particularly those of the Northampton and Newport Pagnell regiments, 'when the Seidge was at Worcester'. Drayton was typical in being required to send unspecified contributions to maintain these regiments 'when they lay before Worcester'; and as further illustration of the continuing cost to these small communities, Luddington was paying £1 8s. per week on 18 June to Major Whitbread's regiment under Colonel Starr 'at the Leger before Worcester', and a further £3 per week towards the men's wages, while Binton was doing much the same. As at Banbury, the besieged garrison at Worcester defended ferociously while stocks of food and ammunition lasted, but their situation was hopeless, and when news came of the fall of Oxford and Fairfax threatened to arrive, the desperate Royalists had no option but to surrender, on 23 July. Shortly after, when in August Parliament took the grand symbolic step of ordering all Warwickshire forces, apart from small garrisons at Warwick and Coventry, to disband, Stratford and the countryside as a whole must have breathed a great sigh of relief as people everywhere could set about contemplating the slow return to normality. In retrospect, Stratford had doubtless escaped the worst, but few could easily forget the recent events in which they had been embroiled. Shortly after, one Stratford official commented on events with typical English understatement as he acknowledged that policing the neighbourhood had perhaps been stressful of late: 'for wach and ward the times hath bin troublesome'. With greater emphasis, one of the Earl of Middlesex's stewards found a surprisingly modern inflection in scrawling a postscript to his own summary of one individual's experience which could have been echoed by many: 'I have lent money to both sydes, bene plundred by both sydes, bene imprisoned by both sydes. A mad world!'[17]

CHAPTER 12

After the Event

Normality is not easily or quickly restored after four years of war, and there were those for whom danger and violence had become addictive. Some of the drifting ex-Royalists, rather than returning to boredom and poverty in their villages, joined foreign ventures or enlisted in the new army being raised for service in Ireland. A few, cynically – or romantically – took to the road as 'highwaymen', to use the new term. 'Captain' Jemmy Hind, a saddler's son from Chipping Norton, was the first from the area to become notorious. Unrest was everywhere; as reported earlier, the county Quarter Sessions had been suspended for the last three years, and the authorities complained of 'the general disposition that is in the people to tumults and insurrections'.[1] It would be an exaggeration to claim that Stratford was a shattered community, for it had escaped the worst. It had never been permanently occupied, it had, as already said, enjoyed the luxury of a relatively stable local government during the war, and as long as taxes continued to be paid the military authorities in Warwick and Coventry had not interfered with the local management of affairs, as had happened elsewhere. It had been spared the wholesale destruction of Banbury, the major disruption of Warwick, and the chaos and vandalism of Worcester. Above all, without town walls or a fortress, it had not been besieged. Yet there remained a legacy of discord, pent-up resentment and real suffering which could not be eradicated overnight, but which – since distress is not quantifiable – is not easy to estimate. A return to normality is by definition less dramatic than its opposite, and is consequently less well documented, and the records offer only sparse hints of the mood in Stratford in the aftermath. Certainly the town's ruling council was still in place as the war petered out, though attendance at meetings had declined, and the curate, though approaching the end of his term of office, was continuing to deputize for the absentee vicar. Market and fair were still, apparently, thriving, and sales of horses at the fairs of 1646 were particularly good. Yet reminders of the recent conflict were everywhere. Though there are no statistics, not all sons and husbands had returned. The market hall stood roofless, the bridge unusable, the mills silent with the sluices destroyed, barge traffic probably seriously reduced if not completely suspended, and the stately Milcote house a charred and plundered ruin. Rents had been difficult or impossible to collect, and the wealthy William Combe was unlikely to have been the only citizen reluctant to pay in full for tithes rented from the corporation. The Earl of Middlesex's estate manager at Stratford, Robert Fawdon, spent years attempting to recoup rent arrears from the wily Combe, concluding that he would

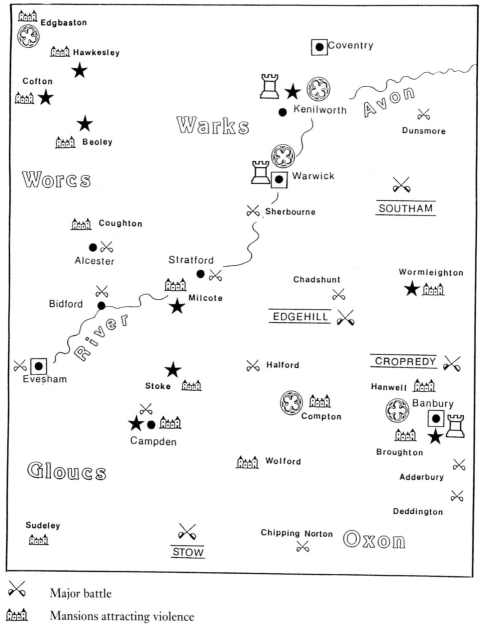

Map 8. Violence in the Stratford District.

pay little 'as long as these troubles last', and was fearful of the effects of the bad example on other tenants. Above all, devastating for the many poverty-stricken who had taken no part in events, the poor relief fund had dried up. Stratford's outlying villages, legally obliged to contribute to the coffers, as well as the new Earl of Middlesex, had been using the war to evade their responsibilities for contributing to poor relief. Money from tithes formerly allocated to 'pious uses' had been appropriated to maintain the soldiers at Warwick, and at a time of increasing vagrancy and what the authorities themselves described as 'a great dearth' and as always hitting the poor especially, Stratford's corporation admitted starkly in 1649 that 'the number of extreme poor people is so great that the rest of the inhabitants of the borough are not able to relieve them'.[2] For by a cruel irony of fate, the first peacetime harvest, that of 1646, was the worst for years, and worse was to come. Violence indeed must occasionally have broken out in the fragile post-war peace as some continued to settle old scores. William Greene, the troublesome collarmaker who bludgeoned Thomas Sharpe 'with a great Clubb' in the street, is unlikely to have been the only citizen prepared to disturb the peace. Sharpe implied that riotous behaviour was not uncommon in Stratford, since Greene had, he claimed, 'severall tymes raysed the rabble people of the said Towne against the Parliamt Souldiers', and an official report admitted that the town's watch authorities were finding the time unusually 'troublesome'. With a succession of very bad harvests and rocketing food prices between 1646 and 1650, the poor relief system dislocated and vagrancy increasing everywhere, for most people the post-war period across the Stratford countryside cannot have been a comfortable one. The Warwickshire Justices of the Peace handled nearly three times as many poor relief cases for the Commonwealth period (1649–1660), as pre-war.[3]

The immediate priority for Parliament was obviously to consolidate its victory over the Royalists, with at least three unavoidable consequences for Stratford's people: the maintenance of a degree of militarization as a precaution against further unrest; the continuation of heavy taxation, which was as necessary as ever; and the intensification of measures against former enemies. Militarily, things improved, but only marginally. It is true that instructions were given to disband armies, apart from small garrisons to be kept, along with stocks of gunpowder, at Warwick and Coventry, so that some fears were allayed and civilians were less likely, in theory at least, to be required to billet soldiers. But this brought its own problems. The regiments to be disbanded were often simply turned adrift without arrears of pay, and so shabbily treated were they that were was widespread revolt and mutiny. The plight of the soldiers at Warwick was as serious as any: they were acknowledged to be 'in great distress', 'very much in arrear of pay due' in 1647, and the situation had not improved in 1648 when the 'sad and necessitous condition of the garrison at Warwick Castle' was again highlighted.[4] The numbers of destitute in the Stratford–Warwick district, already high, were therefore further increased, quite apart from the burden of genuine war-wounded desperately needing relief. Petitions from these swelled into an avalanche with which the Coventry treasury struggled to cope in the immediate aftermath of the war. One of them, doubtless typical of many, from Paul Spooner of Nuthurst, near Tanworth-in-Arden, is moving in its simple eloquence:

Haveing binn a soldiar three yeares and upwards in the parliament servis, [he] wass wounded, and is utterly unable to stand, or any waise to get one peny to helpe him selfe; and now beeing disbanded hee hath not any more pay to reseve, nor any meanes of his owne, or freinds that are able to relieve him; his mother beeing a poore old wyddow, and no other meanes to Leive upon but what shee gets by spinning for 2d. a day att whose poore Cottage howse, which standeth upon the wast in the hamlet of Nuthurst; the inhabittants of the said hamlet beeing all togeather unable to alow him any mayntenance, ther beeing in the said hamlet but two freeholders and foure other dwellers that rent small Tenements; and no les then seven poore Cottagers, and all of them reseve allmes.

The county's treasurers for maimed soldiers were busier than ever. There must, too, have been many more war widows in the district than John Barker's at Stratford or Margery Browne at Pillerton whose names are simply not recorded, or like Hester White, who, as reported earlier, petitioned Parliament for relief after the war, having cared for the sick and wounded after Edgehill from her own meagre resources, only to lose her husband, Daniel, two years later at the siege of Banbury and be left utterly destitute.[5]

In any case, the district had not seen the last of the soldiers, for recruiting was now beginning for Fairfax's new army, with Thomas Basnet at Coventry promoted to treasurer for 'the new British Army in Ireland'. The countryside was not yet at peace. Warwick Castle was still being used as the major regional prison for potentially dangerous 'persons of quality' – there was even a plan to imprison the king there – rumours of plots to seize it were abroad again, and such was local apprehension over 'the Restlesse indeavours of the Cavileers and Malignants to raise a new warre against the Parliament' that Warwickshire gentry petitioned Parliament strenuously against what they considered the 'untimely disbanding' of the army. The fact was that, in spite of the welcome demobilization programme of 1646, there were more soldiers scattered throughout the countryside than collected together in the New Model Army, all nominally under Sir Thomas Fairfax, the only commander above the rank of colonel to be retained. Some of these were reported in the Stratford district, at Alderminster, from September to December 1646. Others imposed themselves on Shakespeare's granddaughter Elizabeth at New Place in April 1647, when she was mourning her husband and living on there alone with her mother Susanna, one of them being implicated in stealing deer from the estate of the prominent local Justice of the Peace Greville Verney at Compton Verney.[6] There were doubtless many more making nuisances of themselves in this way in the post-war period, but once the townspeople of Stratford had submitted their claims for wartime compensation, in March 1646, we are deprived of detailed confirmation. It is often unclear what missions these soldiers, like those who tore up the baptismal register at Hampton Lucy in 1646, were pursuing – unless they were belatedly returning from action at Worcester or Oxford – but there is no doubt that raucous and unruly troops continued to visit village and town during this period. Besides those at Alderminster already noted, others spent two weeks in October at Luddington, and yet more, under Whalley and Swallow, were there in November. The situation did not noticeably improve for years. In July 1648, when Royalists were still holding out here and there, Cromwell again passed through the district, possibly through Stratford itself, on his long march north to Scotland. A scathing royalist journalist was probably not far wrong in contemptuously describing his troops as 'tatterdemallions' quartering 'up and down in Worcestershire', since even a parliamentary source admitted that at Kineton and Warwick at the end of July, although 'cheerfull', 'his Foot [are] as yet without shooes and stockings'. Hardly had Cromwell moved away when in August disturbing news came of a desperate force of two hundred royalist cavalry 'now lying about Mr Spencer Lucy's house' (Charlecote), commanded by the same Joseph Wagstaffe who had been active earlier at Stratford, now knighted for his pains, recently escaped from parliamentary imprisonment in London and evidently intent on insurrection. Details are obscure, but it looks as though the adventurer Wagstaffe, described by a contemporary as 'a man of jollity and mirth' and therefore not, perhaps, the best person to lead a successful armed coup, was hoping to liaise with Sir Henry Lingen, of the local royalist family, busy in July and August in Worcestershire and Herefordshire in what turned out to be a feeble attempt to seize Hereford.[7] Mutinous rabbles were still rampaging through Warwickshire as late as 1649, after the execution of the king, when the London authorities, justifiably anxious over 'the pressure upon the people, both by the charge of free quarter and yet more by the insufferable insolencies and incivilities of many unruly soldiers', sent several urgent warnings to their commander, Colonel John Reynolds, to discipline them. The situation continued much as before until the so-called 'Second Civil War' came to an end with the Worcester campaign of 1651, when Cromwell stayed overnight in Stratford on 26 August on his way to Worcester and another general levy was ordered on the inhabitants of the town to supply provision to General John Lambert, whom he had sent on ahead. Only after that, perhaps, could peace be said finally to have gradually descended on the countryside.[8]

During this unsettling limbo somewhere between war and peace, the general financial plight of the county was dire. In February 1647 in a reasoned and eloquent analysis of the situation, the Warwickshire commissioners protested to Parliament how unfairly the county had been treated and how it could not meet its countless obligations without urgent help. It was even expected to pay its share of the expenses towards demolition work outside the county, as at Banbury Castle. Yet at the same time the authorities were genuinely sensitive to charges of illegality and corruption against their representatives and responded by pursuing culprits. Bishopton was one village prepared to lay charges against one soldier whose conduct had particularly angered its inhabitants, warning the authorities: 'It is conceived that a great charge will come in against Capt. Potter, both for plunder & takeing & sellinge of horses, and in respect he hath left his Comand. It would be requisite that he were enjoyned to put in securety.'[9]

Stratford's corporation struggled valiantly to reassert civilian normality, recoup war losses and, perhaps, redress the balance away from Parliament a little within the limits of its resources. In 1647, despite the relative emptiness of the coffers, it agreed to reimburse those forced to give money to the king's forces 'as the Company shall thinke fitt', on condition that 'they brought in their bills'. One who lost no time in complying was Baldwin Brooks, who within weeks submitted a request for £9 2s. 6d. (having already contributed £13 4s. to the parliamentary side, he claimed). Later, in August 1649, the corporation refunded fifteen residents a total of £41, a considerable sum in the circumstances, 'because ther is noe other way of gettynge the same in an ordinary way, beinge monys laid out in the middest of the warrs'. Whether designed to do so or not, the system seems to have worked to the benefit of royalist sympathizers who had no doubt given voluntarily to the king, for among the recipients were some, like William Lindon and Nicholas Ryland, who were about to face serious charges of helping the enemy, and others, like Baldwin Brooks, Thomas Horne and Richard Smart, likely to be neither parliamentarian nor indigent. But, interestingly, the list of recipients also included a few other names missing from the town's official claims list, like Goodwife Whittle, Joshua Wheeler and Walter Dubice. The protracted process continued as late as 1653, when the chamberlain was sent to Coventry to try to obtain repayment of a further £173 lent to Parliament, and the following year the bailiff was still trying to recover money lent by both the corporation and private individuals to Parliament. In all this, those influential or articulate enough to exploit the system were clearly at an advantage, both during the war and after. If former Royalists were benefiting now, they had probably been deliberately targeted a short while ago. While Captain Thomas Wells's men had often been reported plundering in and about Stratford from royalist homes like those of William Lindon, Richard Smart and John Woolmer, the Parliamentarian Thomas Nash for his part had received £4 4s. 10d. at one point for Wells's 'assignation' – in other words, probably, lodging him while his troops were so engaged. As for the apolitical humbler residents, there is nothing to indicate whether their genuine losses were ever recuperated; but this is unlikely.[10]

Meanwhile, the parliamentary authorities were strenuously engaged in their own programme of redistributing wealth on a vast national scale by pursuing former enemies, making a start on confiscating church property and intensifying legal proceedings against 'delinquents' and 'scandalous' ministers by sequestering their estates and assets. Most former Royalists had little option but to accept reality, plead guilty and try to negotiate the best deal they could in the circumstances by 'compounding', or paying a flat-rate fine based on the value of their real property, which freed them of further fines or levies. The authorities summoned witnesses, sifted information received by well-placed local observers and judged each case on merit. Many were so clear-cut as to be hardly worth contesting, and this was so with a number of Stratford's cases, where information from a local informer, Joseph Collett, condemned Thomas Dighton, Thomas Hitchcock, Edward Wagstaffe, John Woolmer and others. Dighton admitted 'delinquency', as the term went, in taking sides for the king, leaving home (about the same time as the vicar) and remaining in Oxford until its surrender in 1646. Hitchcock's case was still clearer, since he had even worn a sword 'constantly when hee rode abroad' and had tried to 'raise the town and country' against Lord Brooke's delegate, Colonel John Needham, during the eventful days of January 1643. Like Dighton, he too had apparently spent more time in the royalist garrisons at Worcester and Oxford than at Stratford. The case of Edward

Wagstaffe at Bridgetown might have appeared more marginal, since he begged restoration of property rents leased to him by Thomas Greene of Tanworth, sequestered through Greene's recusancy, and the case was deferred. But further information left little doubt, and the charge-sheet was indeed heavy:

> He was in actuall service agaynst the parliament & did hold Intelligence & Correspondencie with the Late Kinges partie, & did Frequent the Late Kings quarters & garrisons, Videlicet: Oxford, Banburie, Compton howse [Compton Wynyates], Hauxlie howse [Hawkesley, Kings Norton], hartelburie Castell & Woorcester & Evisham & divers other garrisons, and this he did in the yeares 1642, 1643, 1644, 1645 & 1646, or some of them, & did appeare at the Comiss. of Array with the Yearle of Northampton & alsoe Raysed the Townesmen of Stratford agaynst Collonell Nedham.

Thomas Earle of Ailstone, likewise accused on the testimony of Collett, had been the active royalist spy who, as already reported, had played a major role in aiding the Earl of Northampton at the outset in provoking the encounter near Warmington. John Stew (another resident absent from the list of claimants for compensation) had sent money, a horse and arms to the king. Nicholas Ryland and William Hiccox had both also been 'in actuall armes for the late Kinge under the command of the Earle of Northampton att the Comission of Array' and had then gone on to 'march in armes to Warwick and Stonley'. Thomas Greene the Justice of the Peace was charged with equally serious crimes:

> Beinge a Justice of peace there [at Stratford] he did call for the inhabitants, & force or procure them to bringe out and stand to theire armes, and told them the enemy was att hand, by reason wherof the parliament partie was forced to retreate in the yeare 1642 [i.e. early 1643, in the incidents reported in Chapter 5].

William Lindon, too, was alleged to have been an armed militant, a Commissioner of Array and had also opposed Needham. Finally, the case against the former bailiff John Woolmer is especially intriguing. Judging by subsequent events the charges against him were almost identical to those already cited, and equally damning, and accordingly, on 21 September 1646, 'upon hearinge the deposicons that are against John Wolmore and the proofes, it is ordered that [his] estate Reall & personall is sequesterd & his goodes are to be seized & disposed of'. Yet he had nevertheless, at some point, lent the considerable sum of £40 to Parliament, paid in to treasurer Basnet at Coventry, and now, as the war drew to a close and Woolmer was once more bailiff, dramatic new information came to light. Either seeing the error of his ways or, more probably, bowing to the inevitable and wishing to cut his costs, he had apparently performed some unexplained service for the parliamentary armies – probably connected with the siege of Worcester – important enough to persuade the authorities to overturn the previous week's order and allow him to compound for £50, 'in Regard of extraordinary service he did for Sr. Th. Farefax & Sr. Wm. Brereton'. The mitigating circumstances were officially acknowledged on 28 September on receipt of information from Colonel Thomas Rainsborough, the victor at Worcester:

> Upon vewe of the Inventory of the goods & Cattell of Mr John Wilmore [Woolmer] seised by the Collectors upon the Sequestration of his estate, And in Regard of the good offices the sayd John Wilmore hath done for the Parlyamt forces [for] his Excellency Sr Tho. Fayrfax [in margin: '& informed by Colonel Raynsborough'] And in regard of the unvendiblenesse of Many of the goods Inventoryed, he haveing formerly paid Forty pounds to the use of the Estate. It is ordered that the sayd John Wilmore shall pay for his sayd goods and Cattle the some of Fifty pounds. And upon paymt of this moneye the sd John Wilmore to be Restored to the sayd Goods & Cattell . . . And from henceforth he is not to be Troubled or molested for his personall estate in Regard of his Delinquency.

Whether the elderly Woolmer was erratic, wily or simply weak and confused is far from clear, but he got off lightly. Matters did not end there, however, for five years later, on information submitted by the same Joseph Collett which confirmed all the previous charges, the cases against the Stratford Royalists, including Woolmer's, were reopened. The indictment against Woolmer was almost identical to that against Edward Wagstaffe, and was apparently overwhelming. According to Collett's testimony, Woolmer too had spent precious little time at Stratford, preferring the safety of the royalist garrisons at Oxford, Banbury, Compton Wynyates, Hawkesley, Hartlebury, Worcester, Evesham and (as though they were not enough) 'divers others'. He too had been a commissioner 'actually in armes' under Northampton, had offered hospitality to the two peers at the Stratford rally (though that seems to have been overlooked), was alleged to have approved the occupation of the town by the Royalists, 'did endeavoure to raise forces in the Towne of Stratford to oppose Col. Needham' and had the church bells rung for that purpose and, finally, 'did assist ye Lord of Northampton in his seidge against Warwick'. Along with his colleagues, Woolmer immediately petitioned against the charges, on 14 February 1652, after which, regrettably, the cases disappear from view. Motives for Joseph Collett's post-war vendetta against the Stratford group are, as usual in such cases, obscure, but there is a hint of commercial rather than merely ideological rivalry in the fact that he was apparently acting on behalf of a local merchant, Henry Stevens.[11] In addition to the foregoing, other Stratford residents duly appeared in the sequestration lists, including some whose names for some reason do not figure in the town's 1646 compensation claims: Henry Wheeler, William Marten, Nathaniel Onley, Widow Anne Burman and Christopher Smith – the latter, interestingly, having been allowed to return home on 28 July 1646 (presumably from imprisonment) and still struggling months later to pay his £5 ransom.[12] It should be emphasized that all of these names relate only to victims of charges and sequestration orders for Stratford, and that nearby villages within a ten-mile radius of the town provide countless more, including some well-known gentry names: John Browne of Tanworth; Walliston Betham of Rowington; Rowland Bartlett of Dorsington; Richard Canning of Foxcote, Ilmington; Anthony Dormer of Grove Park,

Budbrooke; the Darleys of Shelfield, Great Alne; the Fortescues of Weethley; William Halford of Halford; Anne Griffin of Bickmarsh; William Kempson of Temple Grafton; Spencer Lucy of Charlecote; Sir Charles Smith of Wootton Wawen; Margaret and Blaze Sheldon of Temple Grafton; Anthony Skinner of Aston Cantlow; and Robert Throckmorton of Coughton. Many of these were practising Catholics, the other obvious target for the parliamentary authorities besides active Royalists, and when in 1655 most refused to take the Oath of Abjuration binding them to renounce their religion, many more were added to a lengthening list of enemies of the state.[13] Historians have often tended to concentrate on large landowners such as these, but not all were necessarily able to withstand the harsh penalties imposed, and there was sometimes real hardship. One, not untypical, case is that of Anne Griffin, from Bickmarsh, near Welford. By 1653 her husband Nicholas was dead and she was forced to beg the sequestration authorities for leniency in order to manage her husband's estate and make ends meet. She pleaded for a lower tax assessment, claiming that she was unable to maintain an extended family of twenty on the income remaining after the sequestration fine and other taxes were paid. She had to provide for her elderly parents-in-law, both over seventy, 'ould Mr Griffen and his wife, beinge blinde and not able to helpe herselfe', a brother-in-law and his four sons and two daughters, another widow and her three children, besides herself and her own children. In addition, she claimed, she had particularly suffered 'in regard of great free quarter & the hardnes of her lands & their bordering upon the roade'. The committee eventually acknowledged that she had not received her legal rights of one-third of her rents and that she had indeed a large and helpless family to support. Anne Griffin may not have been entirely innocent, since she had contacts not only with Sir Henry Lingen, an active royalist militant, and William Barnes, another conspicuous local Royalist, but also, perhaps worst of all, with a group of local malcontents led by William Miller, Edward Pratt, Robert and Edward Martin and others. These latter were busy throughout 1646 and 1647 helping the obstructive and tenacious former vicar, Dr Jenkin Bowen, to wrest the Welford tithes from John Trapp in contempt of a recent court ruling. This doubtless explains John Trapp's harshness towards her in forcing her to pay the Bickmarsh tithes. Nevertheless, the affair is illuminating.[14] Taken together, such cases represent a vast buried mass of material which, if sifted and researched, would reveal something of the human cost arising from an ideological war. Most of the important names, though not all, possessed the resources and the resilience to survive the inevitable deprivation, though their distress was often real enough for a time and should not be minimized. Although the eventual outcome of these often tortuous cases, including Stratford's, does not always emerge from the surviving fragments, one thing is clear: that long after the war, when some of the temporary exiles like Thomas Dighton had returned to Stratford, old quarrels were constantly resurfacing, given a new and bitter edge by the events of the war and the subsequent legal wrangles. Stratford is likely to have been even more of a divided community after the war than before it. And lastly, few of the profits arising out of the local victims of sequestration benefited the neighbourhood in relieving genuine need. When the Warwickshire parliamentary commissioners at

Coventry received orders to 'pay in all sequestration money' to the central coffers rather than their own, they protested in no uncertain terms, pointing out the county's quite exceptional wartime commitments (including its recent generous contribution of £1,600 towards the army in Ireland) and its heavy burden of debt. 'We have had nothing for our pains,' the commissioners tartly concluded.[15]

Foremost among Parliament's enemies, naturally, were the many local clergymen who were either active or passive Royalists, ideologically unacceptable, or who for whatever reason had deserted their parish (see Map page 97), and Stratford's absentee vicar, although still serving his Huntingdonshire parish as the war ended, was guilty on all counts. Although, as already reported, Twitchet seems to have retained an interest in Stratford as late as 1645 when he was still leasing the churchyard, there was to be no return, and on 6 November 1646, he was obliged to sign a declaration surrendering the vicarage in order that the corporation 'maie the better procure some Godlie, able and learned Minister to supplie the place of Vicar in Stratford'. On 8 February 1647, Parliament belatedly confirmed his expulsion and appointed a replacement:

> Whereas it appeareth by Certificate from the Comittee of plermt [Parliament] for the County of Warwick That Henry Twitchett Viccar of the parish Church of Stratford upon Avon in the said Countie hath wholy neglected & absented himself from the sd cure for the space of three years last past & betooke himself to the Kings quarters & garrisons, whereby the cure of ye said Church is wholie unprovided of a Minister, And this Comittee have thereupon & upon the Recommendation of the said Comittee referred Mr Alexander Beane to the Assemblie of divines to examine his fitness to officiate the said Cure by whome he is approved . . . This Comittee doe therefore referre it to the said Comittee who are hereby desired & authorized to settle the sd Mr Beane in the said Vicarage & in the quiett possession thereof & of the profitts thereof . . . And in case the same be not sequestered then the said Comittee are desired to proceed against the sd Mr Twitchett according to the ordynance of parliament for sequestration of delinquents.

The order was confirmed the following month, on 2/3 March, in very similar terms, but adding further justification in highlighting Twitchet's delinquency:

> Forasmuch as it appeares amongst other thinges by testimony upon oath yt Mr Henry Twitchett vicar of Stratford was at ye beginning of theise warres in Armes at such tyme as Captayne Needham came to disarme Stratford, & did leave his usuall place of abode and cure at Stratford & betake himselfe to ye Enemyes Quarters & Garrisons etc. It is ordered yt All ye proffitts of ye sd Liveing & Estate shall be sequestred to ye use of ye State.[16]

Bean was confirmed as the new vicar, 'and the Baleife of Stratford is to see this order performed . . . and a letter to be written to ye Chamber of Stratford about this betyme'. From the first of these two documents, it is interesting to note, the authorities were clearly in some doubt as to whether Twitchet had ever, in fact, been

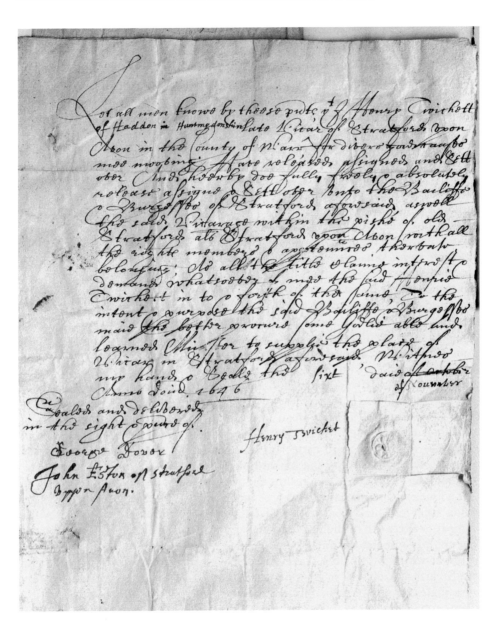

Ejection of Stratford's Vicar. Henry Twitchet was appointed vicar of Stratford in May 1640, but fled the town for his other living at Haddon, Huntingdonshire, as the war intensified in the Stratford district early in 1643. Accused by Parliament not only of dereliction of duty in abandoning his parishioners but (probably unjustly) of resorting to royalist garrisons, he remained absent from Stratford throughout the war. He was eventually forced to surrender his vicarage in Old Stratford on 6 November 1646 in order, as this document explains, to allow 'some Godlie, able and learned Minister to supplie the place of Vicar'. The replacement nominated was the puritan preacher Alexander Beane, a colleague of the Stratford schoolmaster John Trapp. See biographical notes, Appendix 3, pages 161–2.

(The Shakespeare Birthplace Trust)

officially sequestered, and consequently moved to rectify the situation three weeks later, in the second. There is therefore something of an unexplained mystery in why the authorities took four years to clarify what seems to be a clear-cut case of dereliction of duty on Twitchet's part (and also, incidentally, why the vicar should have been allowed to continue unmolested at Haddon, near the East Anglian parliamentarian heartland). One possible explanation may be simply that the sequestration authorities found the Stratford curate an acceptable *de facto* replacement. William Hawling enjoyed the respect of the town's elders and seems, moreover, to have had puritan friends in high places who may well have been influential both in keeping him at Stratford and engineering his transfer to his next parish when Alexander Bean settled in Stratford (see Appendix 3/5). The authorities must have been quite aware that the parishioners of Stratford, far from being 'wholly unprovided' (as the standard jargon had to claim), were being ably served, and the relevant committees could thus devote their energies to more desperate cases. Whatever the truth, Hawling agreed in September 1646 to leave Stratford 'in love', having, it was acknowledged, 'taken greate paynes in preaching', and made way for his successor by vacating the vicarage near the church which he had evidently been occupying for several years. Perhaps through the influence of the Lucy or Fiennes families who had estates in Hertfordshire, Hawling was to complete the remaining years of his ministry in parishes not far distant, ironically, from Twitchet's own place of retirement at Rickmansworth. Tantalizingly silent though the records are on the point, it is perfectly likely that these two middle-aged clergymen, evidently so different in outlook, met in some Hertfordshire village in later years to compare notes on their Stratford experience. At Stratford, meanwhile, their successor, Alexander Bean, was soon to earn a reputation among nonconformists as one of their best preachers, and for many years the voice of Puritanism alone was heard there – at least officially – though long disputes like those involving John Trapp and Jenkin Bowen over the Welford tithes, continuing long into the 1650s and even after the Restoration, came periodically to remind all that nothing was permanently settled, as indeed did the increasing concern over the rising force of Quakerism in the district. For the moment, however, in the immediate aftermath of the war, Puritanism was, if not unchallenged, triumphant. The spiritual war, like the military one, seemed to have been won.[17]

But at what cost, finally? There can, of course, be no accurate final reckoning for Stratford's civil war experience as a whole, though some ultimately meaningless figures can be quoted.[18] The total for the known compensation claims submitted by the town's citizens at the end of the war amounted to about £2,542. More than one-half of this sum related to taxes, 'contributions' and loans, and the remainder of more than £1,000 to free quarter, requisitions and theft. These claims related in fact to two main categories of imposition which could be described as either official or unofficial – those sanctioned by more or less formal legal decisions taken by central or local government committees in order to prosecute the war against the Royalists; and those other accidental burdens, incurred irregularly month by month as a volatile situation evolved. Among the former were the official taxes like the Poll Tax of 1641, still in force as the war began, and much that has already been illustrated in the foregoing chapters: the regular and notorious 'assessments', especially those sums collected by John Bridges' officers to maintain the troops at Warwick and which alone amounted to nearly £900 for Stratford; a much-resented 'excise' levied on basic living commodities, especially meat and beer, which lasted, according to Thomas Scriven in High Street, 'for 2 yeare wanting a month'; occasional levies for a variety of purposes through 'warrants' issued by local commanders like William Purefoy, and which there was no gainsaying; and (the most contentious issue of all) the obligation to provide free quarter to passing regiments upon some vague promise of later reimbursement of costs. But there was no knowing where such obligations would end in such an unprecedented situation, and they could escalate overnight when it became clear that taxation was not adequate to cover the costs of the war. It was soon recognized, for example, that to protect the castle's garrison, Warwick town needed fortifying against potential enemy attack, and more than fifty nearby villages were accordingly called upon for 'contributions' towards this new task, including Ashorne, Alveston, Bearley, Charlecote, Hampton Lucy, Loxley, Moreton Morrell, Newbold Pacey, Preston-on-Stour, Snitterfield, Tiddington, Wolverton and Wootton Wawen – all nearer Stratford than Warwick – as well as Stratford itself. Moreover, any newly established garrison in the district inevitably meant additional levies for its maintenance: as soon as Compton Wynyates was seized, George Purefoy instantly demanded money from local villages, some as far away as Alcester, Kinwarton, Weethley and Great Alne.[19] To such burdens were then added others of a supposedly voluntary nature, and therefore called loans or 'propositions', but which were difficult to evade: the generally popular charity donations to relieve the Irish Protestants, the offer of money and plate, and the subscriptions to raise horses for Lord Brooke and the Earl of Denbigh. To all of these, finally, were added others which might be regarded as unfortunate accidents, like having to supply food and drink to passing soldiers and provender for their horses, as well as provisioning temporary garrisons like that at Coughton, guard posts which could be set up literally anywhere at any time and sentinels guarding bridges. There was also the constant requisitioning of equipment, especially arms, teams of horses and carts, tools and, in fact, anything useful, like the four lanterns Francis Smith sent to the Earl of Essex; nursing the sick and wounded; forced labour for self and servants on local defences like those at Warwick and Kenilworth; and, by far the most infuriating of all the consequences of war, the widespread damage to property, the spoiling of grass and crops, the ransacking of shops like Richard Sturley's in Henley Street and the theft of personal belongings. The victims of all of these acts readily attempted to assess their losses in precise financial terms, but the figures inevitably remain incomplete, since, as pointed out in the Introduction, only half of Stratford's householders submitted war claims which have survived – the 120 or so included in the town's 'first booke', about one-half of those assessed in the Hearth Tax imposed some twenty years later. Well-known names are missing, therefore, including some of the town's elected officers at the outbreak of war as well as known Royalists who evidently fled, like Thomas Dighton, Edward Wagstaffe, Thomas Clopton and (probably) the former bailiff, Nathaniel Duppa.

Other conspicuous absentees for whom no obvious explanation suggests itself include the affluent Combes, Sadlers and Quineys, and, likewise, no vicar, curate or schoolmaster is represented. Unlike Shottery and Old Stratford, which obligingly noted the name of residents 'whose bills are not in', there is no indication of which of Stratford's residents did not meet the deadline for submitting claims. Even those submitted must represent a conservative estimate, since, for most people, record-keeping was an unfamiliar pastime and after a lapse of time memory was inevitably defective: thus Francis Smith's claims were only, as he carefully pointed out, 'of what hee can well remember', Richard Mountford 'cannot sett forthe the particulers' and Baldwin Brooks was also unable to 'set down' precise figures. To these problems could sometimes be added even more insuperable ones, such as that described in a delightful note from the anonymous Temple Grafton representative explaining apologetically why its own submission was particularly deficient, the constable having 'died suddenly, and all his accounts lost. Besides, the Inhabitants of the parish, not knowing that these things weare to be accountable hereafter, did not beare the same in mynd soe well as they might have done.' Further careful enquiries were made, but to no avail: 'We can find no maner of writing about it, for George Biddle he died suddenly, & we can have no resolution from his wife, she is ignorant in this busines'. Finally, it must not be forgotten that even those claims submitted relate almost entirely to damage and losses suffered at the hands of only one of the two sides, the parliamentarian, ignoring the other, despite the fact that many parishes paid taxes simultaneously to both sides, as Leamington, Milcote, Lighthorne, Packwood and Tachbrook Mallory all make clear. Lighthorne spoke for all such villages when its constable wrote in a bitter postscript to its submission: 'Wee have paid allmost as muche to the Garrison of Banbury unto the Kinges army in Weekeley taxe, besides other payments & plunder which they have forced us to pay.'

In any case, the financial reckoning touches on only one part of the equation of war, the tangible part. How to quantify the human distress, the genuine impoverishment? Of course, some in the Stratford district, as elsewhere, had no doubt managed to do well. These included not only those like John Brooks the mercer, as already noted, but also the Warwick merchants supplying unusual quantities of coal for the vast fireplaces at Warwick and Kenilworth from the north Warwickshire fields, together with unknown local traders with lucrative contracts for supplying the troops with shoes, leatherwear and clothing. About these, some of whom must have readily adopted the rascally Pistol's scheme for war profiteering ('I shall sutler [hawker] be/Unto the camp, and profits will accrue': *Henry V*, II.1), little information emerges from the local records. But these few were outnumbered by the many for whom the war simply became a nightmare of unprecedented taxation and harassment impossible to assess. What of the effects of insecurity, duress, fear, bereavement; the loss of freedom to move safely on the highway, of independence and earning ability through economic stagnation, slumped land values or constantly ruined crops; the desperate scrimping in a village rendered threadbare by passing armies; the breakdown in neighbourly trust; the threats of extortion or arson; the increased resort to violence in street, stable and barn; the split families; the widespread sense of grievance; the intolerable looting of every conceivable possession? None of this can be computed. Yet such things are continually glimpsed, lodged between the lines in the scrawled contemporary manuscripts. They are what the war came to mean to countless ordinary people. For what marked the war was perhaps not, after all, the lurid and sensational, the Roundhead versus Cavalier spectaculars beloved of Victorian painters and modern fancy-dress 're-enactments' featuring dashing Rupert and imperturbable Cromwell, but the disruption and interference in people's lives and the sheer grinding, demoralizing weight of constant exaction, harassment and insecurity. Shakespeare's Henley Street neighbour, the glover William Shaw, had five cattle suddenly driven away for some unspecified default and was obliged to go searching for them; Thomas Nash, not exempted by his known parliamentary sympathies, had to spend valuable time 'drying up the fordes about Binton' to assist carriages going to Evesham; William Greene had his horse shot dead by one of Sir Thomas Fairfax's men for some unexplained crime; Richard Sturley's Henley Street shop was broken into and his wares stolen; Edward Wells lost his valued Bible and two pewter chamber pots; and John Hill at Binton had his good pair of buckskin breeches stolen. Disruption was constant, yet always unpredictable – like the sudden invasion of a Snitterfield home by 'a corte of garde at my house foure dayes and foure neights, Thirtie men and thiertie horse', emptying the house of hay, coal and candles.

So for a short while the civil war so much dreaded by Shakespeare came to his own countryside, even to his family and old homes in Henley Street and at New Place, and spared few, not even the relatively affluent and influential. William Combe, well versed in legal and financial dealings as he had always been, was reported by a relative after the war to be 'farr in debt, and all the land that he hath about Stratford is sould or now upon sale.[20] No doubt town and countryside recovered surprisingly quickly, and Stratford, too, revived. But war had also permanently scarred the landscape in spectacular ways, not least in destroying magnificent buildings that Shakespeare had known. Warwick still stood, but Banbury Castle was demolished and Milcote had vanished as though it had never been, soon to be followed by Kenilworth, reduced to a gaunt ruin on Parliament's orders in 1649. Curiously, the John of Gaunt whom Shakespeare only a short while before had imagined predicting England's shameful conquest of itself in an earlier civil war had been lord of Kenilworth. It was as though the dramatist had recalled this later, in virtual retirement at Stratford, as he looked northwards one day across Arden to the great Castle whose unforgettable Elizabethan pageant he is likely to have seen as a boy holding his father's hand, before voicing his final poignant prophecy. Like the gorgeous palaces of Wormleighton and Milcote, Kenilworth's cloud-capped towers simply dissolved into the thin post-war air.[21]

Appendix 1

SIR WILLIAM DUGDALE'S LIST OF PARTISANS, STRATFORD DISTRICT, 1642 *(within approximately ten miles)*

Royalist

Beaufoy, Henry, of Emscote
Betham, Walliston, of Rowington
Clarke, Simon, of Broom Court, Bidford*
Clarke, William, of Oxhill
Clopton, Thomas, of Clopton
Dighton, Thomas, of Stratford
Dormer, Anthony, of Grove Park, Budbrooke
Fortescue, William, of Weethley
Green, Edward, of Little Alne
Griffin, Edward, of Bickmarsh
Halford, William, of Halford
Kempson, William, of Ardens Grafton
Kempson, William, of Hillborough
Knight, Nicholas, of Ullenhall
Knight, William, of Rowington
Knotsford, Fulke, of Studley
Lee, Robert, of Billesley*
Loggins, William, of Butlers Marston
Lucy, Spencer, of Charlecote*
Mordaunt, Charles, of Walton, Wellesbourne
Peers (Pierce), Thomas, of Alveston
Rainsford, Henry, of Clifford Chambers
Randolph, Ferrers, of Wood Bevington
Sheldon, Brace, of Temple Grafton
Skinner, William, of Shelfield, Kinwarton
Smith, Charles, of Wootton Wawen
Stainford, John, of Salford
Throckmorton, Robert, of Coughton
Underhill, Thomas, of Loxley
Walsingham, Maurice, of Exhall, Alcester
Waring, Maurice, of Oversley

Parliamentarian

Abraham, William, of Butlers Marston
Bentley, Charles, of Little Kineton
Bosevile, Godfrey, of Wroxall*
Bridges, John, of Alcester and Warwick
Brooke, Lord (Robert Greville), of Warwick*
Conway, Lord Edward, of Ragley†
Cookes, Henry, of Snitterfield
Fullwood, Thomas, of Little Alne
Lucy, Richard, of Charlecote
Middlesex, Earl of (Lionel Cranfield), of Milcote†
Nash, Thomas, of Stratford‡
Peto (Peyto), Edward, of Chesterton*
Sambidge (Sambach), William, of Pillerton
Shirley, Charles, of Ettington†
Somerville, Edward, of Edstone†
Stoughton, Anthony, of Warwick*
Throckmorton, Clement, of Haseley

* Active in organizing military rallies in the summer of 1642
† Noted by Dugdale as having withheld horses and men from the King
‡ Noted by Dugdale as a captain

Appendix 2

STRATFORD RESIDENTS SUBMITTING COMPENSATION CLAIMS, 1646 *(Source: PRO: SP. 28/136/51; BL: Add 28565)*

The modern spelling of names has been given; in doubtful cases the original form is given in brackets.

Abbot, William
Ainge, Francis
Ainge, John
Ainge, Thomas
Atwood, Nicholas
Baker, Peter
Baker, Richard
Barton, John
Baxter, John
Beck, Ember
Beddom, Benjamin
Beddom, John*
Bellamy (Ballame), John
Benson, William
Billing, Francis
Bradley, John
Brandon, John
Bridges, Henry
Bridges, Philip
Bromley, John
Brooks, Baldwin
Brooks, John
Budd, Philip
Bumpus, Jane
Cale, George
Careless, John
Castle, Richard
Cawdrey, Henry
Clarke, Walter
Cleaver, Thomas
Cook, Edward
Cooksey, Thomas
Davies, John

Davies, Thomas
Dawson, Nicholas
Durham, Robert
Edkins, Stephen*
Edwards, Richard (SP.28 only)
Fitzhughes, Robert
Fossaker, Fulk*
Francis, John
George, Clement (SP.28 only)
George, John
Godwin, Edwin
Godwin, Ham
Gray, Richard
Green, Thomas
Green, William
Green, William, junior
Halford, Mrs Alice
Harrington, Henry
Hathaway, Edmund
Hathaway, Priscilla
Hiccox, Jane
Hiccox, William*
Hicks, William
Higgins, William
Hill, Thomas
Holland, Peter
Hornby, Alexander
Horne, Simon
Horne, Thomas
Hunt, John
Ingram, Richard
Jackson, Richard*
Johnson, Michael

Lane, William
Lindon, William
Loach (Loche), John
Loach (Loche), William
Lock, George
Lord, Edward
Lucas, Clement
Lucas, Thomas
Miles, William
Mills, William
Molineau/Mulliner (Mullinex), John
Molineau/Mulliner (Mullinex), Peter*
Molineau/Mulliner (Mullinex), Robert
Morrell (Marrell), Richard
Mountford, Richard
Nash, Thomas (SP.28 only)
Norman, Jane
Perkins, John*
Perry, Thomas*
Phillips, Richard
Pratt, Henry
Price, Alexander*
Reddle, Thomas
Rogers, Edward
Rutter, John
Ryland, John
Ryland, Nicholas
Scriven, Thomas
Shaw, William
Smart, Michael
Smart, Peter (joint return with Richard Smith)
Smart, Richard
Smart, William
Smith, Francis
Smith, Jane
Smith, John
Smith, John ('late of Stratford': SP.28)
Smith, Richard (joint return with Peter Smart)
Spires, John
Sturley, Richard
Taylor, Thomas
Tibbot, Abraham
Tibbot, Thomas
Tibbot, William
Tomlins, Henry

Tumbrell, John*
Walker, Thomas
Walker, William*
Ward, Richard
Washbrook, Robert
Wells, Edward
Wheeler, Elizabeth
Wheeler, John
Whiteland, John
Whittle, Robert
Wilson, Mrs Margery
Woolmer (Wolmer), John

SHOTTERY AND OLD STRATFORD
(Source: PRO: SP.28/136/50)

Barber, John
Bird, Thomas
Burman, Clement
Burman, Eleanor
Burman, Elizabeth, widow
Burman, Thomas
Burman, William
Cotterell, John
Earl, John
Earl, Robert
Hathaway, John
Richardson, John
Such, Stephen
Townsend, John
Tyler, Richard

Noted as not submitting a return from Shottery and Old Stratford

Barnett, Francis
Smart, John
Watson, Thomas

(There are no returns from Bridgetown, Clopton or Welcombe.)

* Separate draft bill preserved at SBT. BRU 15/17

Appendix 3

BIOGRAPHICAL NOTES ON STRATFORD CLERGY
(in chronological order of service at Stratford)

(1) Thomas Wilson *(c. 1568–1638) Vicar 1619–38*

Ancestry uncertain, but likely to have been son of 'Dean Wilson' of Worcester (see below). If so, perhaps born Hampton Lucy *c*. 1568 (see below), BA 1588, MA 1591. Early career unknown, perhaps diocesan official with William Warmstry (registrar to Dean and Chapter and father of Thomas Warmstry, who later coveted Wilson's living at Stratford). Perhaps related to Henry Wilson, vicar of Bengeworth, Evesham, 1599, but no evidence. Appointed vicar of Stratford 1619 'from Evesham'. Lived in Chapel Yard, not vicarage (Brinkworth). Incumbency marred from outset by bitter controversy and violence, excommunicated 1625–6, temporarily suspended (see résumé *VCH* III, 281; *CSPD* 1635–36; and especially Hughes). Acknowledged learned, zealous and son of respected scholar. Attempted reforming crusade at Stratford, possibly even responsible for breaking font in which Shakespeare was baptized (Rowse). Member, though not apparently leader, of active radical puritan circles in Warwickshire under patronage of Lord Brooke, with wider links, e.g. William Gouge and Sir Robert Harley in London. Children baptized Stratford 1620–30s, last Jonathan baptized and buried same day 24 Aug 1638. Both he and wife treated by Shakespeare's son-in-law, physician John Hall (*Select Observations*, IV, LXXVI). Relationship with curate Simon Trapp and schoolmaster John Trapp unknown, though on one occasion he sat on the stairs of the pulpit to prevent Simon Trapp from preaching a funeral sermon for an alderman's wife (Hughes). Died 'wearied of suits', possibly plague victim, Dec 1638, leaving widow, Ann, who suffered damage to property in fire 1641 who was buried Stratford 27 Oct 1642. Not buried Stratford, no known will. Death followed by vacancy of 18 months before successor appointed.

Father: probably distinguished puritan scholar Thomas Wilson of Kendal, Westmorland, where there were many Wilsons, including clergyman, in Tudor times. Fellow of St John's, Cambridge. Campaigned against images, urging they be 'defaced, taken away and utterly destroyed' (Strype). Vicar of Wasperton 1543–54, Wolverton and Ansley, all Warwickshire, 1554. Fled persecution during reign of Queen Mary, active in religious controversies at Frankfurt, where listed as student 1555–6. Ordained deacon on return to England and canon of Worcester 1561. Rector of Hampton Lucy 1567–86, where advowson held by Sir Thomas Lucy, puritan parish as early as 1537, 'first sign in Stratford of the approach of the Reformation' (*VCH* III, 276). Prebend of Worcester 1571, possibly on recommendation to Queen Elizabeth of relative Dr Thomas Wilson, her Secretary of State and later Dean of Durham. Dean of Worcester 1571–86. Married Dorothy Banister, many children including 3 sons Samuel, Robert and Thomas living at death and all intended for ministry. Died 20 Jul 1586. Buried Worcester Cathedral. Will of Wolverley, Wcs, bequests to sons. Fullest biography in Wood and Nash.

(2) John Trapp *(1601–69) Master of school and puritan scholar*

Of old Worcestershire family from Defford as early as 1560s (a John baptized 1570). Probably cousin of Simon the Stratford curate. Baptized Croome d'Abitot, Worcs., 7 Jun 1601, son of Richard. (Many sources including *DNB* perpetuate error in Foster contradicted by parish register.) Probably attended school Worcester. BA 1622, MA 1624. Married Mary/Marie Gibbard, 11 children. Early ties with local gentry but increasingly with radical puritan circles. Appointed usher Stratford school 1622, master 1624. Occasional preacher at Luddington chapel through patron Viscount Conway of Ragley, who paid his salary. Treated by physician John Hall (who wrote of 'his remarkable piety and learning second to none') for 'hypochondriak melancholy' (*Select Observations*, LXXXI), 1635. Relationship with vicar of Stratford Thomas Wilson unclear. Secured living of Weston-on-Avon 1636 through Earl of Middlesex, signing all works as 'pastor' of Weston from then on. Salary increased by town several times in 1630s. Intimate with zealots like John Bridges, Joseph Hawksworth, etc., and also Willis gentry family who emigrated to New England puritan settlement. In 1638 dedicated first work to the Countess of Middlesex. With new vicar Henry Twitchet collected for Distressed Protestants in Ireland 1641–2. Took parliamentary Covenant 1643. Taken prisoner by Royalists 11 Jul 1643 as queen arrived Stratford but released following day. In 1644 replaced ejected Jenkin Bowen as rector of Welford, but apparently not confirmed until 1646. In Sept 1644 attacked by Royalists while preaching at Welford, taking refuge after in Warwick Castle for 18 months and serving as garrison chaplain until at least Jan 1646. Still at castle May 1646. On returning to Stratford 1646 confirmed rector of Welford though disputed by Jenkin Bowen, remaining there until 1660 when Bowen reinstated. 1648 signed Warwickshire Testimony against religious compromise. In 1650 transferred position of master of school to son-in-law Robert Dale, complaining his salary not being paid. In 1654 appointed Warwickshire Commissioner by puritan authorities for ejecting scandalous ministers, working alongside new vicar Alexander Bean. In 1655 appointed to recommend godly ministers to serve in Ireland. In 1656 published *Commentary on New Testament* dedicated to John Bridges, other editions dedicated to Sir Thomas Rous, William Combe and John Ley. In 1652 son John pupil of celebrated divine Robert Harris at Oxford. In 1660 conformed to new regime and remained vicar at Weston and Luddington until death. Died 17 Oct 1669. According to Grosart, buried at Weston.

(3) Simon Trapp *(1601–42) Curate*

Of same old Worcestershire family as John, from Defford in Elizabethan times. Probably cousin of John. Baptized Defford 17 Aug 1601, son of Nicholas of Kempsey, Worcs. Probably attended school Worcester. BA 1623, MA 1626. Appointed Stratford curate at least 1624. Attended Vestry throughout 1620s, 30s, keeping low profile during vicar Wilson's turbulent period. Witnessed physician John Hall's will 1635. Continued as curate during 2–year interim after Wilson's death 1638. Relationship with Wilson unclear. 1636 unwilling to deputize for Wilson in vicar's absence in London. 1639 hint of reservations of town council concerning his continuing as curate, but who promised to 'deal courteously' with him. Last attended Vestry 17 Oct 1641. Died aged 40, buried Stratford 25 Jan 1642, register entry by William Hawling who replaced him as curate. Curiously, no reference to relations with cousin John.

(4) Henry Twitchet *(c. 1602–59) Vicar 1640–7*

Of old Hertfordshire family since at least 1580s at Bishop's Stortford, Watford, etc. Born Watford *c.* 1602, perhaps son of Henry (died 1627). Many Twitchet baptisms Watford district early 1600s. Matriculated Emmanuel College Cambridge 1618. Ordained London 1625 aged 23. Married Margery Jackson St Albans 1629. 1639 rector of Haddon, Huntingdonshire. Vicar of Stratford 1640, allowed in Apr to add Stratford to Haddon for 4 years. No previous known connection with Warwickshire. Stratford vicarage being extensively renovated for him Feb 1640, officially installed May 1640. First recorded attendance at Vestry 2 Feb 1641 with Simon Trapp curate. With John Trapp collected for Distressed Protestants in Ireland 1641–2. Signed Haddon registers from 1641.

Son Henry baptized Stratford 21 Mar 1641, buried 28 May 1641. Jul 1641 to have lease of chapel orchard for life if continuing as vicar and resident. Alleged by Puritans to be royalist. Fled Stratford for Haddon in crisis of Jan–Feb 1643, perhaps taking temporary refuge at Banbury or Oxford. Curate William Hawling substituted in interim 1643–7. Daughter Mary baptized Haddon Aug 1644. Sequestration not made official until 1647, for having abandoned cure and joined Royalists. Replaced at Stratford by Alexander Bean 1647. Remained Haddon until 1650–1, signing registers, though retaining interest in Stratford until at least Jan 1645, when still leasing chapel orchard and churchyard. Left Haddon *c.* 1651 to retire to Hertfordshire where family still resident. Died Rickmansworth, buried 24 Dec 1659. Left widow who died Rickmansworth 1677.

(5) William Hawling *(c. 1608–83) Curate 1642–7*

Born *c.* 1608 son of Robert of Gloucester. BA 1603, MA 1633. Early career unknown. Appointed curate Stratford 23 Feb 1642 to replace Simon Trapp, died recently. Attended Vestry throughout war, apparently substituting for vicar and occasionally described as minister. Young family, baptisms of Mary 1643, Susanna 1647. Commended by town council for preaching and conscientiousness. Left Stratford on appointment of Alexander Bean to become vicar of Broxbourne, Hertfordshire, 29 Oct 1647, perhaps through patronage of Puritan Richard Lucy of Charlecote, lord of manor of Broxbourne. Later vicar of Great Amwell, Herts, perhaps through patronage of John Fiennes, Lord of manor of Great Amwell. Remained Amwell until death in 1683. Conformed to Act of Uniformity at Restoration despite being nonconformist (Calamy) and being charged with baptizing without godparents 1665. Vicar also of nearby St Margarets, 1666. Died Amwell 7 Feb 1683 aged 75. Will Essex 1683. Buried under choir stalls Great Amwell.

(6) (Samuel) Wills *(c. 1612–84) Occasional preacher c. 1644 in absence of curate*

No Christian name given in sole Stratford reference found to date to 'Mr Wills', but likely to have been Samuel Wills. If so, son of Richard of Coventry, born Coventry *c.* 1612. BA 1631, MA 1634. Vicar of Croxall, Staffs, 1637. Vicar of Wendover, Bucks, 1643, but most of war years in London, vicar of St Helens, Bishopsgate, where very active preacher, regular fast sermons. 'A person of calm and peaceable temper' (Calamy). Became leading Birmingham Presbyterian when rector of St Martin's, Birmingham, 1646 through influence of Lord Saye and Sele, Thomas Hall (vicar of King's Norton) and Simeon Ashe (militant parliamentary chaplain). Served as assistant to Warwickshire commissioners 1654 with John Trapp, Alexander Bean, etc., with whom likely to have had close if occasional relationship. Governor of King Edward's School Birmingham 1654, but 'gon out of town' by 18 Mar 1662 after ejection from St Martin's *c.* 1661. Preacher St John's Deritend, Birmingham, ejected Dec 1662. Held presbyterian meetings at home in Coventry and later Hampton-in-Arden 1669. Died 1684 Shropshire aged 73. Sons living Stratford 1716–17.

(7) Alexander Bean *(1614–c. 1662) Vicar 1647–62*

Son of Daniel of Attleborough, Norfolk, baptized 28 Aug 1614. BA 1633, MA 1636. Early career obscure. Apparently appointed vicar of Highworth, Wilts, 1646, by puritan Assembly of Divines, though no diocesan record and not ordained Salisbury diocese. Appointed vicar of Stratford 8 Feb 1647 to fill vacancy left by flight of Henry Twitchet. Occupied vicarage vacated by curate William Hawling. Associate of leading Warwickshire Puritans John Bryan, Thomas Dugard, John Trapp, Obadiah Grew. With Trapp and Wills signed 1648 Testimony opposing religious compromise. First wife Mary died Stratford, buried 30 Mar 1648/9. Member of active Kenilworth presbyterian group in 1650s and with Trapp and Wills assistant to Warwickshire commissioners disciplining scandalous ministers 1654. Son Obadiah (baptized in homage to Grew?) Stratford 3 Dec 1652. 'Studious, highly esteemed for judicious, useful sermons, one of most celebrated preachers in county' (Calamy). Ejected at Restoration 1662, though Stratford voted him annuity of £6 13s. 4d. and arrears of salary (*VCH* III 281). Continued preaching privately but harassed and died shortly after. Said to have founded *c.* 1662 first nonconformist congregation in Stratford.

Sources

Arbuthnot, G. (ed.) *The Vestry Minute Book of Stratford on Avon*, 1899
Barratt, D.M. *Ecclesiastical Terriers of Warwickshire Parishes*, 1971
Brinkworth, E.R.C. *Shakespeare and the Bawdy Court of Stratford*, 1972
Calendar of State Papers, Domestic, 1635–6
Carter, W.F. (ed.) *The Records of King Edward's School Birmingham*, 1928
Chauncy, H. *Historical Antiquities of Hertfordshire*, 1826
County Record Offices, Norfolk, Wiltshire, Worcestershire
Dictionary of National Biography
Doree, S.G. *The Parish Register and Tithing Book of Thomas Hassall of Amwell* (Herts), 1989
Foster, J. *Alumni Oxonienses, 1500–1700*, 1891–2
Garrett, C.H. *The Marian Exiles*, 1938
Grosart, A.B. *Memoir of John Trapp, M.A.*, 1867
Hughes, A. 'Religion and society in Stratford-upon-Avon, 1619–38', *Midland History*, 1994
Matthews, A. G. *Calamy Revised*, 1934; *Walker Revised*, 1948.
May, G. *The History of Evesham*, 1837
Nash, T. *The History and Antiquities of Worcestershire*, 1781
Neal, D. *History of the Puritans*, 1822
Noake, J. *The Monastery and Cathedral of Worcester*, 1866
Noble, W.M. *Incumbents of the County of Huntingdon*, n.d.
Parish Registers of Croome d'Abitot and Defford, Worcs, Haddon, Hunts, Attleborough, Norfolk
Rowse, A.L. 'Bishop Thornborough, clerical careerist', *For Veronica Wedgwood, These*, 1986
Savage, R. (ed.) *Registers of Stratford on Avon*, 1897–1905
Strype, J. *Annals of Queen Mary*, 1706
Turner, G.L. (ed.) *Original Records of Early Nonconformity*, 1911
Urwick, W. *Nonconformity in Hertfordshire*, 1884, and *Nonconformity in Worcestershire*, 1897
Venn, J. (ed.) *Alumni Cantabrigienses*, 1922–7
Victoria County History
Wood, A. *Athenae Oxonienses, 1813*

Appendix 4

THE KING'S INSTRUCTIONS FOR THE WARWICKSHIRE COMMISSION OF ARRAY, JUNE 1642 (Source: BL E. 154(8), reprinted in: J. Rushworth, *Historical Collections*, London, 1721, IV, pp. 674–5)

Charles Rex

Having by our Proclamations at large set forth the Occasions and Necessity of disposing and ordering the Militia of this Kingdom, and concerning the Legality of our Proceedings therein; We have, in pursuance of that Legal Power, and for the necessary Defence of Us, our Kingdoms, and your Country authorised you our Commissioners, or any three or more of you, by our Commission of Array, to array, and train all the Inhabitants in your County (as well within Liberty as without) which are of Body able, and Estate competent to bear Arms every one of them according to their Estates and Faculties, and to assess and distrain such as are able in Goods and Lands (and bear no Arms) to find Arms for other Men in a proportion suitable to their Estates (so that such Persons as are so arrayed for the Defence of the Kingdom take no Wages, nor Costs, so long as they stay at home) and to dispose of the Persons so arrayed into Regiments, Companies, or other Divisions as shall be convenient. We have also assigned you, or any three or more of you, whereof you *Spencer* Earl of *Northampton*, or you *Francis* Lord *Dunsmore* to be one, to command or enjoyn our Subjects so arrayed, as well to the Sea-Coasts as other places, for Expulsion, Suppression and Destruction of our Enemies from time to time when need shall require.

We have also assigned you, or any three or more of you, from time to time to take view and muster of our said Men, and to proclaim, order and examine, that all our Men so array'd appear in such Musters with their own Arms (not other Mens) under pain of losing them, except only such as are to be arrayed at the Cost of other Men, as aforesaid.

And you are hereby authorized to arrest and attach all such Persons as Rebel or make Opposition, and commit them to our Prisons, there to remain till they be thence delivered according to Law, requiring you strictly upon your Allegiance, that forthwith upon the Receipt hereof, you cause your selves to be well and securely prepared and armed, and call before you at such days and places as shall be expedient, all such Persons, by whom such Array and Defence is to be prepared, so that they may be competently provided, arrayed, and armed; and that they continue in such Array; and also to provide and place Beacons in usual and convenient places, whereby our good People may receive timely Notice of all Invasions and Commotions, so that for defect of such Defence, Array, or Conduct by your Negligence, Damage accrue not to our People in any sort.

And we have likewise given strict Charge and Command to all Earls, Barons, Mayors, Bailiffs, Constables, and all other Officers of the Peace, and all our Liege People, that in all and singular the Premises they aid and assist you.

And to our Sheriff of our County, to whom you are to direct your Warrants, that he issue Warrants to the Constables to assemble our People, at such days and places, as you, or any three of you, shall ordain and appoint, and to keep and detain in Prison such persons as shall be committed for their Rebellion or Contempt herein (as more at large by the Commission appeareth.) And being unwilling in our princely Care for our People, to bring any increase of Charge upon them, we hope for the present it will be sufficient, that you only summon and train the ancient and free-hold Bands of the County (and your number be supplied with sufficient and able Persons) taking special care that they be well arrayed, and under Conduct of such Persons as are Persons of Quality, having considerable Estates and Interests in the County and not Strangers, unless you find it shall be well-pleasing to our People, and for the necessary Defence of the Country to make any Augmentation of their Arms.

And you are to take Notice, That *Recusants* being disabled in Law to bear Arms, are to be assessed to contribute to find Arms for other Men; and if their Tenants that are Protestants bear Arms, you are to receive them. For the better knowledge of your particular Duties herein, you are all to take Copies of these Instructions, and to take Transcripts of our said Commission, the Original to remain with one of those of the *Quorum*; and of your Proceedings herein we expect a speedy and plenary Account.

Appendix 5

INSTRUCTIONS TO THE CONSTABLE OF ALVESTON TO MUSTER FORCES AT STRATFORD, JULY 1642

To the Constable of Alston & Teddington [Alveston and Tiddington]

Whereas we his Mats. Commissioners nominated in a Commission of Array under the great seale of England for the County [of Warwickshire] are authorised to traine and muster the Trained Band of this Countie for the Defense of the Kinge and Countrey; We therefore according to the authoritie thereby given us Doe require you in his Maties name to warne and bringe in all the Trained souldiers both of Horse and Foote wthin your said Constablerie. And in any case any of ye trained soldiers be dead or unfitt for yt service that you doe likewise bringe sufficient supplies to come and appeare before us at Stratford upon Avon upon Friday next beinge the 29th Day of this Instant July, then & there to be exercised beinge compleatly armed; as you and they will answere the contempt hereof at your p[er]ill. You are likewise to give notice to all the Inhabitants of your sd Towne yt as many of them as will then voluntarily offer themselves with such Armes & Weapons as they have to be trained & exercised for the Safetie of his Matie pson, the protestant Religion, the knowne Lawes of the Land, the just Kingdome in this time of soe publique distraction, will be taken to be a verie acceptable service to his Matie and the Kingdome. Hereof we desire you not to faile. Given under our hands ye 22th day of July 1642.

Northampton	Dunsmore
Tho Legh	Simon Clark
Robert Fisher	Will. Boughton
Robert Arden	Roger Feildyng
Richard Chamberlayne	Charles Adderley
	Spen. Lucy
	Robt Lee

Appendix 6

LORD BROOKE'S BANQUET AT STRATFORD, 30 JUNE 1642
(Source: Warwick County Record Office, CR 1886/Box 411/TN 11/1,2)

Chargdes for the Right honble the Lord Brooke att Stratford at the settling the Militia 30th June 1642

		li	s	d
Jun 30	Impris Delived to Mr Whateley one pottle of Sack to the Lyon at	00	02	04
	Itm sent to the Unicorne 2 gallons of Clarett	00	05	04
	Itm sent thither one gallon of Sack	00	04	08
	Itm sent more to the Lyon 1 pottle of Sack	00	02	04
	Itm more 2 gallons of Clarrett att	00	05	04
	Itm more 1 quarte of white wine	00	0	08
	Itm more 1 pinte of Sack at	00	0	07
	Itm a 2 quarte bottle broake	00	0	06
	To the Lyon for my Lord one gallon of Clarrett and one pottle of sack	00	05	00
	Itm more to goodman Lobkins by Mr Brooke for Stratford men 6 quarts of Clarrett	00	04	00
	More sent into the Maydenhead 2 gallons of Clarrett and 1 pottle of sack, Henley men	00	7	8
	More to the Lyon for my Lord one gallon of Clarrett wyne att	00	02	08
	More for my Lord to the Lyon one pottle of Sack, one pottle of white wyne and one pottle of Clarrett att	00	5	00
	Paid for xxiiii mens dynners wch sate at my Lords table at 2s a man	03	8	00
	Paid for 88 mens dynners more at 12d a man	04	8	00
	Paid for the bakeing of 5 pastyes of venison	01	00	00
	Paid for beefe and bread my Lords servants had to breakfast	00	03	00
	Paid for stabling for horses and Oates	00	11	00
	Paid for 2 hoggsheads of beere	02	10	00
	Paid to the Musicioners	00	07	00
	Paid to a Cooke for helpinge ours	00	02	06
	To the poore given	00	04	00
	ex[d]	14	19	07

Appendix 7

The piece (or box) numbers given below should be preceded in each case by the class number SP.28. The full reference for Bidford, for example, is therefore SP.28/183. In italics, those parishes for which no compensation return survives.

Abbots Salford 185
Alcester 201
Alderminster 249
Alveston 183
Arrow
Aston Cantlow
Atherstone-on-Stour

Barford
Bearley
Bidford-on-Avon 183
Billesley
Binton 186
Bishops Tachbrook 182
Bishopton 136/47, 48
Budbrooke
Butlers Marston 183

Charlecote 183
Chesterton
Claverdon
Clifford Chambers
Coughton

Donnington *see* Salford
Dorsington
Drayton *see* Luddington

Edstone 201
Ettington
Exhall 183

Great Alne 182, 185

Halford 186
Hampton Lucy
Haselor
Hatton 201
Henley-in-Arden 184

Idlicote 183, 201
Ilmington 186

Kings Broom *see* Temple Grafton
Kinwarton

Leamington 184
Lighthorne 182
Longbridge 182
Long Marston
Loxley 182
Luddington 183, 185

Milcote 201
Moreton Morrell 201
Morton Bagot 182, 185

Newbold Pacey 185
Norton Lindsey 136/49

Oldberrow 249
Old Stratford 136/50

Appendix 8

SHAKESPEARE BETWEEN TWO CIVIL WARS*

Like his contemporaries, Shakespeare seems to have been exhilarated by the upsurge in national self-awareness, and was endlessly fascinated by England's heroic and turbulent past. Beginning his vast cycle of historical plays (coincidence or not) at about the time of the national euphoria over the defeat of the Spanish Armada, he chronicled both England's pride in itself as a nation, and the fear that whenever it does not remain 'true to itself' (*King John*, closing lines) it can only too easily revert to the anarchy of the Wars of the Roses, when 'England hath long been mad and scarred itself' (*Richard III*, V.5). His historical cycle, viewed as a whole, looks in effect in two directions: most obviously backwards, to a past at once glorious yet often barbaric and shameful, but also, more subtly and covertly, forward, to an uncertain future where national renewal and the triumph of civilized values were far from guaranteed under an ageing Elizabeth every bit as insecure as many of her ancestors. To the theatre-goer, if not to the scholar engaged in close textual analysis, the histories as a whole project the image of a dynamic and proud nation now emerged from the barbarities of remote periods like those of Cymbeline or Lear but still prone, until recently, to tearing itself apart and facing the abyss when honour, virtue and discipline are flouted by tyranny, hypocrisy and greed. Attempts have often been made to go beyond such generalizations and pinpoint Shakespeare's own precise political views, a process seemingly so encouraged by the sheer persuasive force of much of the plays' political argument that it is often difficult not to believe that it is not merely his characters but the dramatist himself who is addressing us directly. Particularly since the Second World War, when Laurence Olivier's superb films of *Henry V* and, shortly after, *Richard III* deliberately projected an uncomplicated patriotic interpretation of the plays, reflecting the eloquence of Gaunt's and Faulconbridge's celebrated 'England' speeches (*Richard II*, I.1; *King John*, V.7), the histories have, nevertheless, aroused unprecedented controversy among scholars, beginning with two highly influential but now widely contested studies – L.B. Campbell's *Shakespeare's Histories* (1947) and E.M.W. Tillyard's *Shakespeare's History Plays* (1944) – which presented a largely conservative, 'establishment' Shakespeare. Since then, as shown by the many commentaries by the editors of individual plays and general surveys of the subject (the latest being the essays by Michael Hattaway and Richard Dutton in *Shakespeare: a Bibliographical Guide*, ed. Stanley Wells (1990)), no concensus has emerged on 'interpreting' the histories other than this: that Shakespeare's political awareness was much more sophisticated than previously supposed, and that a 'radical' Shakespeare is almost as

* I am most grateful to Robert Smallwood, of the Shakespeare Centre at Stratford, for reading this essay and offering much helpful advice. I also record with great pleasure the unforgettable impression made by the many excellent performances of the histories at Birmingham Repertory Theatre, particularly the pioneering sequence of the *Henry VI* trilogy in 1953 at a time when these plays were virtually unknown on the stage.

arguable as a conformist one. In focusing constantly on such burning topical issues as the legitimacy of rebellion against the head of state, regicide, the ruler's accountability to the people, the excessive concentration of power, whether the king is above the law or the law above the king, as well as the fear of national disintegration if such issues were not resolved, Shakespeare under Elizabeth and James was treading dangerously, and anticipating the furious debates of the 1630s to be finally fought over at Edgehill and Naseby. Shakespeare was clearly interested, to say the least, in the abuse of absolute power and in proposals to curb it.

As drama demands tension and confrontation, and as the most extreme form of these is war, it is not surprising that most of Shakespeare's histories are war plays, usually civil war plays, and throughout these, overriding the politics, is the playwright's horror of the sheer barbarity of civil war. This is perhaps most movingly illustrated in such domestic horrors as the butchery of Macduff's children (*Macbeth*, IV.2), the blinding of Gloucester (*King Lear*, III.7), the episodes of the young and old Clifford (*2 Henry VI*, V.2), Clifford's killing of the child Rutland (*3 Henry VI*, I.3), the son killing his father and the father his son (*3 Henry VI*, II.5) and the continuous slaughter of *Richard III*, climaxing in the murder of the young princes in the Tower (IV.2–3). Inseparable from this highly charged treatment of civil war is the theme of the poison of anarchy attendant on rebellion, and Northumberland's classic justification for this, that 'the King is not himself, but basely led/ By flatterers (*Richard II*, II.1; and repeated in *King Lear*), is precisely that used to justify the execution of Strafford and Laud in the 1640s and became the parliamentarian rallying cry during the war. If God had constantly been on England's side in the past, in destroying foreign enemies like Joan of Arc (*1 Henry VI*) and on glorious fields like Crécy and Agincourt (*Henry V*), and in similar national crises in the present, like that of the Spanish Armada, could this be guaranteed in the future if England did not model itself on its 'inward greatness' (*Henry V*, Second Chorus; *cf. Richard III*, V.5)? Could the very land escape the desolation so movingly described by Burgundy (*Henry V*, V.2)? Even without its ultimate horrors, Shakespeare knew what the 'fearful change' of civil war amounted to, in lines which look directly forward to the 'world turned upside-down' catchphrase of the 1640s:

> Rich men look sad and ruffians dance and leap,
> The one in fear to lose what they enjoy,
> The other to enjoy by rage and war,

before reaching the astonishingly prophetic conclusion:

> These signs forerun the death or fall of kings.
> *Richard II*, II.4

Civil war had come close to destroying England's very fabric so often in the past, when it had been touch-and-go whether the people would be governed by the 'unruly waywardness' of kings (*King Lear*, I.1), Jack Cade's rabble (*2 Henry VI*), unprincipled traitors and time-servers (*Richard II*, *Henry V*) or Falstaff's tavern cronies. Each of these represented alternative systems of government which (it is difficult not to conclude) Shakespeare himself rejects, as Hal does Falstaff. This is not to argue for Shakespeare the conservative or royalist, since his portraits of English royalty on the one hand and foreign despots on the other (Julius Caesar, Coriolanus) are almost uniformly unflattering. The very nature and legitimacy of political power which Shakespeare constantly debates was to become central to the events of the 1640s.

To the Elizabethans, the archetypal model for trial by battle and the theme of rebellion was Bolingbroke's challenge to Richard II and his 'evil counsellor' Thomas Mowbray, Duke of Norfolk, in 1398, accounts of which were republished on the eve of Essex's rebellion in 1601 and again, interestingly, in 1641, 1642 and 1643. Shakespeare's own *Richard II*, one of several contemporary treatments of a highly popular subject, is unique among his plays in being the only one known to have been officially censored: the dangerously risky deposition scene (IV.1) allegedly angered the insecure Elizabeth, who is reported to have cried: 'Wot ye not, I am Richard II?' It was only in 1608, after her death, that this scene was published, and further quartos of the play in 1615 and 1634 suggest the play's continuing popularity in the years leading to the civil war. Richard's 'follies' were commonly accepted as 'causing' civil war, and Elizabeth herself was accused of similar indiscretions (*cf.* Campbell, op. cit., pp. 171–2). Now, as her reign drew to its close, to be replaced with one not unlike Richard's, with court favouritism and dilettantism substituted for statesmanship, looking into the seeds of time was a sobering occupation; who could prophesy which grain would grow and which not? How long was the new era of peace proclaimed at Bosworth Field to last? Philip Edwards (*Shakespeare: a Writer's Progress*, OUP, 1987, pp. 124–5) has noted the evident fragility in the dramatist's hopes that the Earl of Essex's campaign of 1599 to crush the Irish rebellion (*Henry V*, Fifth Chorus) might usher in a royal marriage and a halcyon period of peace, a disillusionment expressed in the peculiarly flat words of the play's epilogue, after the previous euphoria of the marriage between England and France, that the child of this union 'lost France and made his England bleed'. Fortune's wheel was turning inexorably, and to Shakespeare, writing his last plays under the new king, and to the generation following, parallels with the past must have been painfully obvious. In the immediate pre-war decade of Charles I's personal rule, widespread corruption, the sales of royal lands and offers of knighthoods to court favourites, together with the Stuart combination of weakness and guile, must have given a new topical edge to John of Gaunt's jibe in revivals of the ever-popular *Richard II*: 'Landlord of England art thou now, not king' (II,1). The peace and plenty promised to Britain at the end of his career and the conventionally obsequious homage to Elizabeth and James (*Cymbeline*, V.5; *Henry VIII*, V.5; *cf. Richard III*, V.5) are too fulsome to allay the suspicion that Shakespeare's farewell to politics had uneasy forebodings. The happy ending of the historical cycle, as one commentator has put it, 'belongs more to the world-as-we-would-wish-it-to-be than to the world as it is' (Edwards, op. cit., p. 110). Twenty-five years after the poet's death, with Ireland once more in revolt and now Scotland too, Essex's son, absolved of the treachery of his father but immediately listed as a traitor, was appointed commander of the rebel forces to spearhead a new challenge to the king as the country again plunged into the misery of civil war.

The extent to which, by 1642, the political nation had become obsessed with medieval precedent has been penetratingly explored by John Adamson ('The baronial context of the English civil war', *Transactions of the Royal Historical Society*, 5th series, 40, 1990, pp. 93–120). A veritable literary vogue for medieval history, already apparent in Tudor times, had increased during the decade of Charles I's personal rule, as the country lurched towards civil war. At Court, the king (who possessed a copy of Shakespeare's second folio, in which he made marginal notes) encouraged a gentleman of his Privy Chamber, Sir Francis Biondi, to compile a vast survey of baronial struggles from Richard II to Henry VII, and this finally appeared in the fraught year of 1641 as *The Civil Warres of England*, translated from the Italian manuscript by Henry Carey, Earl of Monmouth, the lord of Kenilworth (see *DNB*, Biondi). A further local connection was that Monmouth, who dedicated his translation to the king, was related by marriage to Stratford's own lord, Lionel Cranfield, Earl of Middlesex. In May 1641 an essay on Richard II's 'memorable Parliament' was pointedly published (BL E.157/12), July 1642 saw the reprinting of a political speech of 1399 concerning Richard's deposition (BL E.200/51), and, most striking of all, on 12 July 1642, at a time when the Stratford district was alive with political controversy and military preparation, a further tract appeared whose title was both explicit and inflammatory: 'The Life and Death of King Richard the Second, who was deposed of His Crown, by reason of His not regarding the councell of the sage and wise of His Kingdom, but followed the advice of wicked and lewd councell' (BL E.155/15). In the three years 1641–3, Adamson points out (p. 95), no less than fifteen large-scale histories of the Wars of the Roses, plus a large number of shorter ones, were published. The end of the war continued the vogue for seeing topical parallels with earlier precedents: a tract published only weeks before the king's execution referred to earlier 'oppressors' and the depositions of Richard II and Edward II, while denouncing Charles (BL E.536/17).

The onset of the civil war in 1642, Adamson argues, offers striking parallels with medieval baronial conflicts, and the opening moves were widely seen as being set within the aristocratic and chivalric conventions of the Wars of the Roses. It was latter-day barons like Essex (and especially Midland peers) who took the initiative, recruited personal armies, vied for territory and control of the king's arsenals, engaged in local trials of strength, and adopted, at least initially, a chivalric code of archaic formalities and rhetoric. Like Prince Hal's determination to 'try fortune with [Hotspur] in a single fight' (*1 Henry IV*, V.1), leaders issued challenges for one-to-one personal combat, as did Lord Brooke and the Earl of Northampton, or established gentlemen's agreements, as over the

Banbury magazine – promptly violated by more unscrupulous mortals amid much acrimony. Public and private accounts of confrontations were dominated by the doings of these aristocrats rather than emphasis on the issues at stake, forces were referred to not as royalist or parliamentarian but as those of the noblemen, and quotation was readily given from set speeches seemingly modelled on Tudor chronicles and dramas still being reprinted. Adamson's parallels could indeed be multiplied, for the personalization of the conflict in Warwickshire was real enough: 'This cuntrie is full of feares, by reason of the unhappie differences now on foote; for as formerly my Lord Brooke, soe now my Lord of Northampton and my Lord of Dunsmore have their parties'; 'my Lord Compton [Northampton] and my Lord Brooke are in great variance' (KAO U.269/E.126; BL E.109/3). Equally reminiscent of medieval contests were the impressive number of trumpeters invariably attached to each regiment to respect chivalric convention, the distribution of colours, the courteous pleasantries and exchanging of gentlemen prisoners, and scenes of ceremonial pageantry like that at Warwick on 4 August 1642, when the king's herald, Sir William Dugdale, sumptuously robed in his red and gold costume of Rouge Croix Pursuivant, summoned the rebels to surrender amid trumpet calls at the castle gate. As though echoing stage performances, contemporary observers adopted theatrical metaphor, writing of Warwickshire as 'the Stage whereupon these cutting Cavaliers do act daily tragedies' (BL E.112/21), and one of the major participants, Sir William Waller, in his celebrated letter to a former friend now enemy, gave poignant expression to the sense of moving against a theatre backdrop, renewing Shakespeare's image of poor players strutting their brief hour: 'We are both upon the stage, and must act those parts that are assigned to us in this tragedy.'

Shakespeare was well-read, well-versed in local tradition and well aware of the part Warwickshire, and Warwick and Kenilworth in particular, had played in royal history and past civil conflict. Though he did not provide formal stage directions, he set many scenes in and around Warwickshire. He knew that his King John was buried in Worcester Cathedral (*King John*, V.7); that it was at Kenilworth, a favourite royal residence in medieval times, that Henry had received the Dauphin's insulting gift of tennis balls (*Henry V*, I.2; *cf*. Holinshed, and C.A. Cole (ed.) *Chronicles and Memorials of Great Britain and Ireland: Memorials of Henry V*, 1858, pp. 24, 100–101); and that it was to Coventry that Richard II had been brought under armed guard before being deposed (*cf. VCH* II, p. 437) (as, later, it was planned to bring Charles I to imprisonment at Warwick). As it is, his Wars of the Roses present some uncanny premonitions of local involvement in the civil war of the 1640s. As Warwickshire's allegiance had earlier been divided between Yorkists and Lancastrians, so it was again between Royalists and Parliamentarians. In *Richard II* the John of Gaunt who condemns England's 'shameful conquest of itself' (II.1) was lord of Kenilworth, soon itself to be destroyed, while the rebel Mowbray had been lord of several Warwickshire manors, including Kineton, scene of later Edgehill. The play's trial scene (I.3) takes place outside Coventry, which was to become the parliamentary headquarters in 1642; Bolingbroke's rebel army gets lost in the wilds of the Cotswolds (II.3), as Sir William Waller's was to in 1644; and the play ends with news of the destruction by fire of Cirencester (V.6), anticipating its later fate at the hands of Prince Rupert's arsonists in 1643. In *1 Henry IV*, Falstaff and Hal arrive via Daventry at Coventry (IV.2: 'What a devil dost thou in Warwickshire?') on their way to Shrewsbury, Charles I's temporary headquarters in 1642. In *2 Henry VI* the king is at Kenilworth when he enquiries after the rebels (IV.9), as was Charles in October 1642 on his way to confront his own rebels at Edgehill. An ancestor of Charles's inveterate enemy, Lord Saye and Sele, is beheaded (*2 Henry VI*, IV.7); in *3 Henry VI* the kingmaker deposes Edward in Warwickshire after the battle at Banbury (IV.7), later twice besieged in the 1640s; and there is a further confrontation between them outside Coventry, where reinforcements come via Southam, Daventry and Dunsmore (V.1), towns all to play key roles in the civil war of 1642. Even Shakespeare could hardly have imagined the full extent of Warwickshire's involvement in the new conflict after his death, or that its opening scenes would be enacted largely near Stratford – at Warwick, Banbury, Kenilworth, Coventry, Southam, Kineton and Powick – initiated by local rivals across countryside that he knew so well.

Overall, the student of Shakespeare's histories who comes to examine the English civil war often has an overpowering impression of *déjà vu*, or, rather, *déjà lu*. Family loyalties were tragically divided in both: when the Earl of Denbigh was killed at the outset of the war in 1642 and the distraught widow pleaded unavailingly with her son, 'O my dear Jesus, put it into my dear son's heart to leave their merciless company that was the death of his father', or when Sir Edmund

Verney was killed trying to save the royal standard from the rebels among whom his son Ralph was an officer, one is re-reading Shakespeare. In the civil war, the king and Rupert periodically hanged undisciplined soldiers as an example, as Shakespeare's Bardolph is executed for robbing a church (*Henry V*, III.6), while Henry's order that 'in our march through the country there be nothing taken but paid for' was to be echoed repeatedly by commanders on both sides in the 1640s. The civil war accounts are full of Bardolphs, Nyms and Pistols. In Oliver Cromwell's rejection of an army composed of 'old decayed serving-men and tapsters' he was, surprisingly, unconsciously quoting that unlikely military expert Sir John Falstaff, who was ashamed to march through Coventry with 'discarded unjust serving-men [and] revolted tapsters and ostlers' (W.C. Abbott (ed.) *Writings and Speeches of Oliver Cromwell*, I, p. 204; *1 Henry IV*, IV.2). The recruitment at Pitchcroft Meadow, outside Worcester, in August 1642, of 'a great number of men of mean and base quality, having hedgebills, old calivers, sheep pikes and clubs' (*HMC* Portland I, p. 52) resembles nothing so much as Falstaff's celebrated muster in nearby Gloucestershire (*2 Henry IV*, III.2); while Cromwell's reaction to victory at Marston Moor, 'Give glory, all the glory, to God!', is Henry's 'O God, thy arm was here', on the field at Agincourt (Abbott, I, p. 287; *Henry V*, IV.3). Finally, although the circumstantial detail is different, the emotional parting of Charles from his young French queen at Dover, when, in C.V. Wedgwood's graphic description, 'the King galloped along the cliffs to keep her in sight until the last sail had vanished over the wintry horizon' (op. cit., p. 70) recalls the moving separation scene of Richard and his own French queen (*Richard II*, V.1). Faced, like Richard, with captivity, Charles I passed the time by reading Shakespeare. How can he not have been moved at Warwick's counsel to a king anxious to 'read the book of fate/ And see the revolution of the times'?

> There is a history in all men's lives
> Figuring the natures of the times deceased,
> The which observed, a man may prophesy,
> With a near aim, of the main chance of things
> As yet not come to life, who in their seeds
> And weak beginning lie intreasured.
> *2 Henry IV*, III.1

History never repeats itself. But sometimes it comes uncannily close to doing so.

Notes and References

ABBREVIATIONS

Add	Additional Manuscripts series, British Library
BL	British Library
CAM	*Calendar of the Proceedings of the Committee for Advancement of Money, 1642–1656*, 3 volumes, 1888
CCC	*Calendar of the Proceedings of the Committee for Compounding, 1643–1660*, 5 volumes, 1889–93
CJ	*Journals of the House of Commons*
CRO	County Record Office
CSPD	*Calendar of State Papers, Domestic*
DNB	*Dictionary of National Biography*
E	British Library reference, Thomason Tracts
EB	P.E. Tennant, *Edgehill and Beyond: the People's War in the South Midlands*, 1982
HMC	Royal Commission on Historical Manuscripts
KAO	Kent Archive Office, Maidstone, Sackville Manuscripts, Cranfield Papers
LJ	*Journals of the House of Lords*
PRO	Public Record Office, London
QS	S.C. Ratcliff and H.C. Johnson (eds), *Warwick County Records, Quarter Sessions Order Books*, 6 volumes, 1935–53
SBT	The Shakespeare Birthplace Trust, The Shakespeare Centre, Stratford-upon-Avon
TBAS	*Transactions of the Birmingham Archaeological Society*
VCH	*Victoria County History*

Introduction

1. 'Shakespeare, the close of an epoch' (1964), in *History and Hope: the Collected Essays of C.V. Wedgwood*, Collins, 1987, pp. 57–64, 68, 87, 196.

2. R. Savage, E.I. Fripp, L. Fox (eds) *Minutes and Accounts of the Corporation of Stratford-upon-Avon, 1553–1598*, Dugdale Soc. Vols I, III, V, X, XXXV, 1921–90. E.R.C. Brinkworth, *Shakespeare and the Bawdy Court of Stratford*, Phillimore, 1972.

3. The subject of civil war and such themes as divine right, the nature of kingship and treason, the legitimacy of rebellion against the sovereign, social order, patriotism and national renewal were continuously debated throughout the Tudor period, and Shakespeare's debt to the treatment of them in contemporary chronicles and plays is well known. But his own horror and shame at the dehumanizing effects of 'civil butchery' (*1 Henry IV*, I. I) whenever England 'did help to wound itself' (*King John*, V.7) in the appalling descent into mindless anarchy, are so insistently and eloquently presented, especially (though far from exclusively) in the history cycle, as to suggest a personal obsession which in the end seems to outweigh his pride in England's past and to cloud his optimism regarding its future. For further discussion see Appendix 8.

4. KAO U.269/C.292, quoted in C. Russell, *The Causes of the English Civil War*, Oxford, 1990, p. 26.

5. BL Thomason Tracts, 'E' references; useful though very incomplete index by G.K. Fortescue, British Museum, 1908. PRO: mostly SP.28/136, 182–6, 201. This series has never been properly sorted, let alone indexed; most are boxed haphazardly without internal arrangement (for example, alphabetically or by hundreds) and an individual parish's returns may be split between several boxes. Roughly one-half survive for the Stratford district generally, but nearby parishes in adjoining Worcestershire and Gloucestershire are almost entirely missing. For piece numbers of individual parishes see Appendix 7.

6. PRO SP.28/136/51; BL Add 28565; copies at SBT. The PRO copy is slightly longer than the BL one (62 pages of text as opposed to 56, contains three more names, 123 to 120, including the important Thomas Nash, Shakespeare's grandson-in-law, and concludes with memoranda concerning the town's overall charges). There are minor discrepancies between the two, some rearrangement of material and variations in money totals, etc. The two copies were transcribed by different people, the shorter one almost uniformly by the deputy town clerk, John Beddom (*VCH* Wks III, 235, n.99) and with pages left blank as though for last-minute additions; the longer one less neat, carrying entries written in several different hands and appearing generally more rushed. Entries are listed according to the division of the town into the six wards established in Elizabethan times (Bridge St., Church and Chapel St., Henley St., High St., Sheep St. and Wood St.), so that there is no mention of some streets (e.g. Ely St., Rother St., Rother Market, Greenhill St. and Middle Row). The pagination of each copy is either imperfect or confused. Individual entries in each case are almost, but not quite, identical, except that those in the PRO copy are signed, those in the BL one not. Eleven separate drafts of bills (signed) are preserved at SBT, but they duplicate information and add little new. See Appendix 2 for full lists of names.

7. A survey of 1590 lists 217 houses in the town centre belonging to the lord of the manor (R. Savage & E.I. Fripp (eds), *Minutes and Accounts of the Corporation of Stratford-upon-Avon*, IV, pp. 92–110, Dugdale Soc. I, 1921; *cf. VCH* III, p. 222). The number of houses in Stratford during the civil war may be guessed at as being somewhere between this figure and the similar one of 200–230 at the Hearth Tax of the 1660s–70s, and one would need a similar number of compensation claims to gain a full picture. The total number of houses (i.e. including hovels, labourers' cottages, etc. not liable for Hearth Tax) was roughly double (*cf.* also Thomas's estimate of 420 in 1730: Dugdale *The Antiquities of Warwickshire Revised*, ed. W. Thomas, 1730, p. 697). The poorer section of the town's inhabitants would have been unlikely to send in compensation claims, even though they would certainly have suffered from the war in one way or

another. The total adult population of the borough is suggested by the vicar Thomas Wilson's claim of 1636 that he had 2,000 communicants (*CSPD* 1635–6, p. 415).

Chapter 1

1. BL Add 70002 f. 104, dated 19 May 1636. The precise link between Wilson and Harley is not yet clear, but Harley was a great patron of puritan ministers and Wilson's letter goes on to remind Harley of his brother's willingness to serve Harley 'if you be not yet provided'. Harley had Warwickshire connections through his brother-in-law Viscount Conway from whom Lord Brooke, the influential local Puritan, was renting Ragley in the 1630s. Brooke, who had family links with the Conways and was also distantly related to Lord Saye and Sele, had suggested to Harley a suitable minister for the Ragley living. In London, Harley lived in the notoriously puritan parish of Blackfriars where William Gouge preached. Another Warwickshire contact of Wilson, John Ley of Warwick, dedicated a work to Lady Harley and Lady Alice Lucy of Charlecote (*CSPD*, 1631–2, pp. 112, 120, 404; 1633–4, p. 8; 1637–8, p. 144; *DNB*; J. Eales *The Harleys of Brampton Bryan*, CUP, 1990, pp. 61, 65; R.E.L. Strider *Robert Greville, Lord Brooke*, Cambridge, MA, 1958).

2. Vagrancy: *QS*, II, p. 226–7; *CSPD* 1631–3, p. 305; K. Sharpe *The Personal Reign of Charles I*, Yale, 1992, p. 479. Actors: *CSPD* 1633–4, pp. 47–8; J.T. Murray *English Dramatic Companies, 1558–1642*, Constable, 1910, II, pp. 106–110, 163–7. Ben Jonson and Cotswold Games: G. Parfitt (ed.) *Ben Jonson, the Complete Poems*, Penguin, 1975, p. 277, 'An epigram to my jovial good friend Mr Robert Dover'; C. Whitfield *Robert Dover and the Cotswold Games*, Sotheran, 1962. Forest of Arden: P. Levi *The Life and Times of William Shakespeare*, Macmillan, 1988, p. 8.

3. Church courts: Brinkworth, op. cit. Rugby: K. Sharpe, op. cit., p. 748, quoting Robert Woodforde's diary for Feb–Mar 1638. Alcester: S. Clarke *The Lives of Sundry Eminent Persons*, 1683, Introduction; Henley: *QS*, III, pp. 271–2. A. Hughes, *Godly Reformation and its Opponents in Warwickshire, 1640–1662*, Dugdale Soc.

Occ. Papers 35, 1993, pp. 5–6. Bull Ring referred to by Stratford's Francis Ainge in his return. Bowling alley was being repaired 1642: SBT BRU.4/2 f. 164v. Plays and commons: A. Hughes 'Religion and society in Stratford-upon-Avon, 1619–1638', *Midland History* 9, 1994, pp. 60–1. Tavern blasphemy: SBT BRT 4/1/1, 29, 34, quoted in P. Clark *The English Alehouse, a Social History, 1200–1830*, Longman, 1983, p. 158. Welcombe: C.M. Ingleby *Shakespeare and the Enclosures of the Common Fields at Welcombe*, 1885; *VCH* III, pp. 266–8; R. Bearman *Shakespeare in the Stratford Records*, SBT/Alan Sutton, 1994, Chapter 6. Market Hall: PRO C2/P78/34 and C2/P91/27; *VCH* III, p. 226. Mills: PRO C3/449/86. Avon navigation: *CSPD*, 1636–7, pp. 357, 468–9; T. Habington *Survey of Worcs*, Worcs. Hist. Soc., 1895, II, pp. 468–9; there was violence in 1637 over the plans: PRO SP.16/315/79, SP.16/343/67. Church seating: *CSPD*, 1635, pp. 279–80. Brooks v. Susanna Hall: S. Schoenbaum *William Shakespeare: a Compact Documentary Life*, New York/Oxford, 1987, p. 305.

4. Gunpowder Plot: *VCH*, II, pp. 446–7 summarizes local involvement. Sir C. Smith: he demised Old Stratford and Shottery 10 June 1642 to a relative, John Carill/Caryll, of Harting, Sussex, who still possessed them in 1650: SP.23/63 f.272 (*CCC* 1914 carelessly transcribes 'Old Stratford' as 'Stratford'; the lord of Stratford was the disgraced Earl of Middlesex). Catholic scare: *LJ* IV, pp. 439–41, 449, 455; A. Hughes *Politics, Society and Civil War in Warwickshire*, Cambridge University Press, 1987, p. 135; *cf.* R. Clifton 'The fear of popery', in C. Russell (ed.) *The Origins of the English Civil War*, Macmillan, 1973, pp. 159–60.

5. *CSPD*, 1635, pp. xl (full transcript of report on Wilson submitted to the church authorities), pp. 278–9; *CSPD*, 1635–6, pp. 239, 390, 415, 512; *VCH*, III, pp. 276, 281; and especially A. Hughes *Godly Reformation and its Opponents in Warwickshire, 1640–1662*, Dugdale Soc. Occ. Papers, 35, 1993, which gives detailed analysis of the stormy Wilson years with many additional references. Eye infection: J. Hall *Select Observations on English*

Bodies, 1657, Observation IV (original is BL Eg 2065). 'Wearied with suits': KAO U269/E.165 dated 24 May 1637.

6. W. Dugdale *A Short View of the Late Troubles in England*, Oxford, 1681, pp. 95, 117. Barcheston: Churchwardens Accounts, 1635, Wk CRO DR 5/6. Guild Chapel: *VCH*, III, p. 277. Warmstry: E.199(23). 'Poison': E.114(15).

7. Brooke and Laud: R. Ashton *The English Civil War, Conservatism and Revolution, 1603–1649*, Weidenfeld, 1978, p. 118, Brooke and Saye: *CSPD*, 1639, pp. 67–8. The two peers were arrested again the following year as suspected traitors, May 1640, when their homes were ransacked and papers taken: *CSPD*, 1640, p. 152; *HMC* IXth Rpt, II, p. 498. New England: T. Hutchinson *The History of the Colony and Province of Massachusetts Bay*, ed. L.S. Mayo, 1936, I, pp. 410–413. Willis and Huitt: G. Wyllys *The Wyllys Papers*, Hartford, Connecticut, 1924.

8. Catholicism in 1630s: K. Sharpe, op. cit. p. 842; C. Russell *The Fall of the British Monarchies, 1637–42*, Oxford, 1991; and for Warwickshire, *VCH*, II, p. 45; D.F. Mosler 'Warwickshire Catholics in the civil war', *Recusant History*, 15, 1981; A. Hughes 'Warwickshire on the eve of the civil war: a county community?', *Midland History*, 7 (1982). Badger: *CSPD* 1603–10, p. 246, quoted in E.I. Fripp *Shakespeare's Haunts near Stratford*, OUP, 1929, p. 131. Bishop of Worcester: *HMC*, Salisbury VI, pp. 265–7. Lady Dudley: C. Oman *English Church Plate*, Oxford, 1957, pp. 147–8, 225, 269.

9. Dugdale, op. cit. Conventicle: E.77(33, 34); E.17(10, 11).

10. Plague: outbreak at Old Stratford and Haselor, *QS*, II, pp. 34, 58, following those in Worcestershire in 1637, *CSPD*, 1637, p. 391, when lectures were suspended; Wilson's son John also died at this time. Harris: SBT BRU 2/3.C.14, 30, 166, 182; W.D. (William Durham) *The Life and Death of Robert Harris*, 1660, pp. 27–8. Middlesex: KAO U269/E.165; SBT BRU 2/3 C.179. Salisbury: KAO U269/E.166; W. Prynne *Canterburies Doome*, 1644, p. 362; *QS*, VI, p. 23. Salisbury was vicar of Clifford since 23 Nov 1609: PRO Inst. Bks.

11. *CSPD*, 1640, p. 53; SBT BRU 2/3.C.14, 30, 135, 164, 166, 167, 175, 182, 196; BRU 4/2, ff. 159–62; G. Arbuthnot (ed.) *The*

Vestry Minute Book of Stratford-upon-Avon, 1617–1699, 1899, pp. 54–5. Dugard: *Diary*, BL Add 23146, ff. 98sqq., dated 1640–1, when Dugard seems to have been preaching at Stratford and Twitchet at least once, 29 Sep 1640, at Warwick, deputizing for Simon Trapp. Huntingdon: Twitchet apparently signed the Haddon registers continuously 1643–50, baptizing his daughter Mary there 25 Aug 1644. His rectory there is probably the building described in a 1725 glebe terrier at Huntingdon CRO. I am grateful to Dr P.C. Saunders, Deputy County Archivist of Huntingdon, for this information.

Chapter 2

1. Conway: cf. Fulk Reed's letters in *CSPD* 1630s passim. Sandys: SBT BRU 2/3. C.126, 200; *CSPD*, 1636, pp. 449–50. Duppa: KAO U269/E.122, 127. Coaches: J. Taylor *The Carriers Cosmographie*, 1637. Woad: Visct Conway, Earl of Middlesex and Edward Peyto were among local woad-growers; cf. J.M. Martin, 'A Warwickshire market town in adversity: Stratford-upon-Avon in the 16th and 17th centuries', *Midland History*, 7, 1982; J. Thirsk *Economic Policy and Projects*, Oxford, 1978, pp. 5, 169; *CSPD*, 1636, p. 371; and esp. B.M. Baggs 'Woad accounts for the manor of Chesterton, 1638–41', *Dugdale Soc. Misc.* I, 1977. Coal: *CSPD*, 1645–7, p. 430 (the reference is to Nov 1645, but north Warwickshire fields had been supplying coal to the Stratford district and beyond since Elizabethan times at least, and coal merchants at Warwick in particular built up a thriving business during the war: cf. *EB*, p. 97).

2. Great Tew: Clarendon *History of the Rebellion and Civil Wars in England*, 1888, III, pp. 178–90, and *Life*, I, pp. 37–45; cf. R.A. Anselment 'Clarendon and the Caroline myth of peace', *Journal of British Studies*, 23/2, 1984. Broughton plotting: *EB*, p. 9. *The Complete Prose Works of John Milton*, Yale, 1953, I, p. 585, 'Of reformation in England', 1641; Milton later praised Lord Brooke in glowing terms in *Areopagitica*, 1644, ed. H.B. Cotterill, Macmillan, 1949, p. 44.

3. For the general deterioration, cf. K. Sharpe, op. cit., pp. 906–9 and A.J. Fletcher *The*

Outbreak of the English Civil War, Arnold, 1985. Stratford Ship Money: SBT BRU 2/3. C.140, 145, 153–4, 167, 169, 183; in Warwickshire, *CSPD*, 1635–40 passim and *VCH*, II, pp. 447–8. Stratford's William Combe and Sir Thomas Lucy were summoned to the Privy Council and removed from office in 1639 and Combe kept in custody, probably over opposition to Ship Money: Hughes *Politics, Society and Civil War*, pp. 115–6. Stratford and Old Stratford were also among 9 parishes refusing to co-operate over Coat and Conduct Money for the maintenance of troops: PRO SP.16/456/12. 1640 unrest: *CSPD*, 1640, pp. 210, 327 (the disreputable Col. Thomas Lunsford affair: desertion, assaults, fatalities). Stratford corporation records dated 17 June 1640, SBT BRU 2/3.C.186.

4. R. Baxter *Reliquiae Baxterianae*, ed. M. Silvester, 1696, pp. 28–9; *cf.* Sharpe, op. cit., pp. 632–3. Irish refugees: *cf.* Kenilworth churchwardens' accounts, CRO CR 2134 f. 20. John Woolmer the Stratford bailiff paid in £85 19s 0d in Sep 1642 collected for this cause: SP.28/136/51 f. 334, and further collections followed.

5. Petitions: E.135(27); *LJ*, IV, p. 575; BL 669 f. 4(14, 82); *cf.* Fletcher *Outbreak*, pp. 208, 213, 217–8. Fire: S. Porter 'Fires in Stratford-upon-Avon in the 16th & 17th centuries', *Warwickshire History*, 3(3), 1976. Plot: W.H. Coates (ed.) *The Journal of Sir Simonds D'Ewes*, Yale, 1942, pp. 144, 146, 172; *LJ*, IV, pp. 439–41, 449, 455; Hughes, *Politics, Society and Civil War*, p. 135. Unlawful assemblies: *CSPD*, 1641–3, p. 166; *QS* II, p. 116; Fletcher *Outbreak*, pp. 215–6.

6. Worcs: Fletcher, *Outbreak*, pp. 215–6, quoting Birmingham Ref. Lib. 398265–7, Hanley Court MSS Box 5. Stratford chamber: SBT BRU 2/3.C.203 dated 7 Jan 1642. S. Trapp: SBT BRU 2/3.C.220; BRU 4/2 f. 173. Falstaff: *1 Henry, IV*, II.4. Wyllys, op. cit., p. 9. On the economic situation generally, *cf.* M. James *Social Problems and Policy during the Puritan Revolution*, Routledge, 1930, passim. Wood felling: *CSPD*, 1639–40, pp. 599–600; *cf.* R.G. Albion *Forests and Sea Power*, Harvard, 1926, pp. 127–30. Kenilworth: *HMC*, Vth Rpt, p. 64. Warmstry: E.180 (24), *Pax Vobis, or, a Charme for*

Tumultuous Spiritts, 1641. Lord Brooke: *VCH*, VIII, 459.

7. Irish: SP.28/183/22 and SP.28/201 (several lists). Petition: *LJ*, IV, pp. 577–9 (12 Feb 1642). Edward Hyde, Earl of Clarendon *History of the Rebellion*, Oxford, 1888, I, pp. 271–2. For an important analysis of the whole petitioning process, see Fletcher, *Outbreak*, Chapter 6. Lord Brooke: *LJ*, IV, p. 625; *CJ*, II, p. 426. York: E.154(45).

8. C. Carlton *Going to the Wars*, Routledge, 1992, pp. 33–9. William Combe: *QS*, II, pp. xxxii and Appendix I; *CJ* II, p. 602; SP.28/246. Knyvett: *The Knyvett Letters, 1620–1644*, ed. B. Schofield, Constable, 1949, p. 101. Caryll: *CCC*, 1914. Warwickshire Commission of Array: R. Hutton, *The Royalist War Effort 1642–1646*, Longman, 1982, pp. 5–6. (Text reprod. E.154(8); *cf.* in J. Rushworth *Historical Collections*, 1721, IV, pp. 674–5; see Appendix 4).

9. *CSPD*, 1641–43, p. 343. Parliamentary Militia Ordinance: *CJ*, II, p. 602. Money and plate: *LJ*, VI, pp. 196–8. Evesham: SBT BRT 4/1/1, Early Sessions Papers, 24. Coventry: *LJ*, V, pp. 164–6, J. Barker letter to Brooke, 25 Jun 1642; E.114(1), E.202(9, 12); BL Add 11364, Annals of Coventry, f. 14 and Add 14827 f. 144; *cf.* Hutton, *Royalist War Effort*, pp. 19–21. Bellringers: Wk CRO CR 1886, Box 411.TN 11/2. Lord Brooke: 'A Worthy Speech made by the Right Hon. the Lord Brooke', July 1642.

10. Stratford banquet: Wk CRO CR 1886, Box 411.TN 11/2 f. 29 (see illustration). Chamberlain: SBT BRU 4/2, f. 165.

11. Earl of Northampton: *CJ*, II, p. 662 (8 Jul 1642). Royalist Commission of Array: SP.19/146 f.17 (instructions to Alveston and Tiddington; see illustration). Stratford Royalists: *CAM*, 1423, 1427, 1420, 2816; SBT BRU 2/3 C.437, 443. Dugdale: Northampton Record Office, Finch-Hatton MS 4284 (see Appendix 1). 'Meadow beyond Stratford': SP.23/170/153, Kittermaster case. Woolmer: KAO U269/E.126, R. Fawdon to Earl of Middx, 1 Aug 1642. For the post-war charges brought against these inhabitants, see Chapter 12, pp. 146–8.

12. Sharpe v. Greene: SP.24/75, dated 20 Jul 1649. Betrayal of Stratford: SBT BRU 2/3. C.209. Coat and Conduct: PRO

SP.16/456/12 (see n. 3 to chapter 2). Tibbott: SP. 19/21/246; *cf. EB*, p. 26.

13. Estate musters: *cf. EB*, pp. 23–4 for the little-known Earl of Northampton ones at Winderton, Brailes and Tysoe. Propaganda: BL 669 f. 6 (50), 'A true relation of the Lord Brooks setling of the Militia in Warwickshire'; *cf.* similar one reprinted in *QS*, II, xxxii Appendix; V.F. Snow and A.S. Young, *The Private Journals of the Long Parliament*, Yale, 1992, III, p. 181. Thomas Johnson: E.109(3), 'A letter from Sambourne', 4 Aug 1642. Milcote: KAO U269/E.126, 1 Aug 1642. Wages: E.109(3), E.202(32); *CSPD*, 1641–3, p. 361. M. Ashley, *The English Civil War*, Alan Sutton, 1992, p. 65.

14. Warwick Assize: E.202(15, 26, 27), information dated 26 Jul; BL Add 14827 f. 144; *LJ*, V, p. 422; Fletcher, *Outbreak*, p. 366 quoting House of Lords Rec. Off. Main Papers for 21 Jul, Reeve to Lord North. Stratford: SBT Chamberlain's Accts BRU 4/2 ff. 164–5; BRU 2/3.C.209 dated 3 Aug 1642.

15. Lt. Round: SP.28/136/40, QM Round's accounts; SP28/253B, 'The answer and defence of John Bridges'. Rowington: SP.28/185 f. 80. Lord Brooke: E.109(3). 'Cockpit': E.108(26), *Terrible Newes from Leics, Wk & Staffs*, 21–27 Jul 1642.

16. Brooke–Northampton confrontation: E.109(19), 'A Famous Victory . . .'; E.109(35); E.202(21); SP.19/157/142 (calendared *CAM*, 1413); KAO U269/E.126, R. Fawdon to Earl of Middx, 23 Jul and 1 Aug 1642. Combe: KAO U269/E.115, T. Combe to Earl of Middx, 3 Mar and 29 May 1643. Holy Trinity: KAO U269/E.126, 1 Aug 1642. King: 78 *HMC*, *Hastings* II, p. 86, Sir Edw. Nicholas to Earl of Huntingdon, York, 1 Aug 1642. Banbury: *CSPD* 1641–3, p. 367, 9 Aug; E.202(33), E.239(7).

Chapter 3

1. Warwick siege: *cf. EB*, pp. 34–9; *QS*, II, Introduction, p. xxxi. Coventry: E.202(39). Kenilworth: *QS* II, Introduction, p. xxxi. Kidderminster: R. Baxter *Reliquiae Baxteriana*, ed. M. Silvester, 1696, p. 42. John Smith: E.53(10). John Court: SP.16/539/347. Stratford recruits: SBT BRU 4/2, f. 175. Parliament's appeal: C.H.

Firth and R.S. Rait (eds.) *Acts and Ordinances of the Interregnum, 1642–1660*, HMSO, 1911, I, p. 6. Nash: SP.28/136/51. Quineys: SP.28/201. Bryan's accounts, 5 Apr 1647. Fetherston: M.W. Farr *The Fetherstons of Packwood in the seventeenth century*, Dugdale Soc. Occ. Papers 18, OUP, 1968, pp. 6–7.

2. Donations: *cf.* Fletcher, *Outbreak*, p. 338; SBT BRU 2/3 C.209a. The Stratford details are compiled from several sources: John Bryan's accounts (SP.28/182 and 201, later printed *LJ*, VI, p. 196) and the claimants' own returns in the Stratford books. There are some discrepancies between them; *cf.* also *VCH*, III, p. 235. Warmstry: SP.28/201 (2 separate references).

3. Horses: in addition to Stratford's own accounts, *cf.* SP.28/201 (which includes the Nash reference). Wootton: SP.28/182, Warmington accounts. Mr Hunt: SP.28/201. Livestock: SP.28/253B, 'The answer and defence of John Bridges'.

4. Greene: SP.28/201 and 215, Sequestration lists. Snitterfield: SP.28/4 f. 97. Royalists: for many, *cf. CAM* and *CCC*, indexes. Smith: see previous n. 4 to Chapter 1. Clarke: *CAM*, 493, *CCC*, 1134. Gibbs: SP.19/21 f. 209 (*CAM*, 1077). Charlecote: SP.28/183. Aston Cantlow: Nathaniel Wharton letter, 26 Sep 1642, reprinted *CSPD*, 1641–3, p. 392.

5. Fears: Milcote: KAO U269/E.126, 1 Aug 1642. T. Johnson: E.109(3), 'Some speciall passages from Warwickshire', 4 Aug. E.111(11), 'A letter out of Warwickshire', 8 Aug. Fetherston: M.W. Farr, *The Fetherstons of Packwood*, Dug. Soc. Occ. Papers 18, 1968. Falstaff: *Henry IV*, Pt 2, V.3.

Chapter 4

1. Siege of Warwick: *EB*, pp. 34–9. Southam: *EB*, pp. 43–7. Walker: SBT BRU 15/17, and *cf.* Stratford claims; it is unclear why Walker should be the only resident contributing in this way. Milcote: KAO U269/E.126. Grove Park: E.118(13).

2. Soldiers' progress across Warwickshire: see the letters of the subaltern Nathaniel Wharton, reprinted *CSPD*, 1641–3 pp. 379–400, and most recently by Partizan Press, Leigh-on-Sea, Essex, 1989, ed. S. Peachey. Lady Monmouth and Milcote: KAO U269/E.126, R. Fawdon to Earl of Middx, 23 Sep 1642.

3. Coughton: BL E.240(23), *c.* 22 Sep (preceding the action at Powick Bridge). A post-war report of 21 Apr 1648 claimed Sir Robert Throckmorton was 'driven away from his howse at Weston [Bucks], his howse at Coughton made a garason and the gatthows dismantled and the hows quit ruined': CRO CR 1998 Box 86/26. Worcester: C.V. Wedgwood *The King's War, 1641–1647*, Collins, 1978, pp. 123–4; P. Hughes, 'Property and prosperity: the relationship of the buildings and fortunes of Worcester, 1500–1660', *Midland History*, XVII, 1992, esp. pp. 50–4; Letter of A. Trevor to Marquis of Ormonde, *A Collection of Original Letters & Papers*, ed. T. Carte, 1739, I, p. 15; R.E. Sherwood *The Civil War in the Midlands*, Alan Sutton, 1992, pp. 9–10. Milcote: KAO U269/E.126, 9 Oct 1642.

4. Rupert: Lord Wilmot to Rupert, 1 Dec 1642, in E. Warburton *Memoirs of Prince Rupert and the Cavaliers*, Bentley, 1849, II, p. 74. N. Fiennes, 'A most true & exact relation of the battel', BL E.126(38).

5. Essex's proclamation: G. Grenville *Some Memoirs of John Hampden*, 1832, II, pp. 257–61. All village details quoted from SP.28 (see Appendix 7 for references). Nash: SP.28/254 *passim*.

6. Brooke: L. Whitaker, Diary, BL Add 31116, read in House of Commons 22 Oct.

7. Baxter: *Reliquiae Baxt.*, 1696, p. 43. For the battle of Edgehill, see P. Young, op. cit.; (detailed on strategy, armies and personnel, but few details on impact on civilian community, for which *cf. EB*, chapter 4).

8. H. Whyte: SP.16/539/358 (calendared *CSPD*, Add 1625–49, p. 693).

9. Wounded: SP.28/253B; *CJ*, III, p. 187; SBT BRU 4/2, f. 175.

10. Milcote: KAO U269/E.126, 30 Oct 1642; SP.28/246. Barford: SP.28/241.

11. H. Ingram: SP.28/185; *HMC*, IVth Rpt, p. 270; *EB*, p. 118; R.M. Ball 'After Edgehill Fight', *Bulletin Inst. Hist. Research*, 67/12, 1994. Milcote: KAO U269/E.126, 14 and 19 Nov.

Chapter 5

1. Speech: E.84(35). The Long Parliament's notorious 'Nineteen Propositions' had been published 1 Jun (reprinted with comments in J.P. Kenyon *The Stuart Constitution, 1603–1688*, CUP, 1966) and the king had replied with a dignified 'no' on 18 Jun. *Cf.* Wedgwood, *King's War*, pp. 100–101. Warwickshire Quarter Sessions: *QS* II, Introduction, pp. xxiv–v, 125–6.

2. Milcote: KAO U269/E.126, 14 Nov. Round: SP.28/136/40 (see Chapter 2, p. 8). Lord Saye: E.244(3); *EB*, pp. 75–6. Royalist raiding: E.83(10), E.84(6, 10), E.88(20), E.246(25, 42), E.244(26–34), E.85(9), E.86(4, 5). Banbury district: *cf. EB*, pp. 76–83. Wagstaffe: E.244(30), E.246(19); *DNB*; see later comments, Chapter 12, p. 145.

3. Stratford's 'fortifying': P. Styles (ed.) 'The genealogie, life & death of the Rt. Hon. Lord Brooke', *Dug Soc. Misc.* I, OUP, 1977, p. 184. Peyto: Castle Ashby, Northampton MSS CA 1083/15; Dr R. Bearman points out that the Peyto family owned land at Drayton, on the Avon near Luddington: *cf. VCH* III, p. 266.

4. Confrontation: E.86(22). John Lewis and George Wincoate: SP.28/201. Earl of Northampton: E.85(9).

5. E.85(9), Speciall Passages, 10–17 Jan 1643.

6. Thomas Combe: KAO U269/E.115, Combe to Earl of Middx, 3 & 18 Mar, 29 May 1643. Fawdon said unambiguously that Combe was 'intimate' with Col. Bridges and the Coventry committee.

7. Brent: E.246(19), E.89(10), E.90(7). Rupert: E.88(3, 17), E.89(10), E.244(30), E.246(2, 3, 16).

8. Warwick Castle: E.86(3). Robert Arden: SP.28/298 Pt.3, f. 558 (anonymous and undated but *c.* 14 Jan 1643).

9. SP.28/136/1, 2, 3, 4), Col. Needham's accounts. Bryan: SP.28/201. Church bells: SP.19/158 f. 69 (see Chapter 12, p. 141). Kenilworth: SP.28/185.

10. Twitchet and Dighton: KAO U269/E.126. Fawdon to Earl of Middx, 10 Feb. For further discussion of these and others fleeing Stratford, see Chapter 12, p. 141. Twitchet's flight: BL Add 35098 f. 36v.

11. Lord Brooke: Firth & Rait, op. cit., I, pp. 53, 55; *LJ* V, p. 520. J. Hunt: SP.28/136/30, Hunt's accounts. Warwick Castle: E.86(3).

12. Wortley: E.89(17), E.90(3, 12), E.92(3, 20). Northants: E.86(39). Lord Brooke's build-up: SP.28/298/3 ff. 493–570; *cf.* also accounts of treasurer Rowland Wilson, SP.28/139/3 covering this period (refs to Coventry but not Stratford); E.86(41).

Cromwell: P. Gaunt *The Cromwellian Gazeteer*, Alan Sutton, 1987, p. 88. Coventry and Northampton: E.86(41), E.90(3), E.91(5, 19), E.92(3), E.246(20).

13. Wortley: E.89(17), E.90(3, 12). Stratford's occupation: E.91(19). Wagstaffe, etc.: E.89(17), E.246(19); I.G. Philip (ed.) *The Journal of Sir Samuel Luke*, Oxford Rec. Soc., 1947–53, p. 20, report of 3 Mar 1643.

14. Jealousies: 78 *HMC, Hastings* II, pp. 94–5, Sir E. Nicholas to Col. H. Hastings, Oxford, 25 Feb; Warburton (*Memoirs of Prince Rupert and the Cavaliers*, Bentley, 1849, II, pp. 103–4) notes how allies fought among themselves to seize the best quarters. Croker: BL Add 18980 f. 58; *cf. EB*, pp. 100–2. Wortley and Crisp at Stratford: E.92(3, 20). John Bridges consultations: SBT, Chamberlain Thomas Horne's accounts, 1643, BRU 4/2, f. 175.

15. The account which follows is compiled from several contemporary versions of events which, although varying in detail and emphasis, agree on essentials: E.91(19), E.86(41), E.92(3, 20), E.246(19, 20, 29, 33, 37, 38); *CSPD*, 1641–3, p. 449; 78 *HMC, Hastings* II, pp. 94–5; P. Styles (ed.) 'Genealogie of Lord Brooke', pp. 184–5; SBT, 'A true relation of the death of the Lord Brooks', Access. 4342. The account given in *VCH*, III, p. 235, is based solely on E.91(19), 'The last week's proceedings of the Lord Brooke', 21 Feb 1643. Maj. Castle: SP.28/136/23A and 23G. It seems unwise to assume, as *VCH* does, that Lord Brooke's advance followed the line of the modern Warwick–Stratford road. An admittedly solitary reference to 'the fight by Snitterfield' (SP.28/184) almost certainly relates to these events, and suggests that the Parliamentarians may have followed the old Warwick–Bishopton road, the route also probably taken by Sir William Waller's men after Roundway Down (see page ??). Royalist account: E.86(41). Market Hall: PRO C2/P78/34, C2/P91/27; *VCH*, III, p. 226; built 1634–5; a subscription to repair it was opened 1653 and repairs completed by 1661. It was demolished in 1767 and replaced by the present Town Hall on the corner of Chapel St. and Sheep St.

16. SBT Acc. 4342, 'A true relation of the death of the Lord Brooks'; *cf.* P. Styles, 'Genealogie', p. 184.

17. Northampton and Dunsmore: see Chapter 2 page 11–12. Maidenhead: of the two almost identical entries, BL Add 28565 is the clearer.

18. Cooke: S. Schoenbaum *A Compact Documentary Life*, pp. 291–2 and M. Eccles *Shakespeare in Warwickshire*, p. 114, quoting Cooke's own account in his Preface to John Hall *Select Observations on English Bodies*, 1657 (original is BL Egerton 2065). There is no other reference to this episode, but a brief note buried in SP.28/201 refers to a Capt. Smith quartered at Stratford under Lord Brooke and William Lindon's Stratford bill includes a claim for 10s. for quartering soldiers of Col. John Bridges' Warwick garrison 'sent by Captaine Smithe', so Cooke may have been part of this unit. Cooke was still being paid as 'chirurgion' to Warwick garrison in Sep 1644: E.101/612/64.

19. Greene was the royalist 'malignant' from whom the large sum of £15 was taken early in the war (SP.28/201, John Bryan's accounts), attacked Thomas Sharpe the parliamentary soldier in the street (see Chapter 2, pages 15–16) and had a horse stolen from him by one of Sir Thomas Fairfax's men.

Chapter 6

1. 'Contention': T. May, *The History of the Parliament of England*, 1647, reprinted 1812, ed. F. Maseres. Denbigh: *HMC*, IVth Rpt, pp. 259, 261.

2. Milcote: KAO U269/E.126, R. Fawdon to Earl of Middx, 14 Mar 1643, and ib. E.120, Wm. Croft of Todenham, *c.* Jun 1643. Shipston: E.89(10), E.96(2). Rupert's raiding: I.G. Philip (ed.) *The Journal of Sir Samuel Luke*, Oxford Rec. Soc., 1947–53, p. 55; *cf.* E.247(21).

3. E.99(5, 21), E.247(19, 21); N. Wallington *Historical Notices of the Reign of Charles I*, Bentley, 1869, II, p. 163 (18 Apr 1643). Ann Kempson: SP.28/184, Temple Grafton.

4. KAO U269/E.126, R. Fawdon to Earl of Middx, 20 Apr 1643.

5. T. Combe: KAO U269/E.115 and ib., Wm. Croft, E.120. Baddesley Clinton: SBT DR3/711 (transcribed in H. Norris *Baddesley Clinton, its Manor, Church and Hall*, 1897, pp. 34–6).

6. E.247(26); Pierce (or Peers) was listed as a prominent Royalist by Dugdale (see Appendix 1); *cf. VCH*, III, p. 286.

7. Ilmington: E.105(17) and Wallington, *Historical Notices*, II, p. 164. Tredington: BL Harl 6804 ff. 78–9; J.W. Bund (ed.) *The Diary of Henry Townshend*, Worcs. Hist. Soc., 1920, II, pp. 102–5; *cf. EB*, pp. 106–7.

8. PRO C3/449/86; *VCH*, III, p. 269; sluices had been made at various places on the Avon, including Bidford, Welford and probably Stratford too: T. Habington, *Survey of Worcestershire*, Worcs. Hist. Soc., 1895, II, pp. 468–9. Coal was also probably being transported along the Avon; though there are no clear civil war references to this, large quantities of coal from the north Warwickshire fields were being supplied to Warwick Castle and coal was piled at Barford (wharf?) in 1645: *CSPD*, 1645–7, p. 430.

9. KAO U269/E.120, E.126, letters of R. Fawdon and W. Croft to Earl of Middx, May–Jun 1643.

10. Coventry committee assessments: E.90(26). Milcote: KAO U269/E.126, 20 Apr 1643; BL Harl 158 f. 277.

11. Stratford figures taken from those cited in the residents' claims and last folio of SP.28/136/51; *cf. VCH*, III, p. 235; SBT BRU 4/2, f. 175, Milcote: KAO U269/E.252. Shottery and Old Stratford: SP.28/136/50. 'Pious uses': BL Add 28565, f. 23, note of the Chamber's contributions.

12. KAO U269/E.126.

13. Queen's correspondence: Comte de Baillon *Henriette-Marie de France, Reine d'Angleterre*, Paris, 1877, pp. 481–99 (some translated in M.A.E. Green (ed.) *Letters of Henrietta Maria*, 1857). Journey: Clarendon, *History*, III, p. 19; *CSPV*, 1642–3, pp. 283–305; W.A. Day (ed.), *The Pythouse Papers*, 1879, pp. 48–9, H. Percy to Rupert, 29 Apr 1643. Gossip: E.63(1). Warburton, *Memoirs of Prince Rupert*, II, pp. 229–30. I.G. Philip (ed.), *The Journal of Sir Samuel Luke*, pp. 113–4.

14. Cotswolds: KAO U269/E.126, R. Fawdon to Earl of Middx, 17 Jun 1643. Queen's approach: E.60(17), E.63(2).

15. Purefoy: E.62(13), E.56(11); H.T. Cooke *Notices of the Church of St. Mary and the Beauchamp Chapel*, Warwick, 1845, p. 63; Dugdale, *Antiquities*, I, p. 445, and *The Restoration of the Beauchamp Chapel*,

1674–1742, Oxford, 1956, pp. 17–18 (accounts of 4 Oct 1682).

16. Queen: Baillon, op. cit., pp. 489–90; Warburton *Memoirs of Prince Rupert*, II, pp. 224–7; *VCH* Wcs III, p. 184; BL Add 18980 f. 82, Sir E. Nicholas to Rupert, Oxford, 8 Jul 1643. Chipping Campden: ib., f. 84, 12 Jul. Warwick: SP.28/253B; SP.28/136/13.

17. Milcote: KAO U269/E.126, R. Fawdon to Earl of Middx (dated 7 Aug but relating to earlier events).

18. Trapp: *Wyllys Papers*, p. 61, Trapp to Mary Wyllys, Stratford, 16 May 1644; Trapp, Dedication to John Bridges, *Commentary on the New Testament*, 1656.

19. The tradition goes back to information given by the then owner of New Place, Sir Hugh Clopton, to Lewis Theobald, repeated in Theobald's Preface to *Works of Shakespeare*, 1733, which says that the queen preferred New Place for the reason given; later repeated verbatim by R.B. Wheler, *History and Antiquities of Stratford on Avon*, 1806, p. 135. The allegiance of Shakespeare's immediate relatives is a vexed question without conclusive evidence. As said, the poet's son-in-law John Hall was one of the puritan vicar Thomas Wilson's only important allies, though this did not prevent him in his professional capacity treating many 'Royalists'. Of his wife Susanna's politics (assuming she had any), nothing certain is known. A seventeenth-century wife would normally defer to her husband's views, but she has long been suspected (though on somewhat slender grounds) of catholic leanings (*cf.* S. Schoenbaum *William Shakespeare: a Compact Documentary Life*, p. 286), 'witty above her sex' (epitaph in Stratford church) hints at some independence, and she is thought to have given a historical work (perhaps from Shakespeare's own library) as a present to one of Prince Rupert's officers, Richard Grace, quite possibly on this occasion. But she had also invited Lord Brooke's surgeon, James Cooke, to examine her husband's medical case-book (see Chapter 5, page 60). Similar mysteries surround the Nash family. Thomas's allegiance is not in doubt, since, along with William Combe, he was a member of the wartime parliamentary sub-committee meeting regularly at Warwick

(SP.28/254, passim), so the tradition of the royal visit to his house might appear highly suspect. But he was often absent from home, may well have preferred the safety of Warwick as the queen and Prince Rupert arrived in Stratford, and would have been powerless to prevent the occupation of New Place in any case. Interestingly, after his death in 1647 his widow Elizabeth married a staunch royalist, later knighted by Charles II for his loyalty. Cf. Schoenbaum, pp. 291–2, 305, 318–9; Eccles, pp. 114, 143. For Grace, the officer in Rupert's regiment, later colonel, see P. Young *Edgehill 1642*, Kineton, 1967, p. 208; *Hertfordshire County Records*, I, p. 153; Schoenbaum, p. 305; L. Fox, *In Honour of Shakespeare*, Jarrold / SBT, 1972, illustration, p. 140.

20. Rupert: E.I. Fripp, *Shakespeare's Stratford*, Oxford, 1928, p. 9 note; at the Bear, one of Stratford's best inns, recently, and perhaps still, owned by Thomas Nash. Chamberlain: *VCH*, III, p. 254, n. 73. Banquet: SBT BRU 4/2 ff. 175–6; the arithmetic is clearly wrong. Queen's reception: *cf.* Baillon. Milcote: KAO U269/E.126, R. Fawdon to Earl of Middx, 7 Aug 1643 and 17 Dec 1644. Charlecote: A. Fairfax-Lucy, *Charlecote and the Lucys*, OUP, 1958.

21. I.G. Philip *Letter Books of Sir S. Luke*, pp. 113, 117. Kineton reunion: E.61(11), E.62(3). Bonfires: Luke, op. cit., p. 117. Royalist quarters: ib., pp. 114–21.

Chapter 7

1. Snitterfield: SP. 28/201. Temple Grafton: SP.28/184. Milcote: KAO U269/E.126, R. Fawdon to Earl of Middx, 31 Aug 1643.

2. Gloucester: E.67(13), E69(15), E.70(10), reproduced in J. Washbourn (ed.), *Bibliotheca Gloucestrensis: a Collection of Scarce and Curious Tracts*, 1825. Milcote: KAO U269/E.126, 31 Sept 1643.

3. Supplies: *LJ*, VI, pp. 218–19 (10 and 16 Sep 1643), *CJ*, III, pp. 277 (16 Oct), 284, 294–5, 305. Northampton: E.67(22), E.69(25), E.74(1, 4, 21), E.76(3); G. Baker *The History and Antiquities of Northampton*, 1822–30, II, pp. 175–6, 322–3 ff.

4. Coughton: E.77(22, 23): W. Hamper *The Life, Diary and Correspondence of Sir William Dugdale*, 1827, p. 56; Warwick CRO CR 1998, Box 86/26. SP.28/253B, A.

Yarranton's Testimony, and E.81(6, 23, 30). Milcote: KAO U269/E.126, Jan 1644.

5. Coventry: *HMC* IVth Rpt, p. 264; BL Add 11364 f. 16. River crossings: BL Add 18980 f. 162; Add 18981 f. 76, Vavasour to Rupert, 1 Mar 1644; *CSPD*, 1644, pp. 29–30, 29 Feb; *cf. EB*, pp. 151–2.

6. Troops: E.34(21), SP.28/184; Temple Grafton (Broom); E.252(18); *CSPD*, 1644, p. 60; plus the reports from the villages among SP.28/182–6.

7. *Oxford English Dictionary* dates the noun from 1643 (though this could certainly be pre-dated) and the verb from 1632.

8. E.34(21), E.35(1, 23).

9. H.G. Tibbutt (ed.), *The Letter Books of Sir Samuel Luke, 1644–45*, Bedfordshire Hist. Soc./HMC, 1963, p. 331, Behr to Luke, Warwick, 4 Mar 1644 (original: BL Eg 785 f. 5); confirmed the same day by John Bridges: 'I believe Maj. Gen. Behr will stay [in Stratford] for further orders'; ib.; E.37(16).

10. Stratford claims. Milcote: SP.28/201, SP.28/246.

11. H.G. Tibbutt, op. cit., p. 331, Behr to Luke, Stratford, 6 Mar 1644.

12. W. Hamper *Life of Dugdale*, p. 63 (dated 20 Mar but surely earlier?); H.G. Tibbutt, op. cit., p. 331; *cf. CSPD*, 1644, p. 67, Earl of Denbigh to Parliament, Coventry, 23 Mar 1644. Rupert: E.37(16).

13. E.37(21, 24), E.252(14); *CSPD*, 1644, pp. 64, 70, Sir E. Nicholas to Rupert, 21 and 24 Mar. Chadshunt: E.36(6), E.37(21), E.252(23) and Beesley, *History of Banbury*, Nichols, 1841, pp. 354–5. Chipping Campden: E.252(17), and W.A. Day (ed.), *The Pythouse Papers*, 1879, p. 25. It is unclear whether this is the same skirmish involving Behr, already reported, or a further one. Wasperton: Warwick CRO CR 2017/C9/67.

14. Hamper *Life of Dugdale*, p. 64; *cf.* BL Add 18980 f. 144, Vavasour to Rupert, 12 Apr 1644.

15. H.G. Tibbutt, op. cit., p. 334, John Bridges to Luke, Warwick, 16 Apr 1644.

Chapter 8

1. Royalists: Clarendon *History*, IV, p. 462; BL Add 18981 ff. 182, 185. Parliamentarians: *CSPD*, 1644, pp. 237, 293. Cropredy: see *EB*, pp. 171–85.

2. Denbigh: *CSPD*, 1644, pp. 91, 97, 161–2. King: R. Symonds *Diary of the Marches of the Royal Army*, ed. C.E. Long, Camden Soc., 74, 1859, p. 25.

3. Rupert: E.47(5). Wellesbourne: Hamper *Life of Dugdale*, p. 67. Leycester's Hospital: Warwick CRO CR 1600/LH 51/7; *cf.* E.G. Tibbits 'The hospital of Robert, Earl of Leicester, in Warwick', *TBAS*, 60, 1936, letters of 10 May and July 1644.

4. Milcote: KAO U269/E.126, 22 May. Denbigh: *CSPD*, 1644, pp. 91, 97, 161–2. Thomas Warde: *HMC*, IVth Rpt, Appendix, p. 266.

5. W. Purefoy: *CJ* III, p. 517. Stratford's claims. Chamberlain: SBT BRU 4/2, ff. 175–6. Compton: E.50(35), E.51(2, 10, 14); for details of the impact on the countryside of the new parliamentary garrison, see *EB*, pp. 164–70.

6. Lobbying: E.7(20), Aug. 1644 Denbigh: *CSPD*, 1644, pp. 161–2 (14 May) and E.47(5, 10). Acock: *HMC*, IVth Rpt, Appendix, p. 266. 13 May: E.47(27).

7. Clothiers: *LJ*, IV, p. 257; E.53(11). Margery Davies: *HMC*, IVth Rpt App., p. 267. Lucy: ib., p. 67. Stow: KAO U269/E.126, 7 May 1643. Evesham: R. Hutton *The Royalist War Effort*, Longman, 1982, p. 99. For impact on trade generally, see M. James *Social Problems and Policy during the Puritan Revolution*, Routledge, 1930, and for impact on Severn valley, I. Roy, 'England turned Germany? The aftermath of the civil war in its European context', *Trans. Royal Hist. Soc.*, 28, 1978, pp. 133–40.

8. Dover's Games: details are obscure, though they are assumed suspended by June 1644 when R. Symonds noted 'Over the Cotswold Downes, where Dover's Games were', *Camden Soc.*, 1859, p. 15. The claim repeated by P. Rushen and C. Whitfield in their histories of Chipping Campden that the games were stopped by William Bartholomew, the vicar of Campden, seems implausible, since he was claimed by Parliamentarians to be a Royalist, and Dover's Hill was not in his parish. More relevant is the fact that the prominent Puritan Lord Saye was Lord Lt. of Gloucestershire, and that the manor of Weston Subedge, in which the games took place, belonged to the Fiennes family.

9. Conway surrendered to John Bridges at Warwick 10 Apr, *CSPD*, 1644, pp. 113–4; Hamper's *Life of Dugdale*, p. 64, Chandos at the same time, *LJ*, VI pp. 518, 578 and Leicester shortly after: E.252(50), 19 Jun, and Hamper, op. cit., p. 69; *cf.* 77 *HMC*, VI, pp. 554, 558. Earl of Middx: M. Prestwich *Cranfield: Politics and Profits under the Early Stuarts*, Oxford, 1966, pp. 568–70. Smith: *CCC*, 1913–1915; PRO C.203/4; SP.28/215 f. 53, T. Basnet's Sequestration Book.

10. Worcester: R. Howell 'Resistance to change: the political elites of provincial towns during the English revolution', *The First Modern Society: Essays in Honour of Lawrence Stone*, ed. A.L. Beier, CUP, 1989, p. 438; and S. Bond (ed.) *The Chamber Order Book of Worcester, 1602–50*, Worcs Hist. Soc., 1974, pp. 358, 364–5, 370–1, 375, 381.

11. John Eston and William Lindon in 1652 and 1656–7 respectively: SBT BRU 2/3. B.256, C.362, 437, 443, D.23; *cf. VCH* III, p. 236, n. 11.

12. *Wyllys Papers*, op. cit., pp. 76, 87, 95, G. Willis to mother Mary, 9 May, 1646: he has not paid any contribution towards the lecture for about 2 years, 'it being not kept weekly, but there being a monthly sermon preached, ye vicar & towne do threaten to sue for it; I feare there wilbe trouble about it'.

13. SBT BRU 2/3.C.220 (6 Sept 1643); BRU 4/2. f. 173; ER1/77/3 f. 104, Mar 1645; BRU 2/3. C.234 (wife).

14. A.G. Matthews *Walker Revised*, Oxford, 1948, for brief notes on persecuted clergy. Bowen: KAO U269/E.106; P. Carter 'Clerical taxes during the civil war and interregnum', *Bulletin of Inst. of Hist. Research*, 67, June 1994; PRO E.401/1928 ff. 60, 62 (Michaelmas 1643); BL Add 35098 f. 138; SP.28/136/18, T. Baldwin's deposition; KAO U269/E.112, W. Chandler to Earl of Middx, 12 June 1644.

15. Trapp: *Wyllys Papers*, op. cit., pp. 61, 80, Trapp to Mary Wyllys, Stratford, 16 May 1644 and 2 May 1646; E.13(9), 17 Sep 1644; compare the parliamentary account of E.256(15); 'Dedication' to John Bridges of his *Commentary on the New Testament*, 1656; tithes: BL Add 15671 ff. 154, 176v, 204v; stipend: SBT Wheler MSS (1649?).

16. SBT BRU 4/2, ff. 175–6. 'Mr Wills' is probably Samuel Wills, a leading Warwickshire Presbyterian: see Appendix

3/6. Hawling: see Chapter 8, page 99;
SBT BRU 2/3. C.205. Bowen's
reinstatement: *cf. VCH* V, p. 193.

Chapter 9

1. The siege of Banbury is described in some detail in *EB*, pp. 186–200. Henry Cooper: KAO U269/E.117, 19 Aug 1644.
2. Gerard: BL Add 18981 ff. 166, 177, 222–3. Evesham: E.46(9). Massey: *CSPD* 1644, pp. 383, 386. Stevens/Stephens: presumably one of the prominent Gloucestershire puritan family of Chavanage, Eastington, Lypiatt and Sodbury, one of whom, Nathaniel (1589–1600) was a conspicuous MP during the war and a parliamentary colonel of horse. Another member, Thomas, was High Sheriff of Gloucestershire and had a son of the same name. One Thomas, probably this one, commanded a regiment of horse under Waller, was taken prisoner by the Royalists and recommended for an exchange at Oxford in July 1643, *CJ* III, p. 159; *cf. LJ* VI, p. 626, was at Gloucester with Col. Edward Harley's regiment June 1644 and later made Governor of Beverston Castle. Significantly, there were Warwickshire links: Nathaniel married Catherine Beale of Priors Marston and one Thomas married Catherine, daughter of Stratford's William Combe, *Visitation of Glos.*, 1623, Harl. Soc., 21, 1885, pp. 151–2; *Visitation of Glos.*, 1682–3, Exeter, 1884, pp. 174–8; *Trans. Bristol & Glos. Arch Soc*, 22, 1899. Archer: *HMC* IVth Rpt, App., pp. 269–70.
3. Petition: *HMC*, IVth Rpt, App., p. 29; *LJ*, VII, p. 5; E.256(15).
4. Massey: *CSPD*, 1644, pp. 511–2, 17 Sep; E.256(8,9).
5. Cheshire: E.16(3, 4) (royalist account), and E.13(18), the parliamentarian.
6. E.13(18). *HMC*, VIth Rpt, App., p. 29; *LJ*, VII, p. 5.
7. Bridges: H.G. Tibbutt *The Letter Books of Sir S. Luke, 1644–45*, Beds Hist. Soc./*HMC*, 1963, pp. 382, 391. Pont: E.18(6); Tibbutt, op. cit., pp. 80, 336, 391; E.18(1, 4, 6, 7, 10, 16); SP.28/256, Pont's accounts. Pont's death is carelessly dated by Bridges as 17 Sep instead of 17 Nov.
8. Compton: E.16(5). Henley: E.18(2). Warwick: E.19(8), E.21(8), E.22(18).
9. Stratford: SP.28/136/18, T. Baldwin's accounts. Nash and Tibitts: E.21(17). SP.28/254, *passim*. Archer: E.21(27, 29). Parliamentarians: Tibbutt, op. cit., p. 382; E.18(7), E.21(11). Civilian angle: KAO U269/E.126.
10. BL Add 18981, ff. 334–5, 338 (Rupert correspondence, Dec 1644); *Perfect Occurrences*, 23 Jan 1645; *CSPD*, 1644–5, pp. 253, 255, 267; SP.28/183, Alveston.
11. E. Carey-Hill 'The Hawkesworth papers, 1601–1660', *TBAS*, 54, 1929–30, p. 28 (incorrectly dated); KAO U269/E.126, R. Fawdon to Earl of Middx. The long account quoted conflates two of Fawdon's accounts, that of 17 Dec 1644 and (in square brackets) that of 18 Jan, for additional detail: E.21(36, 37).
12. For Middlesex, see the detailed biography by M. Prestwich, *Cranfield: Politics and Profits under the Early Stuarts*, Oxford, 1966. In Trapp's eyes Milcote was irredeemably tainted with evil associated with Catholicism. Recent occupants had included the notorious Catesbys of Gunpowder Plot fame, the poet Fulke Greville, murdered in 1628 (see *DNB*), and the worldly and corrupt Middlesex. The destruction of the house was, he claimed: 'commonly looked upon as a speaking monument of God's just judgement against Sacrilege and Perjury': *A Commentary upon the Twelve Minor Prophets, by John Trappe, Pastor of Weston-upon-Avon*, 1652. Milcote inventory: KAO U269/E.228/10.
13. Compton: E.21(37) (warning); J. Vicars, *Magnalia dei Anglicana*, 1646, IV, pp. 99–102; E.238(12), E.268(1, 9, 13), E.269(3); Henry James, *English Hours*, 'In Warwickshire', 1905.
14. Lark Stoke: BL E.89(10), E.90(7), E.246(19), E.266(24), E.271(16), E.274(17), E.282(7); Vicars, op. cit., IV, pp. 106–8 (account of John Bridges, 8 Feb 1645).

Chapter 10

1. KAO U269/E.201, R. Fawdon to T. Bellamy, 26 Jan 1645, and E.126, to Earl of Middx, 10 Feb and 7 Apr 1645.
2. Banbury: *cf.* A. Beesley *The History of Banbury*, Nichols, 1841, pp. 397–407; H.G. Tibbutt *The Letter Books of Sir S. Luke*, passim. Chipping Norton: N. Wallington

Historical Notices of Events Occurring Chiefly in the Reign of Charles I, 1869, II, p. 246.

3. Stratford district: H.G. Tibbutt, op. cit., pp. 251, 690; BL E.260(12); KAO U269/E.112, R. Chandler to Earl of Middx. Plague: references to plague are intermittent from spring 1645; payments to relieve victims paid in May: SBT ER1/79/4 f. 20; see n. 11 below.

4. Loxley: E.270(33). Halford: H.G. Tibbutt, op. cit., p. 205; Beesley *The History of Banbury*, pp. 398–400. Sherbourne: BL E.278(27, 31), E.281(3).

5. Losses: KAO U269/E.104, E.121, Apr 1645. Neutralism: *cf*. R. Hutton 'The Worcestershire Clubmen in the English Civil War', *Midland History*, 5, 1979–80. Bisbey: *Wyllys Papers*, p. 97, letter of 21 Aug 1646.

6. BL E.284(25). For the royalist march north, see *EB*, pp. 215–7, 246–9.

7. For the little-known episode of Cromwell in Warwickshire, see *EB*, pp. 248–56. Bishopton: SP.28/136/48. Chipping Campden: E.284(23, 25). E.284(14).

8. Massey and parliamentary quarters: BL E.260(39), E.284(14, 17, 22, 23), E.285(4, 9). John Bridges: H.G. Tibbutt, op. cit., pp. 281, 537.

9. Leases: KAO U269/E.126, 5 and 11 May 1645. Evesham: J.W. Bund *The Civil War in Worcestershire*, 1905, pp. 159–61 (who, like most commentators on this episode, is unaware of the contribution from the Warwickshire forces); *Virtue and Valour Vindicated*, London, 1647. Milcote: KAO U269/E.126, E.201, E.204, 1, 5, 16 Jun 1645.

10. Naseby: M. Ashley *The Battle of Naseby and the Fall of King Charles I*, Alan Sutton, 1992; and G. Foard, *Naseby, the Decisive Campaign*, Pryor Pubs., 1995. Radbrook: BL Landsdowne MSS 578/23, reproduced in J.H. Bloom *History of Preston-on-Stour, Warwickshire*, Hemsworth, 1896, p. 35. Catholics: R.F. Tomes 'Gloucester Royalist Families', *Trans. Bristol and Glos. Arch. Soc.*, 12, 14, 1887–90.

11. Plague: *QS*, II, pp. 128, 147, 190–1; there had been major outbreaks at Old Stratford and Haselor (1638), Haselor again (1641), Worcester (1637, 1643, 1644), Oxford (1643–4), Stow (1644, 1646), etc. The first recorded plague death at Stratford in 1645 was for 11 May, the last 13 Oct, at least 70 victims dying of it in all. Combe: KAO U269/E.126, 11 Aug 1645; SBT BRU 15/13/131; ER1/79/4 f. 20.

12. Cromwell: *HMC*, IVth Rpt, App., p. 273, Samuel Kem to Earl of Denbigh, Culham, n.d., (this letter is clearly out of chronological sequence, and refers not to Dec 1645 as assumed by *VCH*, III, p. 235, n.98, when Cromwell was in fact in the south-west, but to this period).

13. *LJ*, VII, pp. 463–4.

Chapter 11

1. Scots army: *CJ*, IV, p. 205; S.R. Gardiner *History of the Great Civil War, 1642–1649*, 1886–1901, II, p. 263; *LJ*, VII, p. 464; *CSPD*, 1644–5, pp. 611–2, 622–3.

2. H. Townshend, *Diary of Henry Townshend, 1640–1663*, Worcs. Hist. Soc., ed. J.W. Bund, 1916, II, p. 236; R. Ashton *Reformation and Revolution, 1558–1660*, Harper Collins, 1958, p. 326.

3. Scots in Warwickshire: 29 *HMC*, XIIIth Rpt (Portland I), pp. 233–4, Leven to Scottish Commissioners, Alcester, 8 Jul 1645. Purefoy: *CSPD*, 1644–5, pp. 622–3; Purefoy was present at the siege of Hereford: ib., pp. 244, 263, 265.

4. BL Add 18982, ff. 68–9, Sir Edw. Nicholas to Rupert, Oxford, 11 Jul; Gardiner, op. cit., p. 263. Gell: *CSPD*, 1645–7, p. 12.

5. Fawdon: KAO U269/E.126. Stratford: BL Add 18982, ff. 68–9, 11 Jul.

6. BL Add 18982, f. 71, Sir Edw. Nicholas to Rupert, Oxford, 21 Jul.

7. Quarter and arrears: *CSPD*, 1644–5, pp. 611–2, 25 Jun. Northampton: *CSPD*, 1645–7, pp. 5, 34. Leven: 29 *HMC*, XIIIth Rpt, pp. 233–4, Alcester, 8 Jul 1645.

8. Hereford: *CSPD*, 1645–7, p. 56. Return march: 29 *HMC*, XIIIth Rpt, I, pp. 259, 265. BL E.301(8).

9. BL Add 18982, f. 68, 11 Jul. Invaders: E.296(33). Combe and Nash: SP.28/254, f.108.

10. Poyntz: *CSPD*, 1645–7, pp. 102–4, 109, 122; BL E.300(2, 9, 11, 17), E.301(2, 8); 29 *HMC*, XIIIth Rpt, I, pp. 259–60. Mutiny: ib., p. 260.

11. BL E.301(2). Hereford: 29 *HMC*, XIIIth Rpt, I, p. 264. Huntingdon: BL E.298(26); *cf. VCH*, Huntingdonshire, II, p. 19–20.

12. BL E.300(3), E.264(18), E.303(34, 36). Charlecote: BL E.302(6). Rugby: BL

E.296(23). Stratford: BL E.303(34). Oldys: J. Walker *Sufferings of the Clergy*, 1714, II, p. 323; *cf. EB*, p. 237.

13. Stratford bridge: *QS*, III, pp. 26, 45–6, 63, 116–7, 159; SP.21/22, f. 93 (*see illustration, page 134*) calendared *CSPD*, 1645–7, p. 241); *VCH*, III, pp. 224–5. Maj. Castle: SP.28/185, James Castle's accounts. The Stratford antiquary R.B. Wheler *History and Antiquities of Stratford on Avon*, 1806, believed it was the second arch from the east end which was destroyed. Repairs: *QS*, III, pp. 26, 46, 63; Sargenson signed a receipt for £20 'in full discharge for the erecting of a new arch in the Bridge according to an order made in Sessions' on 19 Apr 1653 (SBT: ERI/80/13; illustration in L. Fox *In Honour of Shakespeare*, Jarrold/SBT, 1972, p. 94). In view of its importance to the town's trade and the fact that apparently only one arch of Stratford bridge was destroyed, it seems likely that it was patched up long before proper repairs were carried out in the 1650s. As yet, however, no clear evidence has emerged to confirm this, or to suggest to what extent the footbridge at the mill was used as an alternative. Halford: *QS*, III, p. 61. For other bridges, *cf. EB*, pp. 151–2. Barford: provision was sent, e.g. from Bishops Tachbrook (SP.28/182). Coal: *CSPD*, 1645–7, p. 430; *cf. EB*, p. 97.

14. SP.28/254 f.33; R.N. Dore *The Letter Books of Sir William Brereton*, Rec. Soc. of Lancs and Cheshire, 1984, 1990, II, pp. 332, 335, quoting letters of 10 and 11 Dec 1645, with interesting comment.

15. Stow: good résumé in F.A. Hyett 'The last battle of the first civil war', *Trans. Bristol and Glos. Arch Soc.*, 16, 1891–2, pp. 61–7, based on J. Rushworth *Historical Collections*, 1721, VI, pp. 139–41, and Col. John Birch's own account in J. Webb, (ed.) 'Military memoir of Col. John Birch', Camden Soc., 1873. Astley: his son Sir Edward visited him there on 6 July to try to secure his release; he was eventually released on 18 July 1646: R.W. Ketton-Cramer *Three Generations: Based on Letters of the Astley Family During the Civil War*, Larks Press, Norfolk, 1922, pp. 22–3.

16. *Cf.* T.S. Eliot 'Little Gidding', *Four Quartets*, 1942, line 26. See R. Van der Weyer 'Nicholas Ferrar and Little Gidding, a reappraisal', and P. Tudor-Craig 'Charles I and Little Gidding', both in R. Ollard and P. Tudor-Craig (eds), *For Veronica Wedgwood These*, Collins, 1986. The king had visited the community in March 1642 and on leaving had asked it to pray for his safe return (op. cit., pp. 168–9). The community survived the war, but was destroyed by parliamentary troops shortly after the king's last visit of 2 May 1646 (ib., p. 170). This visit may have been to seek spiritual guidance, and confirmed his attraction to martyrdom (ib., p. 187).

17. Disbanding: *CJ*, IV, p. 633. (see Chapter 12, page 141). Stratford: SBT BRT 4/1/1/36, Jury Presentment, 1647. KAO U269/E.127, William Hill, steward on one of the Earl of Middx's Glos. estates.

Chapter 12

1. Highwaymen: C.V. Wedgwood *The King's War, 1641–1647*, Collins, 1978, pp. 532–3; Hind later enlisted for Charles II and fought for him at Worcester in 1651: C.V. Wedgwood *Truth and Opinion*, Collins, 1960. *QS* II, pp. xxiv, 125–6. Unrest: *CSPD*, 1648–9, p. 192.

2. Stratford: *VCH*, III, p. 236. Combe: KAO U269/C.249; ER1/1/108; Hughes *Politics, Society and Civil War*, p. 266. Vagrancy: *QS*, IV, pp. 185–6. Poor relief: *QS* II, pp. 57–8, 128, 189, 205; III, pp. 36, 37, 44, 62, 104–5; IV, pp. 59, 110, 111, 140, 146–7, 157–8; unpaid poor levies were reported at Temple Grafton, Wellesbourne, Balsall, Bidford, etc.: *QS* II, pp. 128, 192, 249; III, p. 107. Pious uses: Stratford claims, return of the 'Chamber'.

3. Greene v. Sharpe: see Chapter 2, pp. 15–16. Town watch: SBT BRT 4/1/1/36. Harvests: *CSPD*, 1649–50, pp. 94, 125; W.G. Hoskins 'Harvest fluctuations and English economic history 1620–1759', *Agric. Hist. Rev.*, 16, 1968, pp. 18–20. JPs: A.L. Beier 'Poor relief in Warwickshire, 1630–1660', *Past and Present*, 35, 1966, pp. 78, 85, 87, 89–90, 92–4. For a clear summary of the social consequences of the war, *cf.* C.V. Wedgwood *The King's War*, pp. 584–7.

4. Disbanding: *CJ*, IV, p. 633; BL E.515(2); *CSPD* 1645–7, pp. 538, 540; *cf.* I. Roots *The Great Rebellion, 1642–60*, Batsford, 1966; J.S. Morrill 'Mutiny and discontent in English provincial armies, 1645–7', *Past*

and *Present*, 56, 1972: by late summer
1646, Parliament was faced with reports of
mutinies in at least 25 English counties,
including Warwickshire. Warwick Castle:
CSPD, 1645–7, pp. 568, 575; 1648–9, p. 5.

5. War victims: *cf.* many cases, including
Spooner's, scattered in SP.28/248.
Treasurers for maimed: *QS*, II, pp. 179–80
and passim (see index). Hester Whyte (of
Great Alne? *cf.* case of destitute Anne
Whyte, 1647, *QS*, II, p. 180): SP.
16/539/358, (calendared *CSPD*, 1625–49,
Add, p. 639); *cf.* Chapter 4, page 43.

6. Warwick Castle: *CSPD*, 1648–9, pp. 152,
186–7. Petition: E.460(8). New Place: J.O.
Halliwell (-Phillips) *An Historical Account of
the New Place, Stratford upon Avon*, Adland,
London, 1864, p. 117; the robbery at
Compton Verney took place 30 Apr 1647.

7. Cromwell: E.458(3, 10); E.525(9, 11).
Wagstaffe: *CSPD*, 1648–9, p. 261; he was
later involved in the abortive Penruddock
rising of 1655 and then escaped to
Holland; see *DNB*. Lingen (Henry was
father of Roger, of nearby Radbrook):
E.460(18–22, 28, 32, 34–5); E.457(21);
E.461(8, 14, 17, 30); E.525(5, 20, 21).

8. Reynolds: *CSPD*, 1649–50, pp. 94, 111,
125. Cromwell: SBT BRU 2/3.C.344–5,
dated 31 Aug 1651.

9. *CAM*, p. 61, 8 Feb 1647; *CSPD*, 1648–9, p.
193. Bishopton: SP.28/248.

10. SBT BRU 2/3.C.280, 281, 315, 323, 385,
389.

11. For general discussion of this complex
subject, *cf.* I. Roots *The Great Rebellion,
1642–1660*, Batsford, 1966, p. 104, and C.
V. Wedgwood *The King's War*, pp. 510,
584–6. Dighton: *CCC*, p. 1521. Hitchcock:
CAM, p. 1413–4. Wagstaffe: SP.19/158 f.
69; *CCC*, p. 2816; *CAM*, p. 1420. Earle:
CAM, p. 1413–4. Stew: *CAM*, p. 1170.
Ryland and Hiccox: SP.19/158 ff. 170–1
(*CAM*, p. 1427). Greene: SP.23/126 ff.
711–21 (*CAM*, p. 1427). Lindon:
SP.19/158 f. 108 (*CAM*, p. 1423).
Woolmer: SP.19/158 ff. 69 (bells), 108;
SP.28/215, Thomas Basnet's Book of
Sequestrations, f. 78; BL Add 35098 ff. 6,
8. Rainsborough had been in the south
Midlands for some time; in Dec 1645 he
had been sent to blockade Oxford, and
Woodstock had surrendered to him 26 Apr
1646. After the fall of Oxford he was sent
to replace Whalley at the siege of

Worcester, and it surrendered to him 23
Jul; see *DNB* and many refs in J. Sprigge
Anglia Rediviva, 1647. Henry
Stephens/Stevens: although the name is a
common one, it is likely that this informer
was related to the prominent
Gloucestershire puritan family and the
Colonel Thomas Stephens already
mentioned above (n. 2 to Chapter 9).

12. SP.28/215, Thomas Basnet's Book of
Sequestrations, 1649.

13. PRO E.370/106/1, list of Warwickshire
'Refusers and Neglecters to take the Oath
of Abjuration' by those 'suspected to be
Popishly affected & therefore Legally
required . . . to take ye Oath', dated 6 Jul
1655.

14. *CCC*, p. 3076; BL Add 35098 ff. 57, 76,
129; SP.23/170 ff. 103 sqq. Trapp: BL
Add 15670, f. 128; Add 15671, ff. 154,
176v, 204.

15. *CAM*, p. 61.

16. For the effects of the war on clergy
throughout the district, *cf. EB*, Chapter
11. Twitchet: SBT BRU 15/14/9;
Bodleian Lib. MS Bodl. 324 f. 140; I am
grateful to Jeremy Gibson, FSA, for
checking this reference; BL Add 35098
f. 36v.

17. Hawling: SBT BRU 2/3.C.205. Bean: see
Appendix 3/7. Trapp v. Bowen: PRO
E.134/13 CHAS 2/MICH 22; E.134/13 &
14 CHAS 2/HIL 5 (1661–2).

18. The following figures are taken from
VCH, III, p. 235. Statistically, the 1640s £
would be equivalent to roughly £100 today.
But such a comparison, of course, ignores
transformed values, assumptions and life-
styles.

19. Warwick fortification: *cf. EB*, p. 95.
Compton garrison: *cf. EB*, pp. 161–70.

20. Brooks: *Wyllys Papers*, p. 97; and see the
many detailed inventories of cloth,
stockings, clothing bought by George
Willis and carried to Bristol by William
Tony for shipment to New England, from
at least 1639 throughout the 1640s, in
Wyllys Papers. Brooks became bailiff of
Stratford 1649 and rented Mrs Willis's
house and close. Coal: *cf. EB*, p. 97.
Combe: *Wyllys Papers*, p. 122, G. Willis to
Wm Gibbons, Warwick, Jun 1650; for
relation of Combe to Willis, *cf.* Eccles
Shakespeare in Warwickshire, p. 121.

21. In the summer of 1575 Robert Dudley, Earl

of Leicester, entertained Queen Elizabeth extravagantly for nineteen days at his seat, Kenilworth Castle (later to inspire Sir Walter Scott's novel). The earl was also lord of Stratford, where Shakespeare's father was still alderman, and his actors received a generous reward of 17s. from Stratford Corporation, probably for performing there as well as at Kenilworth. Commentators have usually been unable to resist speculating that Shakespeare's two almost identical references to Arion and mermaids singing on a dolphin's back (*Twelfth Night*, I.2; *Midsummer Night's Dream*, II.1) were inspired by boyhood memories of having seen the water pageant which was such a spectacular feature of the Kenilworth festivities described by contemporaries (*cf.* Dugdale *Antiquities*, p. 249): R. Savage and E.I. Fripp (eds) *Minutes and Accounts of Stratford-upon-Avon Corporation*, II, pp. xxxiv, xli–xlii, 77, 105–6, Dugdale Soc. Pubs. 3, 1924; *cf.* Schoenbaum, *William Shakespeare, a Compact Documentary Life*, pp. 115–6. For the post-war destruction of Banbury and Kenilworth castles (and also of Wormleighton in 1646), *cf. EB*, pp. 218–22.

Select Bibliography

Place of publication is London except where otherwise indicated

Atkin, Malcolm *The Civil War in Worcestershire*, Stroud, 1995

Beesley, Alfred *The History of Banbury*, 1841

* Bloxam, Matthew Holbeche *Warwickshire During the Civil Wars of the Seventeenth Century*, Warwick, 1880

Bund, J. Willis *The Civil War in Worcestershire, 1642–1646*, Birmingham, 1905

Carlton, Charles *Going to the Wars: the Experience of the British Civil Wars, 1638–1651*, 1992

Eddershaw, David, and Roberts, Eleanor *The Civil War in Oxfordshire*, Stroud, 1995

Green, M.A.E. (ed.) *Calendar of the Proceedings of the Committee for the Advancement of Money, 1642–1656*, 1888

Green, M.A.E. (ed.) *Calendar of the Proceedings of the Committee for Compounding, 1643–1660*, 1890

Hibbert, Christopher *Cavaliers and Roundheads: The English at War, 1642–1649*, 1993

* Hughes, Ann *Politics, Society and Civil War in Warwickshire, 1620–1662*, Cambridge, 1987

* Hughes, Ann 'Religion and society in Stratford-upon-Avon, 1619–1638', *Midland History*, Vol. 19, 1994

Hutton, Ronald *The Royalist War Effort, 1642–1646*, 1982

Matthews, A.G. *Walker Revised*, Oxford, 1948

Morrill, John (ed.) *Reactions to the English Civil War, 1642–1649*, 1982

Morrill, John (ed.) *The Impact of the English Civil War*, 1991

* Mosler, David F. 'A social and religious history of the English civil war in Warwickshire' (unpublished thesis, Stanford, 1975; copy at Warwick CRO)

* Oldridge, Darren 'Conflicts within the established church in Warwickshire, *c.* 1603–1642' (unpublished thesis, Warwick, 1992; copy at Warwick CRO)

* Ratcliff S.C. and Johnson H.C. (eds) *Warwick County Records: Quarter Sessions Order Books*, Warwick, 1935–53

* Sherwood, Roy *The Civil War in the Midlands, 1642–1651*, Stroud, 1992

Strider, R.E.L. *Robert Greville, Lord Brooke*, Cambridge, MA, 1958

* Styles, Philip 'The borough of Stratford-upon-Avon and the parish of Alveston', *Victoria County History of Warwickshire*, Vol. III, 1946

* Tennant, Philip *Edgehill and Beyond: the People's War in the South Midlands, 1642–1645*, Stroud, 1992

Wedgwood, C.V. *The King's War, 1641–1647*, 1978

* Works referring particularly to Warwickshire

Index of Names

Subject Index